RIDDLE OF THE ROCK

RIDDLE
OF
THE ROCK

The Only Successful Escape from Alcatraz

DON DeNEVI

Prometheus Books
Buffalo, New York

95 94 93 92 91   5 4 3 2 1

Library of Congress Cataloging-in-Publication Data

DeNevi, Don, 1937-
    Riddle of the rock : the only successful escape from Alcatraz / by Don DeNevi.
       p.   cm.
    ISBN 0-87975-647-0
    1. United States Penitentiary, Alcatraz Island, California. 2. Escapes—
California—Alcatraz Island—Case studies. 3. Anglin, John. 4. Anglin, Clarence.
5. Morris, Frank (Frank Lee). I. Title.
HV9474.A4D485   1991
365′.641—dc20   90-26764
                                                                           CIP

Printed in the United States of America on acid-free paper.

This book is respectfully dedicated to Robert, Jr., Marie, Audrey, Rufus, Mearl, Patsy, Carson, Verna, Christine, Mary Nell . . . and their adopted sister, Jeanette.

If Clarence and J. W. Anglin are as warm and loving as their brothers and sisters, they deserve to be free.

"How will you escape it?
By what will you escape it?
That's impossible with your ideas."

Fyodor Dostoevsky,
The Brothers Karamazov, 1880

Contents

Contents

Foreword

I have read and enjoyed this intriguing and well-researched book. It chronicles in great detail an incident that has held the interest of the people of this country for over twenty-nine years. So much material, both written and filmed, has been produced that the escape from Alcatraz has beome a part of prison folklore.

It is my hope as a law-enforcement official that the three subjects of this book will, if they are still alive, be reached by the message the author delivers. The unanswered questions surrounding this signal event are so important that it would be to everyone's interest, including the escapees, that they come forth from their years as fugitives. Only in that way can the books be closed forever on one of the most bizarre and noteworthy incidents in the history of our penal system.

William T. McGivern, Jr.
United States Attorney
Northern District of California
San Francisco, California

Preface

In his narrative, author Don DeNevi offers the very real possibility that Clarence and John Anglin, who escaped from Alcatraz with Frank Morris in early June of 1962, are alive. Less hope is offered for Morris's survival.

Should this be the case, and the three escapees present themselves to me, they can be assured they would be treated fairly, a Federal Defender would be appointed, and they would be housed in a safe and secure facility until all hearings were concluded. The follow-up investigations would be done by the U.S. Marshals Office. One hopes the years of freedom would prove they have been upstanding citizens during this period of time, and that the judge and the Department of Justice would take this into consideration and grant them their freedom in their remaining years.

Meanwhile, to the reader who is about to begin this engrossing account, I say "enjoy." Don has obviously done his homework in assembling every known fact about the details of the escape, fusing them with the unpublished memoirs he assisted Clarence "Joe" Carnes in writing in 1978 and the hitherto unpublished FBI report of the subsequent manhunt. When combined with maps, drawings, rich appendices, as well as never-before-seen photos taken by Alcatraz officers, the book offers one of the most readable prison stories in recent memory. Pivotal to his character development of Clarence and J. W., as John was called, was acceptance by, and close friendship with, the remaining seven sisters and three brothers of the Anglin family in southern Florida.

And, to the three men who have eluded our search during these past 29 years, I say that it's time to come home. Give me a call and let's see if we can work something out.

Richard "Dick" Bippus
Chief Deputy
U.S. Marshal
Northern District of California
(415) 556-3930

Acknowledgments

I am indebted to many people for their interest and contributions to this project. They include Philip R. Bergen, former Captain of the Guard at Alcatraz, whose advice, help, and guidance added immeasurably to the book; Erica Schoenhals Toland, Assistant Archivist, and Karen Berlin Sherwood, Conservation Technician, for the San Francisco Maritime National Historic Park; Dale Cox, Marianna News Chief for WJHG-TV; Judy Canter, Head Librarian, *San Francisco Examiner*; Jeanette Williams; Patricia Akre, Photography and Exhibit Curator for the San Francisco History Room and Archives, Main Library; Charles E. Hopkins, former Alcatraz inmate; Joan S. Moore, daughter of former Alcatraz Lt. Joe Simpson; Tom Duncan, Chief Photographer for the *Oakland Tribune*; Ron Colwak, photo archives, *Tampa Tribune*, Joan Carroll, Associated Press technician, Los Angeles; Eugene Anglen and Nunie Anglen Billbe, Essex, Iowa; Dennis Berry, Chief of the Fugitive Division, U.S. Marshals Office, San Francisco; Mike West, Photographic Assistant, Cominex, Washington, D.C.; Patty Kindberg; Jack Green, Mayor of Columbia, Alabama; Sheriff Haddon, Houston County, Alabama; Patty Kennedy of the Dothan, Alabama, *Eagle*; Eugenia MacGowan, San Francisco; Betty Waller of Cambridge, Ohio; U.S. Attorney William McGivern, San Francisco; Richard "Dick" Bippus, Chief Deputy, U.S. Marshals Office, San Francisco; "Mac" McLendon, U.S. Marshal, Tallahassee, Florida; Sheriff "Johnny" McDaniel, Jackson County, Florida; Joe Brandenburg, Deputy Chief, U.S. Probation Office, Kansas City; Alex Ivanov, Fairfax, California; and Bob Basil, Senior Editor and Lorraine Baranski, Director of Promotions, Prometheus Books. But of all those interviewed, none were more responsive, or yielded greater information, than the Anglin family and Alfred Anglin's widow, Jeanette. The wealth of information provided collectively by the above made my job a pleasant one. The only difficulty was in deciding what to omit. In the end, the omissions outnumbered the inclusions.

Introduction

"If you ever write about me, Don, tell the reader that none of us, including myself, could try to escape unless he first had the courage to deal with his own loneliness. In isolation, I learned to live through the loneliness. Being alive again, I could plot escape. Trying to escape was freedom itself."

Clarence "Joe" Carnes to the author in the summer of 1984

For a boy growing up in the San Joaquin Valley, that vast fertile plain of Central California, there was plenty of time to imagine. The summers were long and scorching hot on the valley floor and the winters little more than drifitng mists and tulle fog. For me, life in my Valley town seemed slow and routine compared with the adventurous life I imagined my big-city counterparts led. To farm kids and small-town boys, San Francisco was The Metropolis, the big city where anything and everything was possible and mystery abounded. And of all the mysteries of the big city, none captured my imagination more than Alcatraz.

Alcatraz—its very name sounded strange and harsh, at least to my childish and un-Hispanic ear. It conjured up a fantastic world of desperate men and steel bars, a hell-hole where prison guards and famous gangsters and dangerous convicts killed each other off for sport, where dark secrets were buried in men's souls, where the unspeakable remained unspoken. Popular radio programs of the 1940s such as "Gangbusters," and movies such as *The House Across the Bay*, *Alcatraz Crashout*, *The King of Alcatraz*, and *The Rock of Despair* fueled my boyhood imagination. The schoolyard where I played during my schooldays became, in my imagination, a fenced prison exercise yard where my fellow "inmates" served out time. The playground was also the place where lurid rumors and chilling stories about prison life circulated freely. The "Battle of Alcatraz," which was what the press labeled the 1946 escape attempt, provided many hours of speculation and grisly story-telling among my peers.

As I grew to adulthood, my fascination with Alcatraz diminished in importance, along with other childhood fantasies, but my interest in the prison system never entirely left me. So, as a somewhat mature young man of twenty studying for a credential in General Pupil Personnel Services, I requested internship at Deuel Vocational Institute. This medium-security prison near Tracy, California, for wards of the California Youth Authority gave me the opportunity to work in the Reception Guidance Clinic as a counselor.

During the course of my work there, I came face-to-face with my long-forgotten curiosity about Alcatraz. One morning I mentioned to a secretary that as a child I had wanted to see the island prison from the inside even though I knew "tourists" were forbidden. She said, "Oh, you want to go to Alcatraz? I'll arrange to have you visit my uncle—he's a guard there. He might even get you into the cellhouse." I knew casual visitors were still not permitted. I took her up on the offer.

On Sunday, May 26, 1962, I met Gene Kessler, an Alcatraz correctional officer, at Fort Mason in San Francisco. He escorted me to the island aboard the prison boat on its regular run. We went to his apartment in the big "Apartment Block" for a chicken dinner. After dessert and coffee the big moment came: Gene asked me if I wanted to tour the cellhouse. It was a quiet Sunday afternoon; the inmates were in the yard, and the Warden was probably taking a nap. I realized that if an unplanned-for civilian were discovered in the cellhouse, my friend would be severely reprimanded.

We passed through security and suddenly I was inside the forbidding building that had once been the focus of my fantasy. It was quiet, mysterious, and it was clean. Somehow that surprised me. The walls were freshly painted and the glazed surface of the concrete floor highly polished. The three-tiered cell blocks were as I had imagined. Inmates' names were displayed on little name-plates at the front of each cell. As we began our walk down B-Block, I noticed two names on adjacent cells that were similar. The names John Anglin and Clarence

Anglin meant nothing to me, but I asked Gene about it. Were they brothers? He said they were. I peered into the dark cells. There was the usual clutter: photographs, books, towels, and articles of clothing in the otherwise stark cells. In one of the brothers' cells, an artist's easel stood with a half-finished oil portrait on it.

"We don't mind if they're next to each other," Gene said. "That way, they can discuss family problems and keep the relationship intact."

As it turned out, the brothers apparently discussed more than their family back in Florida. Two weeks after my visit to the cell-house, John and Clarence Anglin, along with inmate Frank Morris, escaped from Alcatraz. Their sensational break on June 11, 1962, sparked a manhunt unparalleled in Alcatraz history. The escape of "The Tablespoon Trio," and the subsequent manhunt, is the subject of this book.

The escape of the Anglin brothers and Frank Morris captured the attention of the American public and has captured the imagination of writers, fiction and factual, ever since. Several books have retold the story, mostly from press accounts. A 1975 movie, *Escape From Alcatraz*, was based on the 1962 escape. In 1980, NBC produced *Alcatraz, The Whole Shocking Story* for its "Movie of the Week" presentation. The six-hour, two-part film featured Art Carney, Telly Sevalas, and Michael Beck. In 1989 a special episode of the television series "Unsolved Mysteries" reenacted the daring escape. In this presentation, I stated my conviction that the escape had been successful.

Almost thirty years after the escape, the events of that summer night are still the subject of conjecture and mystery. Did the three prisoners make it? Or did they drown in the dangerous waters off Alcatraz?

After all that has been written about the escape, those fundamental questions remain unanswered. Feeling unsatisfied, I wanted to retrace the escapees' steps, learn from their co-conspirators, delve into the numerous files and detailed records. I was determined to discover if somewhere there was a clue, perhaps overlooked, that might lead to a resolution of the mystery.

My quest over the past ten years has taken me many miles and into many homes, where many people have openly discussed with me their experiences and special memories of the events of June 11 and 12, 1962. I will be forever indebted to Officer Gene Kessler for that thirty-minute unauthorized glimpse into the cellhouse, and many others who gave of their time and knowledge.

I was particularly fortunate to make the acquaintance and friendship of Clarence "Joe" Carnes, a former Alcatraz inmate. Over the last sixteen years of his life, he provided me with many insights and his first-hand experience of life on "The Rock" and, in particular, of the 1962 escape. Clarence Carnes was an extraordinary man. In spite of his youthful crimes, he was straightforward and honest, more so, in fact, than some faculty colleagues and college presidents I have known. It is his honesty that has led me to the conclusion, in my mind, that John and Clarence Anglin and Frank Morris did survive their escape from Alcatraz. Clarence told me so. I asked him why he was so certain they had made it. He said, "Bumpy told me. And that's all the reason I need to know they made it." As Clarence believed Bumpy, I believe Clarence. I will present the evidence, the insights of Clarence Carnes, the story of Bumpy Johnson, and the feelings of the surviving members of the Anglin family. The reader can decide.

Don DeNevi
May 1991
San Rafael, California

1

The Riddle

"Man is a very complicated being, and though he knows a great deal about all sorts of things, he knows very little about himself. . . . This may be the greatest riddle of all."

C. G. Jung

On July 6, 1945, when Clarence Victor ("Joe") Carnes first saw Alcatraz, the U.S. Government's so-called "maximum custody—minimum privilege prison" in San Francisco Bay, it was only eleven years old. At eighteen years of age, the youngest person ever confined on the Rock, he wasn't much older than that himself, but he had been convicted of murder and kidnapping. He had escaped from a county jail and a reformatory in Oklahoma and had been sentenced to serve a life sentence, plus 104 years.

Ordinarily in the federal prison system, a youthful offender such as the teen-aged Carnes would have been confined in one of the several federal correctional institutions. If Joe had even come close to matching the pattern of the young law-breakers, he would, most probably, have been committed to one of these less restrictive institutions. Because of the nature of his crimes, the length of his prison sentences, and his record of violence and escape, the young man simply did not match the pattern. He was, therefore, committed to the U.S. Penitentiary in Leavenworth, Kansas, a "close custody" prison for more sophisticated adults, for "observation" and "evaluation."

Again, the teen-ager did not fit the pattern, this time because of his youth, and his obvious vulnerability to abuse by the vicious, sexually deviate element in the prison population.

Carnes served only a few months of his sentence at Leavenworth —but, while there, he had heard innumerable "horror stories" about Alcatraz, "The Rock," the federal government's "escape-proof" prison in far-away California. He had thought, "Oh, it's just another prison"— never suspecting that he was destined to become one of "The Rock's" most notorious inmates.

After much deliberation by the Leavenworth staff, and several consultations with the upper echelon of the Bureau of Prisons in Washington, D.C., it was decided to transfer Joe to Alcatraz for "safe-keeping." It was believed that housed in a single-occupancy cell, and subjected to constant close custody supervision, this unusual inmate would be relatively safe from sexual seduction or assault and, of course, would not be so apt to escape.

When he was transferred to the island prison, largely for his own protection, along with twelve other prisoners, Joe was serving an Oklahoma state sentence of life imprisonment for murder, plus five years for escape, together with a 99-year federal sentence for kidnapping. Seventeen years later, on January 18, 1963, just a few months prior to the official closing of Alcatraz, an older and wiser Carnes, Register Number 714 AZ, with an additional 100-year sentence for murder added to his penalty score, was transferred to the federal prison hospital in Springfield, Missouri.

In the interim, unshakably defiant and increasingly desperate because of the seeming hopelessness of his situation, he had become involved in several escape plots. One of these, the attempted "blast-out" in May 1946, had earned the young man his third 100-year sentence. For him, Alcatraz had not been just another prison, but a "coffin for the living dead."

*   *   *

The Alcatraz Concept, as conceived by J. Edgar Hoover, Director of the Federal Bureau of Investigation, was quite simple, "Build a federal prison that would be impossible to escape from; staff it with a competent no-nonsense warden and well-trained experienced prison officers—and provide the inmates thereof with adequate food, clothing, shelter, medical care, and access to the courts."

"No nonsense" seemed to mean "no privileges and no formal attempt to rehabilitate by formal education or job-training programs, together with strict discipline and the utmost in escape-prevention." As he often said, "There is no possibility of wiping out crime by trying to reform criminals. The house has been burned down. The tree has felt the blow of the ax, and has fallen in the forest. The house cannot be re-erected, nor the tree again point its leaves to the sky."

In their initial reaction to Hoover's proposal, Sanford Bates, Director of the Federal Bureau of Prisons, his three assistant directors, and nearly all of the federal prison wardens were opposed to the concept. But all were political appointees, and their boss, Homer Cummings, was the Attorney General of the United States. In a very short time, all of them seemed to be agreeing that Cummings was correct: It *was* a good idea to confine all of the desperadoes in one so-called "maximum custody-minimum privilege" prison.

If they had asked the officers who were "on the firing line" at the several federal prisons struggling to control the "uncontrollables," there would have been an enthusiastic affirmative response. The prospect of getting rid of some, if not all, of the "big shots," "saboteurs," "arsonists," "murderers," "rapists," and "escapers" was very pleasing. They reasoned that, with these assorted non-conformists out of the prison population, they could reasonably expect less inmate resistance to the rehabilitation programs.

As soon as they realized that they were going to have to include Alcatraz in their "family" of penal and correctional institutions, Bates and his assistants set about formulating plans which, while ameliorating some of the "dumping ground" aspects of Hoover's original concept, would not alienate the very influential director of the FBI. The concept therefore became a compromise. Sanford Bates and his assistants were professionals, dedicated to the eventual rehabilitation of all criminals, not just those who were amenable to discipline and control, but of the "uncontrollables" as well.

By the time the Bureau was ready to open the new prison on

Alcatraz Island in July of 1934, the Alcatraz Concept had been revised to some extent. While Alcatraz would be Hoover's "no nonsense" prison in the sense that there would be no formal rehabilitation program, and no special privileges such as Stroud, "the Birdman," enjoyed at Leavenworth, there would be strong incentives for "good behavior." Nearly all of the privileges available to the inmates of the other federal prisons would be available to the Alcatraz inmates, but they would be tightly restricted to "essentials," and the inmates would have to earn them.

The program at Alcatraz could easily have been called "an attitude adjustment program." The policy was to persuade—or, if necessary, to compel—the so-called "incorrigibles" to modify their totally unacceptable behavior so that, following an intensive retraining period of four or five years, the majority would be eligible for transfer, usually back to the very same prison that had once rejected them. Only a very few were re-rejected and returned to The Rock.

Most of the Alcatraz inmates adjusted their behavior enough to justify a transfer to a less restrictive prison. Carnes did not. Like the other inmates who were isolated on The Rock, he could look across the bay at a free society he could not touch. While other inmates were abandoning their antisocial behavior, and working their way back, escape continued to be foremost in the mind of the man known as "The Choctaw Kid."

When Carnes began his autobiography in 1958, written in his cell on Alcatraz, he began, "Certainly prison has shaped my personality and character. I know I would be a different person if I had never done time. But, how in the hell did I ever get into Alcatraz?"

The route that Joe traveled to The Rock was not too different from the paths followed by many who end up in prison: ignorance, violence, petty thievery, bad company, false pride, the thrill and self-satisfaction of easy money. Clarence Victor Carnes, a Choctaw Indian, was born in 1927 in the eastern hills of Oklahoma. His parents were poor, hardworking, country people. His father was determined to spare young Clarence and his brothers and sisters the arduous life he had known. During the depression of the 1930s, and at great expense to his parents, Clarence was enrolled in a boys' boarding school, where he fell in with a group of students for whom skill at fist-fighting was the way to earn respect. He was so good at it he became a leader among his classmates. He got the nickname "Joe" after a movie was shown at school featuring Joe E. Brown, the famous comedian.

One of the stunts the big-mouthed comedian pulled in the movie was to stuff a whole apple into his mouth. Afterwards, several of the boys tried unsuccessfully to mimic the stunt. Clarence was determined to duplicate Joe E. Brown's feat. He got an apple almost all the way in his mouth when it lodged. He struck it with the heel of his hand and drove it in, to the delight of his friends. They kept laughing as he struggled to get the apple out. Humiliated, and followed by his jeering friends, Clarence had to walk to the school nurse with the apple firmly lodged in his mouth. Even the nurse laughed as she removed it.

Thereafter Clarence was called "Joe E. Brown," "Joe E.," and finally "Joe," a nickname that stuck for the rest of his life.

By the time Joe Carnes was sixteen, he and his friends were stealing regularly. Sometimes they would steal an automobile for a "joy ride." Carnes had a pistol by then, and he decided to use it to get some "big" money. In July 1945 he and a young friend tried to rob a sevice station in Atoka, Oklahoma. The station attendant came at him, brandishing a soda bottle. They struggled, the gun was unintentionally discharged, and the attendant fell, mortally wounded.

While awaiting trial for murder, Carnes and his codefendant broke out of the county jail. They were captured and taken to the state penitentiary for safekeeping. He admitted his guilt and was sentenced to life imprisonment. But his stay in prison was brief.

Carnes and two other inmates escaped from a rock quarry work detail near the state reformatory at Granite, Oklahoma, where he and other young offenders were incarcerated. The escapees stole a car and took its owner along with them across the state line into Texas, where they picked up another captive and drove across another state line into Kansas. When they realized that they had violated the federal kidnap law by crossing state lines, they released their two captives unharmed, and headed back to Oklahoma. They were captured at Boise City, Oklahoma, and again, Carnes did not contest the charges. Tried in the federal court this time, he received a 99-year sentence for violation of the Lindbergh Act, and was sent to the U.S. Penitentiary, Leavenworth, Kansas. His "life sentence" for the Oklahoma murder was to be served concurrently.

He hadn't been at Leavenworth but a few months when he was informed that he was being transferred to Alcatraz. "I had no idea I was going to The Rock," Carnes murmured sadly, "until they came for me in the laundry the day before the transfer train pulled out. Sixteen of us, handcuffed, leg-ironed, and closely guarded by grim-faced armed officers, were in that prison coach that ran so fast and took me so far in three days that it took me eighteen years to get back."

Carnes was determined to "do his own time" on Alcatraz and live from day to day, stay out of trouble, and wait for his opportunity to escape. He soon became known for his calm but powerful personality, his fierce, visceral pride, and uncompromising loyalty. "If Carnes was your friend," former inmate Charles Hopkins recalled, "he would back you all the way. He was the kind who did his own time, quiet and independently. All the old-timers respected him."

To his keepers, Clarence Victor Carnes was sullen and uncommunicative, forever brooding over what had befallen him. He never hesitated to acknowledge his perplexity over his fate, and always presented himself as an inscrutable phenomenon. His sullen demeanor only enhanced the official U.S. Bureau of Prisons' judgment that he was at that point in time an escape risk.

Whatever alchemy was in Joe's soul, it worked wonders on those whose paths crossed his. Those "incorrigible" prisoners facing the formidable waters of San Francisco Bay with an overpowering ambition to escape sensed his innate quality of timelessness that only a "lifer" possesses. He became their legacy of hope. It was precisely this touchstone of their own peculiar tribulations that led determined plotters like Bernie Coy—and, fifteen years later, Allen West—to the quietly determined young man.

Less than six months after his arrival on Alcatraz, Carnes became involved in what some prison personnel would euphemistically call "the riot." Before that forty-eight hour "riot" in May 1946 was over, fourteen officers were wounded and two officers and three prisoners lay dead. (No inmates were wounded. One, James Groves, "faked" a superficial bullet wound, but his false claim was easily refuted.) It had begun, as most violent prison breaks do, many months before.

The long string of events that led Joe to this "blast out" attempt began shortly after he arrived on Alcatraz. He asked permission to work and was assigned to the laundry, known by inmates as one of the few places in the prison where so-called "homosexual" acts could be performed without detection by the prison officers. It wasn't long before young Carnes was "propositioned" by an older convict who, in Joe's opinion, got "too personal." A fist-fight ensued, and when it was over Joe realized he was in for more trouble if he remained in the laundry. So he quit his job and returned to "idle" in his cell. For several months, he did little or no work other than odd jobs like cellhouse cleaning and polishing to earn yard privileges. But mostly he passed the time stretched out on his cot, dreaming of escape.

It was during this time he met Bernard "Bernie" Coy, register number 415 AZ. "He told me he was forty-seven years old," Joe Carnes recalled. "To a youngster of eighteen, that was practically like having one foot in the grave." Coy had false teeth and his dark hair was turning gray. When he didn't shave for a couple of days, his beard would grow out white. His blue eyes were sunken and that, plus his dark eyebrows, gave him a piercing stare. But he was full of energy and, when he walked in the cellhouse he was always in a hurry. "His shoes squeaked on the polished floor of the cellhouse," Carnes said, "and I would always know Bernie Coy was coming when I heard those telltale footsteps."

Coy was tall and thin, almost emaciated, nervous and fidgety. When conversing, he constantly shifted his weight from one foot to another, cracking his knuckles. He would do most of the talking. To Joe Carnes, Coy seemed unusually polite to younger inmates, unlike some of the "old-timers." Carnes recalled, "There was never any talk about Coy being homosexual, although he was probably bisexual, like most habitual criminals who serve lengthy prison sentences."

Carnes's cell in those days was thirteen away from Coy's, on the same tier of the north side of B-Block (the side that faces the "east bay" cities). Coy's job as a deliveryman for the prison library was to distribute books and magazines to the inmates (each inmate was allowed to have in his cell up to seven magazines or books at one time). When the inmates were finished with them, they would drop them on a wheeled table placed at the west end of the main cellhouse on their way to the dining room. Most of the magazines delivered by Coy were prison library property, and the order in which they were distributed was controlled by the prison librarian. Some inmates who subscribed to magazines were allowed to have them passed by Coy to other inmates.

Each day Coy would sort the magazines by cell location and distribute them throughout the main cellhouse, but not in the Treatment Unit, which was "off limits" to all inmates not confined there.

Coy's was considered a good job because it permitted greater freedom of movement than any other work assignment in the cellhouse. To a prison inmate, any freedom was highly prized. Other cellhouse jobs, such as cleaning and polishing floors, restricted the inmate worker to one cellhouse area. Violations of this rule—by "wandering," "loafing," or "visiting"—could mean the "hole" (solitary confinement). Coy did his job diligently; he didn't want to lose it because it put him in an excellent position to prepare for the escape he was planning.

Carnes didn't have any money to subscribe to magazines, so he relied on those that were prison library property. Coy saw to it that Joe got a few of the latest magazines from time to time. If he wasn't in a hurry when he came to Joe's cell, Coy would stop to talk. "Ordinarily this was not permitted," Carnes said, "but the hacks didn't enforce the rule strictly against the library deliveryman." Coy talked about painting. He had the reputation of being the best landscape painter in the "joint" and he encouraged young Carnes to take up the hobby. "It's easy," Coy said, "and it helps pass a lot of time." With the time Carnes had to serve, he might become an accomplished painter. Coy brought pencils and paper to Joe's cell and explained that the first step in artistry was to learn to draw.

"He told me to put a shoe on the table and look at it," he said. "I stared at my shoe and wondered if he expected me to draw anything as complicated as that. Coy said every principle of drawing was in that shoe and if I learned to draw that shoe, I could draw anything."

Carnes drew his shoe for hours every day. Coy would stop by the cell on his magazine route to check his progress and offer encouragement. "I leaned to draw that shoe," Joe said. "To this day I can draw a helluva shoe, but nothing else."

One day Coy stopped by Carnes's cell and asked if he could do him a favor. Joe agreed but wondered what possible favor he could do locked in his cell. Coy said he would be working near a window across from Joe's cell at a certain time and he wanted Joe to "jigger" for him. Jiggering involved the use of two small mirrors positioned on a small wooden board to allow the "jiggerer" to see both ways along the length of the corridor adjacent to the cell. Coy said he would let Carnes know when to start "jiggering," and he gave him a domino board to drop on the floor of his cell if he saw an officer coming.

The day came, and Carnes watched Coy move the magazine table near a cellhouse window across the aisle from his cell. A section of the "detention sash" windows could be opened for ventilation, but a cage of tool-resistant steel bars over each window discouraged any thought of escape. Surely, thought Carnes, Coy couldn't be thinking of something so stupid. Coy sorted his magazines for a long time, while Carnes waited impatiently for the signal to start "jiggering." He finally got the signal and he placed the small mirrors between his cell bars to get a clear view of the cellhouse corridor. He could also see Coy, who didn't appear to be doing anything but sorting magazines. Suddenly Coy jumped atop the magazine cart, reached up, and thrust his hand between the bars and through the open window. When he pulled his hand back he was holding a small paper-wrapped package not much larger than a pack of cigaretes, and he signaled Joe to stop "jiggering." What was in the package? "In some joints," Joe said, "you might ask. But not at Alcatraz. If an inmate wanted you to know something, he'd tell you."

Coy hid the mysterious package among the magazines and went casually about his rounds. Coy asked Joe to "jigger" for him again the following Thursday. Again Joe was willing. Carnes and Coy repeated the performance every Thursday for several months. Coy never mentioned what was in the package. It appeared to be the same package each time, but since he couldn't question Coy, Joe had no way of knowing what it contained. He did suspect that something important was going on.

After the aborted escape attempt in May 1946, which cost Bernie Coy his life, Carnes learned what had been in the package. It was a bar-spreader, an ingenious little device consisting of a steel bolt, washer, nut, and a hardened, tubular sleeve. It was designed to fit between two steel bars and, when the nut was turned by a wrench, the bars would be spread apart. Presumably, each time the bar-spreader was handed to Coy through the open window, the escape was scheduled to take place. But each time something went wrong at the last minute. The bar-spreader was then concealed in a certain cellhouse trash can. An inmate on the trash collection truck would then retrieve and stash it until the following week. Then, on Thursday, the same inmate trash collector waited for Coy's hand to appear at the window and again the wrapped bar-spreader was handed in through the open window.

Coy kept Carnes in the dark about the details of the actual escape plan because at first he wasn't sure that Carnes could be trusted. There was a natural mistrust of the younger inmates at Alcatraz. A young man hadn't been tested, but, sooner or later, he would get into a situation where it would become obvious if he was "solid" or not. Joe was asked to "jigger" for Coy, simply because his cell was in the right position, and as sort of a test of his dependability. Coy had seduced him for that purpose.

Coy's complicated escape plan was well organized by the time Carnes was drawn into it. Joseph Cretzer, bank-robber, murderer, and a co-conspirator in the plan, had spent almost five years segregated in the Treatment Unit for his participation in a 1941 escape attempt, in which he and three other inmates had bound and gagged a shop foreman and the captain of the guards while they tried unsuccessfully to cut through the steel window bars of the workshop. While in the Treatment Unit, Cretzer was friendly with Sam Shockley, who had participated with him in the 1941 escape attempt. Shockley, called "Crazy Sam" by other inmates, was a mentally retarded bank robber and kidnapper who claimed he heard voices inside his head. Shockley's erratic and disruptive behavior had caused him to be placed in the Treatment Unit until a decision could be made about his medically advised transfer to the federal prison hospital in Springfield, Missouri.

The other co-conspirators in the 1941 escape scheme were Marvin Franklin Hubbard, Tennessee kidnapper and robber whose criminal record showed his ability and readiness to use a gun and carry out a criminal plan to the bitter end; and Miran (Buddy) Thompson, kidnapper, murderer, and escape artist from Texas whose vicious reputation of murder, kidnapping, and rape was well known to the criminal elite of Alcatraz.

The conspirators needed another man, someone who could stash important items prior to the escape and be trusted. Since Carnes had demonstrated that he was trustworthy, Coy slipped him a packet of maps and a small book of names and numbers for "safekeeping"— the packet was labeled "LIFE ROUTE." Ostensibly the book contained the names of inmates who regularly received *Life* magazine, but, in reality, it listed the names of everybody even remotely connected with the plot and their respective roles. When Coy finally asked Carnes if he wanted to join the escapees, the young inmate quickly assented, so Coy gave him a dagger made from a steel "divider"—an instrument used in drafting.

The plan was for Coy and Hubbard to overpower the unarmed cellhouse officer, release co-conspirators Cretzer, Thompson, and Carnes from their cells, and for Coy to break into the west gun gallery, overpower the armed officer, get his guns and keys, release Shockley from the Treatment Unit, break out of the cellhouse and work their way down to the dock and sail, aboard the prison motor launch, to the mainland. An overly ambitious plot, with little probability of success—but Coy and Hubbard had studied the problems carefully and were completely confident. (Apparently, Coy and Hubbard kept most of the details of the plot to themselves, informing Cretzer, Thompson, Carnes, and Shockley on a "need to know" basis.)

On May 1, 1946, everything seemed right. Coy and Hubbard expected that Mr. Lageson, one of the two unarmed cellhouse officers, would go to lunch outside the cellhouse at 1:30 P.M. Mr. William Miller, the other cellhouse officer, would be alone in the main cellhouse. When Mr. Miller began his routine "frisk-search" of Hubbard, who (allegedly) was returning to the cellhouse from kitchen duty, Coy, who was nearby polishing the cellhouse floor, quickly came up behind the officer, held a knife to his throat, and overpowered him. Hubbard and Coy took him over to the southwest corner of C-Block and placed him in the first cell (No. 404). Coy tied Mr. Miller's hands behind his back, after taking the officer's uniform pants, keys, and personal property.

When Carnes arrived at the west end of B-Block, Coy had already squeezed into the gun gallery—but Hubbard was still clinging to the gun gallery near where the bars had been spread apart, preparing to climb down. At this point, approximately when Coy was assaulting Mr. Burch in the Treatment Unit section of the gun gallery, the prison steward, Robert Birstow, returning to his duty station in the prison kitchen, reached the west end of Broadway. Carnes and Hubbard captured him and placed him in cell No. 404 with Miller and inmate Moyle.

When guards outside the cellhouse sized up the situation, they called for reinforcements. The inmates planned to escape through one of the roof skylights and go across the roof and down to the armory, where they would get enough weapons to take over the entire prison. When the alarm sirens went off, Cretzer, enraged and frustrated, began shooting the hostages in the cells. Shockley went completely berserk and yelled at Cretzer to kill them all. Most of the inmates went back to their cells when they heard the siren, certain that the plan could not succeed.

As Carnes would later tell the author, "The men began to return to their cells. Coy motioned for me to go back to the kitchen area with him. Hubbard was also with us. I had no idea what he was up to. Maybe there was an entrance to the tunnel from there. I knew there had been some digging back there sometime before, though I had not known what they had in mind. Maybe that was it. They were trying to get into the tunnel. And maybe they had now succeeded and this was where we were going. I really wanted to go to my cell, but a man with a gun had said, 'Come on!' and I went.

"When Coy began shooting out the kitchen windows at the towers, I knew with a sick feeling that it was all over. And I knew, too, that there had never been any tunnel. It did not occur to me to become angry. It was shock and horror that I felt. And the more so as we got into the cellhouse. We met Shockley and Hubbard, who apparently had heard shooting inside the cellhouse (I hadn't). Then we saw Cretzer's face. Hubbard asked in a tone that already knew the answer: 'Where's the guards?' 'They're dead,' said Cretzer. 'I just shot them.'

"I was stunned. I looked over at Coy guarding the recreation yard door with the rifle. Seeing the questioning look on my face, he lowered his eyes, nodding. Cretzer had a twisted smile on his face. Although he was now calm, he had gone berserk when he hadn't found the key to the yard. He had rushed over to cell 403, where six officers had been huddled on the floor. With Shockley and Thompson screaming, 'Kill the lousy screws! Shoot the sons-of-bitches! Shoot the bastards! Don't leave any witnesses!' Cretzer had placed a .45-caliber Colt pistol on the crossbar of the cell, begun screaming, and emptied two clips into the helpless men.

"Now Cretzer looked at me. He took the large kitchen knife Hubbard was holding and handed it to me. He ordered, 'Kid, go in there and cut the throat of anyone still alive.' In a daze, I opened the cell door and went in. There was blood and carnage everywhere. Officers Weinhold, Lageson, Miller, and Corwin were badly wounded; Burdette and Bristow were playing dead. As I looked around, Cretzer stepped over in front of cell 402 and shot Simpson in the back and Baker in the legs. Sundstorm was on the floor unhurt, but Cretzer thought he was dead.

"I emerged from 403 and said, 'Joe, they're all dead in there.

You got 'em all.'

" 'Check this other cell. Kill any still alive.'

"After remaining a few minutes in which I whispered to the guards to stay on the floor playing possum, I emerged and nodded. Cretzer then left the area with Coy.

"The sequence of events and details which developed after this are a bit hazy in my mind. There was walking and running back and forth from D to C; men had begun to come back out of their cells after it was evident the guards were not coming in immediately. One fellow had gotten a youngster in a cell and was committing oral sodomy on him. We learned later that he had the complete cooperation of the youngster. Anyone who permits this, or commits sodomy on another, is not a homo. This epithet is reserved for the passive role in sodomy, or the man who commits oral copulation.

"My attorney for the trial in 1946 asked me why I did not go to my cell when the siren went off, knowing obviously the break-out had failed. I told him the truth. I was afraid that they might become angry and come to my cell with the guns. It was not until I saw the others go to their cells that I went. By then, the hacks had been shot. At one point, Coy had motioned me to go with him to the kitchen area and, though I had wanted to go to my cell, I had gone with him.

"I told my attorney this. But telling the same thing on the stand in court was another matter. It was the false pride of the young. And he had not impressed me on the importance of this part of my testimony, so that when he questioned me about it I gave another answer. I would not admit fear in public. A moment of stupidity and ignorance, and I was convicted of murder, which, in a legal sense, at least, I was innocent of. I specify 'legal sense' because there is no escaping the responsibility that I had in the affair. I always come back to the one point: If I had not been in the thing, if I had refused to come out of my cell, if I had said no to Coy, would the thing have come off at all?

"But, the main thing is that I did not have on a uniform or any part of one, as some guards later said. I did have a club Coy had gotten from the gun cage. I did not hit or hurt anyone. I was not present at the first shooting. I feel I saved the lives of nine officer hostages, and this fact ultimately saved me from the gas chamber at San Quentin."

(Fourteen unarmed guards stormed through the front gate of the cellhouse and rushed down to B- and C-Blocks. The escapees fired at them from atop C cellblock, but the officers persisted in their search for the captives. One of the captives called out to guide them to the bloody scene in cells 402 and 403. Three of the captive officers were unhurt; one was shot in the face, one shot twice in the legs, and the others more seriously wounded, one fatally by the murderous gunfire that Cretzer had poured into the two crowded cells.)

By then, Coy, Cretzer, and Hubbard had already decided to die. It was odd how it happened. Coy asked Carnes what he was going to do and Carnes replied, "I don't know." Shockley had returned to the Treatment Unit, muttering, still half-crazed. Thompson had gone back to his cell in the main cellhouse. There were just four escapees left. For a moment, Carnes considered dying with the other three escapees. He recalled years later: "I thought it might be best if I died then. But there is always the optimism of the young. Old age and death are an eternity away."

Carnes knew if he survived, the least he could expect was a long term in lock-up. Maybe ten years. Before he could speak again, Hubbard said calmly, "I'm going to check out. This is all of it for me." Carnes knew what he meant, that he was going to die. Coy said, "Yeah, I am too. They'll never get their hands on me." Cretzer said, "We'll save one clip for ourselves, in case we need it."

Carnes recalled, "The odd thing about this scene was that they were so calm. It was like they were discussing some ordinary thing."

The group was silent for a few moments. Then Carnes made his decision. He told Coy he was going back to his cell. Coy shrugged. "All right, Old Man," he said. "Good luck to you." Joe Carnes thought it was ironic that Coy, the oldest of the group, called him, the young-

est of the group, "Old Man." As an afterthought, Carnes asked Coy
what he wanted him to do with the maps and the book of names.
Coy said, "Burn it." Carnes put the maps and book on the floor
in front of C-Block and touched a match to the little pile. They silently
watched as years of planning went up in flames.

As Carnes started toward his cell, he knew he had to cross
Broadway, where he would be in the line of fire if the east gun gallery had been manned. Coy told him to run for it. He did, and made
it safely across the broad corridor. "Sorry it turned out this way,
Old Man," Coy called to him. Carnes raised his hand in acknowl-
edgment and then ran to his cell and closed the door. He never saw
them again. Coy, Hubbard, and Cretzer retreated into the C utility
corridor, where they would make their last stand.

(Lt. Phil Bergen, soon to become Captain of The Guard, would later
write, "The battle, and it *was* a battle, raged on, *without let-up*, for
more than two days. We didn't have the slightest idea as to the location
and condition of the officer hostages. There was no way to find out!
When we rushed the gun gallery, Harold Stites was drilled through
the kidneys and died a few minutes later. I, myself, managed to pick
up four little hunks of iron, but otherwise was unscratched. Who
knows how the battle would have ended if it wasn't for General Frank
Merrill's Marauders, more than sixty heavily armed combat Marines,
who came over from Treasure Island. They drilled holes in the roof,
dropped grenades. Coy, Hubbard, and Cretzer were found riddled
with grenade fragments and rifle bullets in C Block's utility corridor.")

*   *   *

Clarence recalled asking himself thousands of times, "Why would
I not kill? And why the sickening horror of what occurred? Well,
only three years before, I had begun serving time. I had never known
criminals to this time (juvenile delinquents, yes, but not hardened
criminals), and I believed in God. I had been attending church services
regularly as part of my upbringing; I had been going to Bible classes

up to vacation time the year I first got in trouble, when I was sixteen. Like every kid, I had seen murder and such on the movie screen, but that is not part of reality, nor does one ever expect it to become reality. It is like a daydream, and not a part of real life. I had not been conditioned at any time in my life to accept the fact of killing another human being. That killing in Atoka, I knew, was an accident, though under law a murder. But I had not intended his death. The idea of just deliberately killing someone without real cause, like defending your life, was not part of my thinking. My family was religious and at one time my father had been a preacher. And now what was happening there was a nightmare!

"To this day, when I talk of that incident, I get upset, nervous, and don't feel so good. The shock of what happened left its mark on me, though it is not as it was immediately afterwards, the few years following. Back then, my voice would practically leave me when I talked of it and, consequently, I didn't speak of it when it could be avoided.

"I have been asked many times through the years by curious inmates, many of whom said they would rather be dead than in my place, whether I felt I had gotten the better of it when the jury gave me life instead of death as they did Thompson and Shockley. I have always answered this way: 'If I get out of prison before I am an old man, broken in mind and health, then I got the better of it. But, if I am old and my life is over, it would have been better if I had died in the gas chamber with Thompson and Shockley back in 1947.'

"But I never mention that there are other considerations. Most would not understand anyway, and those who tried would undoubtedly come to the conclusion that my attitude was just a lot of high-powered rationalizing. Where there are people, where there is existence, there is living. Who said that the prime motivation of an individual should be the pursuit of happiness, an elusive thing at best, and something that no one can give an adequate definition for? The secret of living is knowing where it's at for you. And one man's happiness may be another man's torture. A psychiatrist once said to me when he stopped at my cell during a visit to Alcatraz, 'You must learn to adjust to the conditions that prevail.' From this viewpoint, a man who adjusts in prison can build an existence for himself that will never be completely satisfying, but will at least save him from the feeling of 'I wish I were dead!'

"You learn to deal with hassles, and, as time passes, you come to realize that this is part of living anywhere. Hassles are a part of life. Any other view is just a dream. Prison can never be home, but, from time to time, a man may pause and think to himself that life is worth living, even in prison. There are moments. No man anywhere is ever completely contented or happy. And everything is relative. For myself, I have, as one dimension of my existence, read literally enough books to fill a fifteen-thousand-volume library, counting magazines. From the confines of a cell, I have seen life through the eyes of thousands who have lived before; I have been given a view of life and history such as I would never have known otherwise. I have a view of things as they were, or probably were, as they may be in the centuries to come, and I think I have come to an understanding with myself—a thing that is priceless! So if I die before I get out, and, in the instant of my death, I am asked if I would rather have died in 1947 with Thompson and Shockely, I would answer: 'No. I am glad I have lived!' "

2

The Plan

"A mile and a quarter of treacherous water . . . keeps men in Alcatraz."
Opening chorus for a ballad sung by Sonny James
commemorating the 1962 escape

Joe Carnes emerged from his segregation cell in the Treatment Unit in 1952, eager to rejoin the main population again. His legend had grown; there were new inmates who had heard of The Choctaw Kid and his role in the bloodiest escape attempt in Alcatraz history. The older men were impressed that Carnes had done his time in lock-up with courage. He had passed the weeks, months, and years in the company of incorrigibles, killers, and rapists. In spite of that he had not become hardened. He had the respect of most of the men in Alcatraz, including some of the officers. In lock-up he had gotten to know Robert Stroud, the so-called "Bird Man," who had taught him chess and at first routinely beaten him at it. They had played chess every night and eventually Carnes had become skilled at the game and could even beat his mentor occasionally. By the time he was released from the Treatment Unit, he was a chess expert and won the institution chess championship, a title he held for the next ten years.

Carnes was celled on the second tier of C-Block, across from the library, and he was assigned to the library detail. Ironically, he was given the same job Bernie Coy had held years earlier: the book and magazine deliveryman. He learned there had been changes during his time in lock-up. The rules had been eased somewhat. There were more programs aimed at rehabilitation, and, it seemed to Carnes, the inmate population had gotten younger. There was more inmate turnover; men came in, served three, five years or so, and earned their transfer from Alcatraz to another institution. Although there were indications of organized efforts to rehabilitate as well as punish, the official attitude toward the older, long-term inmates (Carnes, with almost 300 years to serve, found himself included in this category, even though he was only twenty-five years of age) was that these men were unredeemable—habitual criminals not worth the time and energy it would take to try to rehabilitate them.

Joe Carnes was faced with a lifetime of soul-crushing tedium in the demoralizing belief that he would never get out of Alcatraz. His family was poor, so it was unlikely they could ever visit him. The only thought that could sustain him was escape, and that thought never left him. Once again Carnes joined the ranks of those who dreamed of escape, who schemed and planned and constantly observed and evaluated all the little details of prison facilities and routine that might provide the key to freedom. It became an obsession with him, but he wasn't desperate enough to get involved in plans that included violence. He had had enough of trying to blast his way out. All that had gotten him had been another life sentence, and it had cost his co-conspirators their lives. A better way would have to be found. Over the years Joe had considered the clever plots and fantastic schemes of many inmates and he had heard the first-hand accounts of men who had successfully broken out of other institutions. Yet, like them, he had never found a way out of Alcatraz.

As the years rolled by, thoughts of escape continued to dominate his dreams, but more practical matters required attention. There was always the remote possibility of a parole. Other long-termers had been paroled; perhaps he would be, too, and return to the free world. In 1960 Carnes applied for a transfer to Leavenworth, hoping his record of eight years of good behavior might be in his favor. He believed the transfer would put him one step closer to parole, maybe as early as 1980.

Then, in October 1961, the siren song of escape reached his ears once more. Again he was approached by men who were determined to escape, men who wanted to know if Joe Carnes, with all his knowledge and experience, would participate in an attempt. But the Carnes of 1960 was a different man from the youth of 1946. Joe had served sixteen years and was a seasoned con. He wasn't about to become involved in a wild, irrational scheme concocted by newcomers, a scheme that might get him killed or, even worse, ruin any chance of parole. He also knew that the prison officers watched him closely, that he was still considered a big risk. Any out-of-the-ordinary movements on his part would cast instant suspicion on him.

But the man who approached Carnes was not a new kid with a wild idea. Allen West was also a smart, experienced con, two years older than Carnes, who knew his way around several prisons. Carnes had known West for some time. He recalled, "West wasn't a bad-looking guy and probably had even been handsome when he was younger." At one time Joe had wondered if West had been a "sissy," a prison "girl," when he was first in prison. He doubted it, and experienced cons like Joe were usually right about that. West was a tough guy, the type who expressed himself with a knife and wasn't afraid of anybody. Charlie Hopkins remembered Allen West in Atlanta, before he had gone to The Rock, and recalled, "West looked like Montgomery Clift, the actor. He liked to make faces like movie gangsters and talk and act tough. Allen West was a guy who liked to get involved in everybody's trouble. I never did trust West nor like him because he was so pushy and egotistical."

Joe Carnes knew West under different circumstances. Alcatraz was not as open as Atlanta, and West had little opportunity to display his tough-guy act. As soon as West spoke to him, Joe knew this was no idle conversation. West was painting cell bars on the middle level of C-Block near Joe's cell as he was returning from his usual magazine rounds. At first Carnes thought West wanted a favor. Usually this meant carrying a message or some contraband object to another inmate's cell, a forbidden act which the library book-magazine deliveryman was often urged to do. West hedged and wouldn't come out and say what was on his mind. Carnes became irritated.

"I know you can be trusted," West said.

"Get to the point."

"I have a way out," West said in a low voice.

Carnes was silent. The words cut deep, deeper than West could have imagined. Carnes knew from his tone that West was deadly serious and that if West told him details of his escape plan, Carnes could be considered a participant. He also knew that West needed him for some reason and was therefore inviting him in on the escape. West looked at him expectantly.

"I'll let you know tomorrow," Carnes said as he continued on his rounds. He had some serious thinking to do. He could imagine what West was thinking, and memories of Coy and the gruesome events of 1946 filled his mind. Was West the type to risk a crash-out? How many other inmates were in on it? Did the hacks already know about it? Was it a trap?

When the cells were opened the next morning, Carnes made a discreet inquiry about Allen West. Could West keep his mouth shut? Joe was satisfied with the answer. In the dining room West caught his eye and gave him a questioning look, as if to say, "Are you with us or not?" Carnes only winked, an undecipherable reply that made West angry. He was testing West's patience. If an escape plan had any chance at all, it must be constructed patiently and thoroughly. An impatient man had the cards stacked against him and would likely blow the whole scheme. And West already had a reputation for being impatient. When he played handball, for example, he couldn't wait to get started or for the next point to be played. When he played bridge, he growled when others took time to study their hands before making a bid. He hated baseball because it was too slow.

An exception to West's impatience was when he played chess. Carnes had often played the game with him and knew him to be deliberate and slow to make his moves. He studied every avenue of attack and defense before he committed himself. If Joe Carnes's theory that you could judge a man's character by the way he played chess was correct, West would be an excellent escape partner. Carnes knew West was one of the most intelligent men in Alcatraz. He was self-educated, well read, good at mathematics and logical thought. And Allen West got things done. Some men Carnes knew had the courage and ability to break out, but they seemed content to just talk about it. If West set his mind to it, Joe believed he would do it.

When Carnes returned to C-Block after completing his book deliveries, he immediately checked his telltale device to see if the hacks had searched his cell. (He sometimes placed a small wad of paper under the cell door or stretched a hair across the gap between the door frame and the door.) Joe's "telltale" told him his cell was undisturbed, but he was concerned that his little chat with West the day before had been noticed and had already brought the heat down on him.

As Carnes shelved books in the library that morning, he continued to reflect on West's invitation. He was sure he knew every avenue of escape from the prison. What was West up to? West's cell was on the lower outside tier of B-Block. It was darker there at night because the light from the exterior roof lamps that flooded some sections of the cellhouse was partially shielded by A-Block and a long shadow was cast across the lower tier of B-Block. When the cellhouse officer made the hourly cell count at night, he looked in on almost totally dark cells. In the early days the officer used a flashlight when counting the inmates, but by 1961 the practice had been discontinued. The officers still carried flashlights but, due to complaints from inmates who resented being awakened by the glaring light, rarely used them when counting. Since the cells across the aisle in A-Block were unused, the occupants of the north side of B-Block had a degree of privacy in their cells. West had probably maneuvered himself into that dark section of B-cell block for some illicit purpose.

West was serving his second term on Alcatraz. After he had finished his first term, he had returned to Florida on a detainer—but he had escaped. Following his capture, he had been sentenced under the Dyer Act (transportation of a stolen automobile across a state line) and returned to Alcatraz. Carnes figured that West had decided to escape because he had more state charges waiting for him after his Alcatraz term.

Joe was intrigued by the thought that West and/or his unknown co-conspirators had discovered something new, something nobody had ever noticed, perhaps a flaw in the prison's security system. Yet

Alcatraz security was reputed to be the tighest of any prison in the world. Purportedly, nothing was taken for granted and no officer was ever allowed to become lax in his duties. Joe remembered with a smile the old stories of the long lost "sealed entrance" to the Spanish tunnel. Surely it wasn't that. But whatever West had in mind, Carnes was certain it revolved around his cell location and his job as a cellhouse painter.

There were only three ways out of an Alcatraz cell—through the cell front bars or, if you lived on the bottom tier, as West did, through the concrete floor or the back wall of the cell. But if West managed to dig through the floor, he would find himself in what remained of the old Army citadel below with no way to get out. In 1946, Carnes had assumed that Coy had found a way through this basement area to the alleged sealed tunnel to the island dock. Once in the basement, he had been led to believe all Coy's group had to do was kick down a thin brick wall and they would be on their way. That, obviously, had not happened. Carnes was convinced that there was no tunnel (actually, such a possible escape tunnel *did* exist, and it could be entered from the old citadel area beneath the cellhouse).

West could dig out through the rear wall of his cell into the narrow utility corridor between the rows of cells. That led nowhere except up. If you climbed to the top of the triple-tiered cellblock you would still be inside the cellhouse, surrounded by concrete and tool-resistant steel bars.

If West did get out of his cell somehow, there would be three avenues of escape from the cellhouse: out an exterior window behind A-Block, through a roof vent above the top of A-Block, or through a roof vent above the top of B-Block. If West tried for the windows along the north wall of A-Block, his problems would be considerable. He would have to get through the tool-resistant steel bars over the window in a matter of minutes; otherwise, the roving lieutenant outside the cellhouse would be apt to spot him. Furthermore, the A-Block window bars were frequently inspected by the cellhouse officer. So West would have to cut through the bars quickly, climb out, replace the bars and seal them somehow so his exit route would be undetected, make his way unseen past the Warden's house, the doctor's house, the officers' apartments, and the children's playground to reach the water. Since no one had ever been able to solve the logistics, no one had ever tried to escape by this route. This left the roof vents above A and B cellblocks as a viable means of egress from the main cellhouse.

If West tried for the B-Block vent he had to get to the top of the cell block. And there were only two ways to do that. If he could get out of his cell via the cell door, West could go around the corner of the block and, assuming he had the door key, go through the steel door into the utility corridor. No one had ever been able to make such a key, although some had tried. Maybe West had succeeded. He was in a position to test such a key while working as a cellhouse painter. And Joe knew West was knowledgeable about locks and keys. From inside the utility corridor it would be possible to climb the sewer and water pipes unseen to the top of the cell block. The vent in the roof would then be within his reach.

A major obstacle to getting out of a cell through its bars was the "shakedown crew." Every few days at random times a special cell-inspection team came around pounding cell bars with rubber mallets. If a bar had been cut, the bar would ring differently from the others. The same team tested the window bars every week or so. But, strange as it may seem, there was no indication that they ever checked the bars in the roof vents. The officers probably thought that since it was almost impossible for an inmate to get to the roof vents anyway, it was unnecessary to check the bars. So if an inmate got that far, he might have a chance to cut, break, spread, or remove the bars.

The other possible route to the vent above B-Block was through the concrete wall at the back of the cell, into the utility corridor, and then up the pipes to the top of the block. The flaw in this plan was that it would be almost impossible to avoid detection of the lengthy digging operation it would take to get through the reinforced concrete cell wall, assuming one had the tools to dig with in the first place.

If by chance West did make it to the top of the cell block, he would find himself completely exposed and entirely enclosed in a cage of steel bars which ran from the top of the cellblock to the cellhouse roof, a distance of ten feet. Assuming he wasn't spotted by an officer patrolling the upper level of the gun gallery, he could get up to the vent and cut the bars and just possibly squeeze through. Of course, information about the diameter of the vents had come from guesses and estimates, since very few inmates were allowed to enter the area atop the cell block.

If West succeeded in getting out of his cell and into the utility corridor, the officers would most likely discover his absence from his cell during one of the hourly bed-checks, probably on the first such check following the 9:30 P.M. "lights out." Thus he would have only about an hour to reach the top of the cellhouse, somehow get through the roof vent and across the roof of the cellhouse, down to the water, and away. An impossibility, Carnes thought. If he got to the roof vent and found the estimates of its size were wrong, or if it had been sealed with concrete as some inmates had said, he would be in the hole for a long stretch, perhaps along with other inmates involved in the plan.

The vent above unused A-Block probably offered the best chance of success, if West could reach it. The bars in that vent, according to what Joe Carnes had heard while he was in lock-up, had not been replaced since the old days and were made of mild steel, like the steel used to reinforce concrete. They could be cut with a homemade hacksaw blade. That must be it, Carnes thought. West knew Carnes had some saw blades stashed away and that was why he had been invited to go along.

Joe Carnes had made the saw blades from three bread knives stolen from the kitchen. The knives were foot-long thin strips of hardened steel that fit into a bread-slicing machine. Of course, Alcatraz had no machine that would require such obvious weapons. In the mid-1940s three dozen blades had accidentally gotten into the kitchen inside a second-hand dishwasher that had been installed. Ordinarily, the guards on the dock made a thorough search of every item that arrived on Alcatraz. But on that day there had been a slip-up. No one knew how it happened, but one drawer of the washer had been overlooked and inside it were the thirty-six knives. The inmates discovered the knives and quickly spirited them off. Joe Carnes had three; he knew Larry Green had two and another had half a dozen. He didn't know what had become of the rest of them. Larry's blades had been used by Whitey Franklin and Joe Cretzer nearly twenty years before, when they had tried to cut their way out of D-Block. The Alcatraz administration had never admitted it, but it had been the greatest lapse of security in Alcatraz's history. At the time, the news media never learned of it. Probably to this day there are several of those blades on Alcatraz, hidden so cleverly that they have remained undetected.

The blades were razor sharp and serrated along one edge with small teeth about a half-inch apart, hardly suitable for cutting through steel bars. But Joe had cut teeth in the back edge of the blades, an arduous task that was typical of his ingenuity.

He had read about electroplating and been fascinated by its possibilities. He learned that he could use electrodes to etch metal, literally cut it to any shape. Even though at the time he had no escape plan in mind, the saw blades might come in handy if, someday, his chances of parole were lost. He managed to acquire a length of electrical wire, which he cut into several pieces. Then he made a simple but effective rheostat to control the electrical current from his cell to the steel blades. He wasn't worried about electrocuting himself because the cellhouse used direct current produced by the Alcatraz powerhouse rather than alternating current from the mainland, and he knew it was safe to handle. His rheostat was a ceramic cup he filled with water. The wires ran from his cell outlet to the cup, thence to the toilet bowl, where the actual etching would take place. He found that by adding a pinch of salt to the water in the cup he could start the water bubbling and the current flowing through the wires. If he added too much salt the water boiled and drew too much current. When that happened, it would blow a fuse at the end of the cell block. To his dismay, this happened several times. Each time the guards replaced the fuse and didn't suspect the cause was Joe Carnes hunched over in the darkness of his cell trying to manufacture hacksaw blades.

The toilet bowl, which would serve as his solution pan for the etching process, had to be sealed to prevent shorts by water coming in contact with the metal pipes connected to it. Joe used wax and masking tape to prevent leaks. He used masking tape cut in the shape of saw teeth to protect the steel blades where he didn't want the etching process to occur. Then came the moment of truth. He slowly applied electric current to the toilet bowl and was astonished to see the metal edge of the blades transformed: He successfully etched the three knives into reasonable facsimiles of hacksaw blades. But the crude teeth were dull and uneven. Much more work had to be done. The initial stages took only a few days. The rest took a year.

Whenever he had the opportunity, he would set up his electric etching system and work on the blades. He used a wooden tongue depressor, which he had soaked in a strong solution of salt water, as a file. He attached one wire to it, the other to the toilet bowl. With a mild current he was thus able to shape one tooth at a time until the blades were capable of cutting through steel.

Few men knew about Joe Carnes's blades, which he kept hidden in his cell. West was one of them. Maybe he had figured out a way those blades could come into play. The vent above A-Block, for example, was made of sheet metal and could easily be cut with Joe's blades. So could the mild steel bars across it. But this, Carnes thought, couldn't be it. The area was in plain view of the cellhouse officer patrolling the tier on the north side of B-Block. In addition, the inmates in B-Block would be able to see West up there sawing away at the vent. And if there was just one rat, or one loose mouth among them, the game would be over quickly. At the minimum it would take two or three nights to cut through the vent bars.

Maybe the roof vent above B-Block was West's target. Joe Carnes had special knowledge about that vent. In 1957 Red Winhoven, an inmate electrician, had worked on it. All the roof ventilators had had suction fans in them at one time. Over the years, as the electric fans had given out, they had been removed. The electric fan inside the vent shaft above B-Block had quit and Winhoven had been sent up there to repair it. He had removed the motor and fan when he found they were beyond repair, and they had never been replaced. Winhoven had also noted that there were two sets of bars inside the vent tube, one set of mild steel bars from the Army days (when the prison had been a disciplinary barracks prior to becoming a federal penitentiary in 1934) and a newer set of tool-resistant steel bars installed in 1933. For anyone trying to get through the vent in a hurry, these would be a tough nut to crack. Carnes doubted if West knew about the tool-resistant bars.

Then there was always the tricky problem of noise. Any attempt to break out of a cell would create a noise. Almost any sound inside the cellhouse echoed and reverberated as though the entire building were a drum. Even well-muffled sounds of digging or scratching or filing could not be entirely eliminated. The cellhouse was a noisy place, filled with the clatter of routine sounds, but an experienced cellhouse officer could readily detect a sound that was not "regular." The regular sounds—the rattle of a window in the wind, the clang of a knocking radiator, even the slapping of a wire on the roof in a high wind, and a thousand others—were familiar to the alert cellhouse officer. In addition, there were the sounds that a gathering of hundreds of men make: talking, whistling, snoring, toilets flushing, the plunk of a guitar, the rattle of a door as someone sweeps out his cell, the tap-tap as someone knocks the ashes from his pipe, the thump-thump-thump as someone exercises in his cell.

Over time all such sounds become normal to the ear and one no longer hears them. But if a strange sound, no matter how soft, intrudes, both officers and inmates will hear it. So any type of noisy work after "lights out" is impossible. And the noise from any surreptitious work during the day must blend into the background. The cacophony of the so-called "music hour" each evening might be a good time for digging and sawing, Carnes thought.

After reviewing all the convoluted obstacles to a successful escape from the cellhouse, Joe Carnes still couldn't figure out what West had planned. Then suddenly it came to him. The key! West must have heard that Joe had a key to the A-Block utility corridor door. Joe had gotten it years before from inmate Edgar Cook as payment for a boxing bet. Cigarettes were the usual medium for payment of bets in Alcatraz, but on one occasion Cook had been short of cigarettes and Carnes had known he had the key. Joe had offered to settle for the key, and Cook had accepted. Immediately Carnes had made three patterns by pasting paper over the key and cutting out the pattern with a razor blade. He had sealed the paper copies in the cover of a library book he'd assigned a false call number to—so that nobody could ever check it out by requesting it from the library card catalogue. Joe still had those paper copies, but he had lost the original, which he had stashed in the bottom of a trash can in the library. The cellhouse orderly had unexpectedly been ordered by the librarian to discard the old trash can since a new can had come in. Nobody but Joe knew the key had been lost. Now it occurred to Joe that West somehow must have heard about the key from Cook, who was no longer imprisoned on Alcatraz.

Carnes was glad he didn't see West for the rest of the day. He still needed more time to reflect on West's offer. There was one element that West had not considered, or had simply ignored. Joe Carnes was "hot." Whenever anything was missing that could possibly be used in an escape, Carnes's cell was the first one searched. West probably figured that since Carnes had been "clean" since 1946, the heat was off. In reality, most of the officers who had participated in the 1946 tragedy were still on duty in 1961. Some of these officers behaved as if the incident had occurred yesterday and they were still seething. Carnes was still the object of their suspicion and animosity. They were convinced he would never be paroled and that one day he would again try to escape.

Maybe West thought that the guards' suspicion of Carnes worked in his favor. They were so attuned to watching Carnes and a few other escape artists that they were unable to accept the fact that times had changed and their suspicions were two decades old. Other inmates, like West, could go about their business plotting to give their keepers the slip.

That night Joe couldn't sleep. He lay on his bunk pondering the possibilities. What would it be like on the outside? To be free and "out there" even for a few days would be worth the effort and the risk. To be out of this tomb of the living dead, to breathe free air again, to be with a woman, to do simple things, to pet a dog, to hear children laughing—what he wouldn't give! He had been sixteen when he had gone to prison, just eighteen when he had been buried alive on Alcatraz. Better to be dead than live even a few more years in this place. Guys like West knew what it was like to live out there and they knew nothing was worth losing that, not even life itself. West, and whoever else was in on the attempt, would rather die than rot in Alcatraz.

After lying awake until past 3:00 A.M., Joe dozed off, only to be awakened a few hours later by the "morning count" bell. He crawled out of bed and stood drowsily at the door of his cell until the count was over, and then he immediately got back into bed for another hour of sleep before going to work in the library. He often missed breakfast by sleeping in. The guards didn't mind.

All through the morning Carnes sat at his desk in the 10,000-volume library, pretending to work. He was tired and irritable and he knew that sooner or later West would show up. Around 11:00 A.M., West appeared at the library enclosure.

"What did you decide, Joe?" West asked in a whisper.

"I need to talk to you first."

"Hell, Joe, what's to talk about?"

"A couple of questions."

Since the library entrance gate in the C-D aisle was no place to talk, they agreed to meet later when they were less conspicuous. West returned to the library that afternoon, ostensibly to paint a radiator near Carnes's desk. After he started painting, Carnes came over to talk, making it clear beforehand that if he didn't like what West said, he reserved the right to walk away. West agreed to his terms.

"I wouldn't get mixed up in a suicide deal," West declared. "This plan will work!"

"First of all," he explained, "you're in a position to hide things for us. The library is a good place—best in the joint. And you can furnish information we may not have."

We? So there was someone else in the plan!

"You may know something we don't and it would mean the difference between success and failure. You know every inch of this place."

Carnes felt a twinge of doubt. How could West be so sure of success if he still had serious questions unanswered? And his statement indicated he was ignorant of the shakedown procedures; otherwise, he would know that the library was subject to the most intensive searches. The officers had years of experience; they knew hiding places even the inmates had forgotten. West should have known that. And who was in on the deal with West? Were they trustworthy? Carnes didn't even want to know who they were at this point.

West continued. "The skeleton plan is this. We'll go out the backs of our cells in B-Block, go up the utility corridor on the pipes, cut the bars in the roof vent and climb through the ventilator shaft to the roof, go across the roof and down the old bakery flue to the ground, and then go into the water."

Carnes's heart sank. The plan sounded simple, but it wouldn't work. It was insane to think you could work on that roof vent without being seen either by the hacks or the stool pigeons. At the first suspicious sound the officer in the gun gallery at the east end of the cell block could climb to the top tier and have a close look at the top of the cell block. And how could they get into the roof vent? This required tools. Getting tools from somewhere in the institution meant involving people. Someone was sure to talk.

Carnes put those questions aside for the moment. He had others.

"What about all the black guys in the cells behind you? They surely will know you're digging into the corridor. Do you know these guys? Will they hold tight?"

"I checked it out with 'Bumpy' and he says everybody down there can be trusted."

That impressed Carnes. He knew that Bumpy Johnson was the acknowledged leader of the black inmates in Alcatraz. He knew him well and played chess with him every weekend in the yard. Bumpy would not ask questions.

"What about the concrete back-wall of the cell? Red Winhoven and Tom Norris tried it years ago. It was too tough to get through."

West drew closer and whispered, "We have two star drills. Carbide tipped."

Carnes was again impressed. "You have to do some pounding to make a hole with those things."

"We'll wrap the drills in a towel or something," West said. "And work slowly with very light taps."

"You've got the drills? Or have they been promised?"

"We have them. They're brand new. Never been used."

So, Joe thought, the story he had heard years before was true. Like the introduction of the contraband bread cutting knives, the drills had gotten into the prison by accident. A shipment of woodworking tools, including drill bits, had come into the furniture shop. Somehow the two star drills had been included in the order by mistake. An inmate carpenter had recognized them as concrete boring tools rather than woodworking tools and concealed them in a safe hiding place. The officials knew only that two drills had been stolen, but they had made only a routine search. After all, what could an inmate do with a couple of drills that would only go through wood? Now it seemed that the drills had surfaced and were in the hands of a man who would damn sure use them.

"What about Red Winhoven and Norris?" West asked. "How come they didn't get out?"

"They planned on going through the floor into the dungeon and out the vent above A-Block. But they had only files. That's all they had, a couple of files. They gave up. Two files aren't enough to cut through a thick concrete door."

West was silent and went back to painting the radiator, no doubt thinking of Winhoven and Norris, two guys who had planned and dreamed and talked just like he was doing now. They had had to give up their dream. After a few minutes, he turned to Carnes and asked, "Any more questions?"

"Yeah. How long will it take to get through the cell wall?"

"I don't know. Longer than the roof vent. We should be through everything by Christmas."

Three months—a long time to have an escape in the works without being discovered.

"What about the roof vent?" Joe asked. "Can you get into it?"

"I may be able to slip past the motor and go up to the bars and work on them."

So West didn't know the motor had been removed.

"You know about the vent?" West asked.

"Yeah. I've schemed on it for a long time. Red Winhoven worked on that vent. He told me I could get through. And you're smaller than me, so you could probably make it."

Then Carnes gave West the good news about the missing motor and the bad news about the two sets of bars blocking the vent. West hadn't heard about the second set. He knew the difficulty of cutting through the tool-resistant steel bars.

"But it can be done," Carnes assured him. "In fact, it has been done. Doc Barker and his pals back in '39. They went through a D-Block window. Right over there." He nodded toward a window in the corner of the library.

"How in hell did he get in the library?"

"It wasn't part of the library then. They changed things after Barker and those other guys got out to make it harder to get to the windows."

He explained the technical details of the Barker escape to West. It had happened before Joe Carnes had arrived on Alcatraz, but some of the participants had told him about it. During the escape attempt by Doc Barker and four others, a window bar had been successfully cut. In those early days, D-Block consisted of old Army cells with mild steel bars, like the ones on A-Block. Henry Young was in a cell in D-Block right across the aisle from those windows in the south wall, and he had a file. Young managed to cut the rivets on his cell door that held one of the horizontal bars that, in turn, kept the flat bars from being pried apart. He was then able to slide the bar up, exposing a length of bar almost two feet long at the bottom of his door. He worked at it until he could raise the bar quickly, lower it quickly, and put dummy rivet heads in place. Then he began the slow process of cutting through one of the bars held by the slat. Every night he filed away at it. At the end of each session, he packed the cuts with putty and painted over them with matching paint he had managed to acquire during his work as a cellhouse painter. He mixed the metal filings with the putty so when the officers tested the bars with rubber mallets, they rang true.

When the bar was free and the slat raised, an opening at the bottom of his cell door was created that was big enough for Young to squeeze through. He would wait for the patrolling officer in the west gun gallery and the one cellhouse officer to move toward B-Block. He would then crawl out of his cell, sprint to the window, and file away at one of the window bars for a few minutes. He timed it perfectly. When the officers were due to return to the D-Block section, Young rushed back to his cell, to emerge and renew his filing when the officers again left the D-Block area. When a night's work was completed, he would carefully conceal the cut, return to his cell, slide the slat into position, and crawl into bed. At the same time, the other four escapees were cutting the bars on their cell doors.

The danger in this repeated performance was that the patrolling officers in the west gun gallery and the cellhouse might alter their patrol pattern and come upon Young while he was sawing at the window bar. One night it happened, just as Young had filled and painted the saw cut and was crossing the aisle to his cell. In the dim light the guard saw a figure in the area between the cell fronts and the outer wall. He contacted the shift lieutenant by phone and said, "There's a man over here out of his cell." Fortunately for Young, the gun gallery officer hadn't recognized him. By the time the lieutenant and the cellhouse officer arrived on the scene, Young was back in his cell pretending to be asleep. The officers checked all the occupied cells in D-Block and found everyone present. The hurried inspection revealed no sign that any bars had been tampered with on the windows or on the cell fronts. The officials arrived at an unusual conclusion: The gun gallery officer needed a rest. He was given two weeks' vacation. And, naturally, the other officers had a good laugh about it. So did the five anxious escapees in D-Block.

Forty days later, after the gallery officer was back from his restful vacation and on duty in the west gallery, he had the last laugh. Doc

Barker and his pals went out through that window one morning about 4:00 A.M. in dense fog. When all was ready, the five escapees slipped out of their cells, removed the cut window bar, forced their way through the somewhat constricted opening, and climbed out.

In a way, that affair would touch upon what was to happen more than twenty years later. Barker and four others made it down to the water undetected and were ready to swim for San Francisco and freedom. They picked up wooden debris along the beach for buoyancy and plunged into the icy water. But there was one among them who couldn't swim. He found a wooden chair on the beach and launched himself into the water hoping the chair would hold him up. It worked for some distance but it became clear he wasn't going to make it. His pals had agreed beforehand they would stick together, and when Barker saw that Young was in trouble, he ordered the swimmers back to the beach to find a better float for him.

By the time they reached the island shore, their escape had been discovered. The prison boat, loaded with armed officers, was already circling the island. Doc Barker refused to surrender and was mortally wounded by gunfire. Another inmate, Dale Stamphill, was wounded, and the other three, including Young, were captured. When the other Alcatraz inmates learned the fate of the escapees, a lesson was learned. Ever since that attempt, the popular feeling among Alcatraz inmates was that if anybody got out, he was on his own. If you couldn't carry your weight, you would be left behind. Every man for himself!

Joe Carnes filled West in on the deficiencies of the Barker escape. "In the first place, they didn't make dummies to leave in their cells to give them extra time. They just jumped in the water hoping the cell count wouldn't happen. If they had left dummies in their bunks, they might have had more time. Damned if I know what they thought. And they didn't have a plan what to do once they got to mainland San Francisco, let alone how they were going to get away from the island."

West looked thoughtful. "Anything else we should know?"

"Yeah," Carnes said. "There's a lot of heat on me. You should know about that."

West was not discouraged. "You decided what you're going to do yet?" he asked Carnes.

The moment of decision for Joe Carnes was here—work for a parole which he might never get, or try for freedom now. A failed escape attempt could mean death—or, worse, *capture*, and many more years in segregation, where he would probably die. He looked directly at West.

"Was there ever any doubt?"

"No," said West. "I know you too well. I knew you'd be with us."

Just three months to freedom.

3

The Key

"Six feet of chambered stone
The nation gives us for a home . . ."
from "Alcatraz," a poem by Ellsworth R. "Bumpy" Johnson

The next morning Joe Carnes awoke from a troubled sleep to another day of his routine existence. He was in a bad mood as he lined up for morning cell check. Then he remembered it was Saturday, and that gave his spirits a boost. Saturday meant a game or two of chess in the yard with Bumpy. He would go to breakfast, return to his cell, wait for the bath line, and then go to the yard. By then it would be about ten o'clock.

In the exercise yard Carnes waited for Bumpy Johnson to come out. Bumpy's tier would be one of the last out today, so Joe waited patiently for him by the "snitch box," the electronic metal detector by the entrance to the yard. In time, Bumpy came out as usual with his chess set tucked under his arm.

The two men played chess every Saturday on the top row of the "bleachers," the concrete terraces in the Alcatraz recreation yard that looked like giant steps leading up from the yard to the blank wall of the prison building. The steps were part of a huge retaining wall and foundation supporting the cellhouse. Inmates used the steps as seats from which they could view the handball courts and softball diamond and, in general, scan the entire recreation yard. The top step was reserved for only the most revered or feared cons, or maybe both. Having earned the privilege of sitting there meant you were always in the sun, if there was any sunshine to be had, compared with sitting on the lower, cold steps, where the sunlight was blocked by the high walls of the yard. From the top step an inmate could see over the walls. There was a panoramic view of San Francisco Bay, the San Francisco city skyline, the Golden Gate Bridge, and Sausalito.

The top step belonged to Bumpy Johnson. Any con who dared join Bumpy and Joe Carnes up there without Bumpy's approval was foolish. Sooner or later he would receive a severe beating or a knife puncture. A low wooden table had already been set up on the top step for Bumpy by inmates who worked in the yard. The table had been made in the prison shop, as had the two wood-and-canvas folding chairs that also awaited Bumpy and his companion for their chess game.

Bumpy Johnson didn't look like the popular image of a gangster. For one thing, he was black, and that didn't fit the Hollywood stereotype, the Cagney or Bogart image. He looked like a common, ordinary guy. Like the rest of the cons that Saturday morning, he had just showered and changed clothes, although the black cotton coat he wore needed to be laundered. This, too, was common among cons since the laundry would wash coats only twice a year.

To Joe Carnes, Bumpy was typical of the gangsters he had known in Alcatraz. They all seemed like ordinary men once they were in prison. At times there were hints that the Bumpy he knew may have been a different person on the outside. And even though he had never crossed paths with Bumpy on the outside, he knew Bumpy Johnson was not ordinary. He was a professional. He had risen in the underworld of Harlem starting in the 1920s until he was king of organized crime there, the self-proclaimed "Robin Hood of Harlem." When Dutch Schultz and his organization tried to take over Harlem in the early 1930s, they had to deal with Bumpy. After a bloody struggle Schultz decided to try elsewhere. There were whispers in Alcatraz that it was Bumpy who had ordered Dutch Schultz's death long after the war was over. Bumpy never talked about it. And Joe Carnes never asked. Once in a casual conversation Bumpy did mention killing in general to Joe: "These guys who have shanks and kill someone, knowing they can't get away with it, are stupid fools. When I've killed, it was decided in a closed room. And when we walked out of there, the man was as good as dead."

But to Joe Carnes, Bumpy Johnson was not a gang boss. He was a chess player and his closest friend. And Bumpy trusted Joe implicitly because the thirty-five-year-old "Kid" knew how to keep his mouth shut. Over time, Bumpy confided his entire life and career to his friend, and Joe always claimed, "Bumpy never once bullshitted me." Joe Carnes knew Bumpy Johnson came from a different world; it is unlikely that, outside of Alcatraz or some other prison, a smalltown Oklahoma boy would ever meet a big-time black gangster like Bumpy Johnson.

Ellsworth Raymond "Bumpy" Johnson was a legend in the annals of black gangsterism, a mercurial, endearing personality, a celebrated racketeer and folk-hero. In the mid-1970s, less than a decade after his death, he became the model for the popular hero in the *Shaft* movies. Yet for those who knew him, those who understood his role in the Harlem underworld, Bumpy was not only the brains and brawn behind the largest cocaine importing scheme of the 1960s, but one of the most vicious drug kingpins in United States history.

In his prime in Harlem, nothing about his appearance particularly distinguished him from hundreds of other criminals encountered on the New York streets and in the police lineups. Totally bald, with a round face, Bumpy was a powerfully built man of average height. Although he always appeared neat and well manicured, he wore dark sunglasses, which made him appear ominous. Unflinching, penetrating brown eyes bore into every passerby. And when he smiled, several gold teeth flashed in utter contrast to his deadly seriousness. A large bump on the back of his head, which he had acquired while playing basketball as a kid, had given him the nickname by which he became known to police, associates, and close friends for the rest of his life.

Ellsworth Johnson was born in 1903 in Charleston, South Carolina, the youngest child in a family of six. His father, William Johnson, one of the directors of the old Negro Federation Bank, had noble intentions for his son. Before Ellsworth was six, his father had fostered in him a desire for learning that would last a lifetime. Bumpy often boasted that by the time he entered kindergarten he had already read Captain Joseph Wilson's *History of the Black Phalanx*, the saga of northern black soldiers in the American Civil War. "That goddamn book was 528 pages long and I read every single fucking page," he told Joe Carnes.

Young Ellsworth was sent to the private Avery Institute of Charleston. After apparently breezing through the elementary grades, he was shipped to Brooklyn at the age of thirteen to live with an elder sister, who promised the boy would finish his education.

When Bumpy arrived in New York during World War I, along with a vast migration of other blacks from the South, he knew he would never return to Charleston. He graduated from Boys' High in Brooklyn and enrolled at New York City College, determined to become the city's first black lawyer. Although he was diligent in his studies, his father and sister were unable to support him after his freshman year. And, to make matters worse, he fought violently with his sister. As a result, he not only dropped out of the pre-legal program, but headed for Harlem, then considered by the New York cops the sin capital of the nation. Here, among the "reefer dens" and "King Kong joints," and amid the mixed mass of petty thieves, pimps, whores, gamblers, and hustlers, he found acceptance and easily adapted to the "wild and free-flowing" life.

At the age of fifteen, Bumpy began his criminal career as a runner for "Big Jim" Watson, a small-time black "policy banker" who would become his mentor. The game of policy was played by placing bets upon numbers selected in a way supposed to be known only to the banker. It was played daily by hundreds of thousands of lower- and middle-income people, who bet pennies, nickels, and dimes. By the time Bumpy arrived in Harlem, there were more than twenty black-controlled policy banks large enough to collect and pay off bets in an area spanning forty city blocks.

With gambling profits growing annually, and the dog-eat-dog mentality of mobsters infringing upon the territories of others, the "Roaring Twenties" in Harlem were a heyday for gunmen. More than four hundred black gangsters died violently within the eight square miles of Harlem between 1925 and the Stock Market Crash of 1929. The gun and razor blade were the final arbiters of all disputes.

Bumpy was intelligent and quick, and soon learned his mentor's shrewdness and savagery. When the popularity of "Big Jim" ended (he was "taken for a ride" in a sedan one day and had his brains blown out by a fellow he believed was his pal), Bumpy changed gangs and went to work for Madame Stephanie St. Clair, a migrant from the West Indies who became the Policy Queen of Harlem in the early 1930s. In addition, he was on the payrolls of Wilfred Brender and Casper Holstein, two other powerful Harlem policy bankers, as a numbers runner. In this milieu of sin, bathtub gin, graft, gangs, and daily deaths, Bumpy fought loyally for his employers like a dedicated lion. Between February 28, 1924, and October 1, 1931, he was arrested seven times and convicted twice, and spent two years in the Elmira Reformatory.

But Bumpy didn't mind. He had had his wealth and success. In fact, that sensation stuck with him throughout his life. He was often spotted by police flashing a "wad" of $20 bills as he casually walked along Seventh Avenue past admirers always eager for a handout. He commented to Joe Carnes one Saturday morning while playing chess in Alcatraz, "Everywhere 'Big Jim' or Casper went, doors opened. People treated them with respect. If you showed money, the world was yours—even for black men."

By 1932, when he was twenty-nine, Johnson had achieved the distinction of being Harlem's most ferocious sidewalk brawler, a human alleycat ready to scratch his way past all the other two-bit hoodlums who stood in his way. In one of the most bizarre and daring feats in Harlem's seamy history, Bumpy took on "Red" Dillard Morrison, one of New York's most feared underworld figures. Their deep-seated rivalry stemmed from an unprecedented all-black gang war over gambling, prostitution, policy, and narcotics territories. One night, the hot-headed "Red" Morrison countered a near-fatal gunshot wound from "Chink" Cunningham, one of Bumpy's bosses, by almost slicing Cunningham's head off. Bumpy, who had set himself up as the personal avenger for the popular "Chink," stormed past scores of hoodlum bodyguards standing outside Sydenham Hospital, had then through a cordon of ten cops, and into the emergency room, where he repeatedly punched Morrison in the face as he lay on the operating table as doctors and attendants stood by in utter horror. When Morrison recovered, he began stalking Bumpy single-handedly through the streets of Harlem. Finally, "Red" met Bumpy face-to-face on 114th Street at Seventh Avenue around two in the morning. There was no conversation, only an instantaneous shootout, in which more than thirty shots were fired and, remarkably, neither man was hit. The battle ended when "Red" ignominiously retreated into a tenement basement.

Bumpy was now "a man of mark." In the minds of most older black mobsters, this shootout had won him his spurs. Unfortunately for Bumpy, the gunshots attracted more than a dozen cops, who arrested him on the spot. For this act of bravado, he was slapped with a felony assault rap, which sent him to Sing Sing for two years. While in prison, he learned to play chess, got into fist fights, read voraciously, and planned his return to Harlem.

When he was paroled from Sing Sing in December 1933, police learned they were dealing with more than just another Harlem big-shot gambler and small time drug-trafficker. His conversations with other gangsters were always deliberate, brutally frank, and sparse, as if small talk cost money. He smoked heavily, loved rich food, and never drank liquor, except for an occasional glass of house wine in the expensive Harlem restaurants he frequented.

Bumpy was proud of relating how he had stood up to Dutch Schultz, the powerful New York beer baron who was maneuvering his men into the Harlem numbers and gambling rackets. According to Bumpy, those rackets were grossing more than $50 million a year from Harlem alone. However, on Black Wednesday in 1931, because of a leak in the Treasury Report of the Daily Clearance House balance, a "hot number," 527, bankrupted the bankers. That is, so many New Yorkers picked the winning number, which had been passed from one friend to another, the big bankers couldn't pay off.

For Dutch Schultz, who had originally believed the numbers racket was penny-ante until he learned what the blacks were raking in, this was the time to wrest control. He told the policy bankers, "I'll give you the dough to cover your losses, but I'm taking control of Harlem. From now on, I'll operate your business and give you a third of the profits." The Dutchman then hired William "Bud" Hewlett, one of Harlem's famed "Elder Badmen," to keep the black numbers bankers in line.

With Schultz entrenched in Harlem, Bumpy was approached soon after his parole by Hewlett, the new strongman for Schultz's syndicate. "You work for Dutch, or you don't work at all. Since I'm chairman of all the rackets here, I'm going to make you my protégé. You'll move up the ladder in the big-time white mob. But you work for us and no one else." Bumpy claimed he had laughed in Bud's face. He said he would never turn against the black numbers bosses for "the Jew bastards," or any other white man, for that matter. He said he had heard that Dutch had sent the Weinberg brothers, Sully and Girch, along with a couple "Kike henchmen," uptown to kill Madame Stephanie St. Clair, forcing her to hide under a pile of coal in her nightclub cellar until they gave up the search. "That wasn't very nice," Bumpy told Hewlett, adding, "I'll see the son-of-a-bitch in hell soon enough."

Ill prepared to fight for control of the numbers rackets, black bankers relented and were quickly absorbed into Schultz's new organizations. But Bumpy soon began a running, sniping campaign against the Dutchman wherever he could. Although he considered it anathema, Bumpy became an "ex-member of the Legs Diamond gang," which was out to silence Schultz for killing their beloved leader. Bumpy again allied himself with St. Clair, serving as her personal bodyguard. Faced with such open defiance and contempt, Schultz stepped back, heeding the advice of his underlings not to "mess with that crazy nigger who don't give a fuck for his life."

On the street once again after Sing Sing, Bumpy took stock of Harlem. The neighborhoods had been hit hard by the Depression, so the first thing he did was to organize bread lines for the hungry. Many of those who received free handouts would pay their respects more than thirty years later at his funeral. It was during this bleak period in American history that he became fiercely nationalistic, demoralized by the suffering of the poor he encountered all around him. "I am very bitter," he told Joe Carnes, "toward a white society which held out a Bible in the one hand and hit you over the head with the other." Deep mistrust of the white race would remain with him for the rest of his life.

There was another story from his Harlem days that Joe Carnes enjoyed hearing Bumpy tell. While Bumpy was in Sing Sing, a handsome young black man from Chicago named Ulysses Rollins wandered into Harlem. Handy with the stiletto, Rollins quickly caught Hewlett's attention. Hewlett was always on the lookout for new talent and "strong arms" to assist his new management responsibilities, so he introduced the midwesterner to the Dutchman, who hired him as one of his "boys." Rollins suddenly became a rising mob star. Not only did the new enforcer have all the money he could spend, but also the pick of any woman he wanted. Bumpy learned about the "foreigner" and began to trail him. Chances are that Bumpy, his narcissism injured, felt *he* was Harlem's top womanizer—and there was room for only one at the top.

It wasn't long before every street person realized that a two-man war had been declared. Never was Bumpy more of a predator. By all accounts, he was absolutely relentless. One night he caught Rollins at "Mom's," an after-hours spot on 141st. With an eight-inch switchblade, he slashed the cornered man thirty-six times. Rollins's left eye was cut away, leaving, according to one detective, "a bloody, grape-like orb hanging by a ligament from its socket."

Believing he had erased his only threat to Harlem's night ladies, Bumpy casually walked off to dinner at "Edmond's" across the street. But Rollins wasn't dead. By some miracle, he survived the jealous onslaught, although he was near death from loss of blood. Doctors at Harlem Hospital felt he was within a fraction of dying. Later Rollins commented, "I just wasn't going to die at the hands of that cocksucker." Less than a week later, still swathed in stitches and bandages, Rollins escaped from his hospital room and borrowed a couple of guns. After an all-night search, he found Bumpy in the old Alhambra Night Club at 126th and Seventh Avenue, where most of the Harlem mobsters hung out and where shoot-outs were so frequent they weren't even mentioned in the *Amsterdam News*.

Inside, Bumpy sat with his back to the wall. He saw the bandaged Rollins in the large wall mirrors at the entrance. Since this was no eerie phantom striding across the dance floor toward him, Bumpy decided that discretion was the better part of valor. He turned his table over and tore through the rear exit leading to 126th Street behind the Harlem Opera House. But Rollins, with only one eye intact, and a pistol in each hand, was already blazing away. Although none of the twelve bullets reached their mark, one managed to tear into the head of a young black girl dancing in the rear cabaret, killing her instantly. Rollins was captured and drew a thirty-year sentence at Sing Sing. Bumpy said he had, upon hearing the sentence, laughed all day.

Bumpy's personality and character were common gossip in Alcatraz. Both friends and enemies agreed he was ill tempered as well as kind, cultured as well as crude, hated as much as loved. Bumpy told Joe Carnes he had no regrets about the course he had taken. In the privacy of his friendship with Carnes, he even sounded philosophical. And, like so many mobsters Carnes came across, Bumpy could be sentimental. But never once did Joe Carnes have to remind himself that Bumpy was a cold-blooded killer who dealt in heroin and cocaine. He also knew Bumpy had strong ties to the Mafia.

Bumpy Johnson's involvement with the Mafia went back almost to the beginning of Prohibition. Bumpy, who maintained that he had foreseen the day when the public would accept Prohibition, knew that even when the government stepped in, the people could not live without liquor. So, he and "Red" Sanford, his best friend from his teenage years, who was as close as any brother could be, had a plan of action ready when Prohibition became law. But Bumpy also realized that he might have problems with the Mafia in New York, who would also be after control of illegal liquor. The two leaders of the Mafia at that time were Salvatore Maranzano and Joe "The Boss" Masseria. Lurking beneath them was Salvatore Luciana, known as "Lucky Luciano." Eventually Lucky would become the top Mafia boss after he had killed off Masseria and Maranzano, both of whom had befriended him. Lucky's lieutenants were Frank Costello, Vito Genovese, Meyer

Lansky, and Benny "Bugsy" Siegel, with Costello responsible for organizing the Harlem rackets.

Fearing for a long time that the Mafia would eventually annex Harlem, Bumpy formed his own black "Mafia." He developed a secret file, known only to Red Sanford. This file contained plans for the defense of Harlem when Costello made his move; it included the names, addresses, habits, and daily routines and schedules of all of Lucky's associates and hired assassins. They would all be hit when the appropriate hour came.

But, on orders from Luciano, Costello did not move directly against Bumpy. This was not because Lucky had feelings for Bumpy Johnson; the Mafia boss had heard about the "Forty Thieves," Bumpy's personal gang of formidable toughs. (A gang in Harlem called the "Forty Thieves" did indeed exist, but whether Bumpy Johnson, as he claimed to Joe Carnes, headed the murderous group, is open to speculation.)

The "Forty Thieves" were entrenched around 140th Street and Seventh Avenue in order to compete with the East Harlem Italian mobsters for the area's gambling, prostitution, and numbers businesses. No longer would the blacks pay off the "Wops." Henceforth, the "Forty Thieves" would recruit and employ their own hit-men and enforcers in order to ensure that the profits from the Harlem rackets would remain in black hands.

Rather than spark a war with Bumpy, Luciano had Costello persuade Joe Logan, Bumpy's black rival, to move against him. Bumpy, foreseeing this possibility, had established a "plant" in Logan's headquarters, someone who would know everything Logan was planning and was trustworthy enough to report back. It was a dangerous game—one error in judgment by anyone would result in death to many. To emphasize this point, and to let all know that no one was moving in without Bumpy's approval, Logan's number-one hitman was blasted into eternity within sixty minutes after the agreement between Costello and Logan was reached. Although it was a stern warning, it was also Bumpy's declaration of war.

Logan was practically hysterical with fear. How had Bumpy known so soon? He knew there was a potential rat in his headquarters and it scared the hell out of him. He called Costello, asking for a meeting in order to call off the deal. But Costello reminded him that when they had met they had shaken hands on the agreement. No, Logan would have to take Bumpy's place or die in the attempt. As he told this story to Carnes, Bumpy always added, "In the underworld, no agreement on a written contract basis is possible, so the handshake and a man's word serves as a contract."

Then, according to Bumpy, the hostilities began in earnest. It was a war of violence, not of words. Murders, hijackings of liquor shipments, bombings, the buying of loyalty or getting it through fear of death, double-crossings, attempts to frame or kill Bumpy, and Bumpy's countermeasures, were everyday occurrences. Bumpy knew he could eradicate Logan at any time, and he relished the anticipated coup. Even at his young age, Bumpy felt he had the instincts of a master chess player. And now, with control of all of Harlem at stake, he considered the war little more than a game of chess. Of course Logan, whom Bumpy considered stupid, was a mere pawn in the game. Bumpy was biding his time, all the while demonstrating his patience and power to Luciano.

From the very beginning, even before war had been declared, Bumpy knew victory would be in the form of peace with honor and the mutual understanding that Harlem would be his. Coexistence with the Italians would be the state of things, at least for the foreseeable future. To achieve this, however, Bumpy knew that he would have to demonstrate his efficacy. He understood that for one Mafia leader to kill another, it had to be approved by the mob's top hierarchy. And it was traditional that the members meet face-to-face. Bumpy was not going to be restricted by such a custom, though. If necessary, he could, and would, assassinate all the "Wop" leaders. Lucky realized that Bumpy already had this capability via his "Forty Thieves." He had learned enough to understand that his foe was neither weak nor ignorant. The war was well under way when Lucky admitted bad judgment in suggesting that Logan rub Bumpy out. Bumpy, who respected Luciano's cunning, knew that Lucky would sooner or later make amends.

Bumpy heard there was disagreement among Luciano's crew about pushing narcotics. Vito Genovese had always been the man who insisted on selling narcotics. And, in years to come, Vito would continually be at odds with Lucky. Bumpy knew about the internal squabble and used this knowledge to his advantage. It was not long before Bumpy learned that Lucky had ordered all his gunners to cease fire and withdraw from Harlem. With this good news, Bumpy decided that now was the time to put "Operation X" into effect.

Operation X was a brilliantly conceived plan consisting of two hits. Logan was immediately killed in his office by one of his top aides (Bumpy's plant). Then Bumpy ordered one of his men, who had been purchasing pure heroin from Vito for almost a year, to buy two more pounds. Vito, of course, had continued to import and sell the drug in spite of Luciano's warning to stop selling the junk. The buyer went to Lucky and complained that the heroin was not pure. The charge had its expected result of creating a rift in Lucky's organization. Luciano was enraged over Genovese's disobedience. But, since Vito had strong support among many in Lucky's mob, Luciano resisted the temptation to kill him.

As Joe Carnes sat in the Alcatraz recreation yard and listened to this tale over and over, it seemed plausible up to this point. That which followed, however, seemed a bit Hollywoodish to him. Still, when Bumpy told the story to his trusted friend, he spoke in a serious tone. With such a close friend, he didn't have to boast, impress, or lie. Hollywoodish or not, Carnes believed the account.

Bumpy next ordered the killing of one of Costello's closest associates while Costello was sitting next to him in the same room. The hit was made through an open window with a high-powered rifle more than half a block away. Bumpy's message was that he could have shot Costello, or any of the Mafia leaders in the room. And, for that matter, his hits could be accomplished in a manner not traditionally Italian. Bumpy would always laugh, "Those Guineas realized there was no defense against this kind of shooting except to crawl in a hole and pull the hole in after you."

Luciano and Costello knew in a flash that Bumpy was behind the slaying, and this was exactly what Bumpy wanted them to know.

He called Luciano the next morning and expressed dismay that rumors implicated him in the murder. As expected, Lucky, who had the mind of a statesman, a mind that could have rivaled the best in international diplomacy, saw Bumpy's game. Realizing that with Logan out of the way he would have to conduct an all-out war with Bumpy's "Forty Thieves" for control of Harlem, Lucky threw in the towel. He was in a precarious situation at the moment and it was all this "nigger's doing." Instead of flying into a rage, Luciano felt a deep respect for his wily adversary. Logan had been a fool. Bumpy was certainly nobody's fool. Who was better qualified to run Harlem for the Mafia than a man who knew how to fight his way to the top?

Bumpy, of course, knew that Lucky would have to conclude three things. First, the price of fighting for Harlem was great: Too much outside publicity would be generated. Second, a man as gifted as Bumpy could bring in millions, so why spend so much trying to usurp control of Harlem? Third, Lucky realized that every major city had a black population. If a black leader respected by the underworld pumped Mafia money into these areas, who could know the beneficial results? The possibilities were intriguing. Once Lucky got to thinking about it, Bumpy knew, he would realize that Mr. Ellsworth Raymond Johnson was the only man for a joint venture.

There was still some unfinished business to take care of—namely, retribution for the Mafia man who had been killed. But who had done it? There was a risk if the wrong man was killed. Lucky pointed out the benefits of peace. He explained that the "Forty Thieves" were a part of a rising black awareness in Harlem and this spirit could fuel an unprecedented conflict lasting decades between the Italians and the blacks, spelling the ruin of everyone. Luciano shuddered at the thought.

According to Bumpy, Lucky called him back later that day and laughed, "Mr. Johnson, I know you had nothing to do with the affair." Bumpy said, "I'm glad you called. There are some things I want to discuss with you. Why don't we get together and talk?" Luciano answered, "Name the time and place."

Bumpy smiled to himself. How sweet victory was! He knew long before Luciano that they would one day become partners. It was inevitable. It was a pity, Bumpy told his friends, that it had taken a war to bring this about. But now, he not only had won the war, but also had won the Harlem empire. The potential for money-making was limitless.

The peace dinner, held in one of Manhattan's "Little Italy" restaurants, developed into a lavish banquet. Not only were all of Luciano's people there, but many out-of-towners, including Joe Torrio and Al Capone of Chicago. Luciano, Costello, and Bumpy talked briefly before the others arrived. And Bumpy, being well aware that Costello needed to save face, volunteered to contribute to a fund handled by Costello to pay off local politicians when needed. It was a very simple pay-off fund, a new concept that the Mafia soon put into regular operation. (In years to come, it would generate millions of dollars annually. When the heat finally came down, during the Kefauver investigations, it became apparent that there had been wisdom in establishing the "fix" with certain political types. As far as the Italians were concerned, there was no problem in placing Mafia money in the hands of "the nigger" for "investment" in the black ghettos of America's other major cities.)

During the banquet, Bumpy, who sat with Luciano and Costello, was introduced. After Lucky explained Bumpy's new position with the mob, he invited his guest to speak. "As the only black man present among all you whites," he began, "I feel like a fig in a bowl of milk." Everyone laughed. Then Bumpy said the usual expected words of goodwill. He concluded, "For years you have been boasting you have a Jewish Mafia headed by Bugsy Siegel. Now you can boast you have your first black Mafia."

Not only was there a roar of good-natured laughter, but there was also genuine acceptance and respect in the faces before him. Bumpy thought, "Whatever lies ahead, it has to be good." Ten years later, he would encounter Lucky in Dannemora Prison, where he would save the life of the Mafia chieftain.

Bumpy told Joe Carnes about those days when he ran around with some of the most socially prominent people in Manhattan. With

a coterie of actors, actresses, producers, composers, and other celebrities and socialites, he loved buzzing the garden and penthouse parties
where, as he admitted, "I was the only nigger gangster they could pet."
They would invite him downtown for all-night drinking and drug
binges, or to Sunday morning brunches on Westchester estate lawns,
while he, in turn, took them on tours of the Cotton Club, the Harlem
Uproar House, the Ubangi Club, Edmond's, "Mom's," the Rhythm
Club, the Turf Club, the Brittwood, Connos, and many others.

In those relatively peaceful days and with the Harlem rackets
prospering under Mafia-controlled Casper Holstein, Max Romney,
Heinz Miro, Alex Pompez, Leo Altman, and others, Bumpy had time
to relax. He had made his peace with Luciano, and now he had time
for numerous affairs with high-society white women who drove over
to Bumpy's apartment on Seventh Avenue in their Stutz-Bearcats,
Marmons, and Rolls-Royces. Bumpy's favorite lover was probably
Helen Lawrenson, who later wrote in her autobiography, *Stranger at
the Party—A Memoir*, "I don't want anyone to think that I used to
sneak up to Harlem for assignations in the manner of many white
women of that era—those cheap Hollywood stars and anonymous
New York beauties who wanted cheap sex thrills with the popular
black gangster. There was nothing clandestine about my love affair
with Bumpy. I loved the man and this was long before it became
a fad for the white woman to love a black man."

Bumpy Johnson's free-wheeling days came to an end in 1937.
On August 31 of that year, Bumpy was sentenced to Sing Sing for
six to ten years for first-degree felonious assault. Bumpy had become
concerned that the traffic in women was fast becoming Harlem's
number-two industry, so decided to take on the street pimps single-
handedly. Without the intrigues and contract murders of the numbers war to occupy his time, he stalked the pimps one at a time.
Some had various parts of their anatomy slashed away, others disappeared, and a few had their brains blown out. His chief target, "New
York Charlie," who had said some unpleasant things about Johnson's
ancestry, emerged from his stronghold one night and found himself
being cut from ear to ear by a lone man who had been waiting in

the shadows. Charlie needed ten months to heal. Bumpy, who was arrested that evening, went to the penitentiary at Sing Sing for the full term.

The *New York Daily Mirror* editorialized, "Harlem is in a state of rejoicing that his reign of terror is over." It was Bumpy's twenty-first arrest and conviction. "They'll be calling me Uncle Bumpy by the time I get out," he joked as he was led away. He would eventually serve the entire ten years, more than one-third of it in solitary confinement due to his violent nature.

"To survive here," he wrote, "you have to be a whole lot of man." White inmates who made the mistake of calling him "nigger" were attacked instantly by the enraged Bumpy, who had fashioned sharp knives out of stolen spoons. Bumpy told one story of how a big-wig white convict had challenged him to a duel in the recreation yard. "But the white dude stole on me. He plunged the knife into my chest when it was given to him. It broke as it hit my chest. The turnkeys grabbed us and took us to the warden's office. Hell, I was not a model prisoner. Before the warden had a chance to open his mouth, I grabbed a marble inkwell from his desk and smashed it in the convict's face."

When Bumpy was released on March 7, 1948, he was forty-five years old. "When I got back to Seventh Avenue," he told Carnes, "Harlem was changed forever. Dewey, the only honest son-of-a-bitch I've ever seen in the D.A.'s office, had broken up all the rackets. All the sinners and evil-doers had abandoned ship as if someone had poured rat poison on the decks." It was true. Most of his buddies were retired, dead, or in prison. There was no welcome, and no one cared that he was home, including all the celebrities and high-society women who, a decade before, had considered him a hero. The Mafia, led by the likes of Vito Genovese, Frank Costello, and Albert Anastasis, was in control.

Bumpy, who had no intention of working with his hands at an honest job, returned to the numbers racket as the quickest avenue to bankroll his depleted savings. Within six months of his return, he was arrested in a gambling raid. Appearing before a Manhattan magistrate, he explained, when asked his occupation, "Your Honor, I am a professional gambler. That's all I've done all my life. There's no other way for me to make a living. That's what I do best and I'm an artist at it." The judge, surprised by such honesty, dismissed Bumpy with the comment, "Anyone that truthful about himself has to have an ounce of goodness in him." Meanwhile, Bumpy knew his rivals were waiting for him back in Harlem.

In the months that followed, Bumpy was shot at numerous times. "Each time," Bumpy said, "my swiftness, knife, and guns got me safety." When his enemies began tipping the New York Police Department on Bumpy's criminal activities, including his daily whereabouts, a number of organized raids occurred. Bumpy then called upon the editors of Harlem's five newspapers and gave them proof that the police, especially the black plainclothesmen, were taking bribes. And, to make matters worse, he claimed that every white cop in Harlem was a racist who had targeted him personally.

Bumpy now started to go legitimate by investing in a cleaning and dyeing business. In October 1949, however, he was again arrested, this time by federal narcotics agents for heading a major drug-selling scheme. He later insisted he had been set up. He once told Carnes, "Dope you keep at a distance. Those raps sting. In 1949, I was deliberately set up, framed, by the Wops, or 'Big Joe' Richards, who took over from Bud Hewlett. Hell, for all I know, it could have even been the FBI. Every nigger in Harlem knows I drove the pushers and pimps out of there."

Carnes always believed him. Selling dope at this stage in his life would have been totally uncharacteristic of him, especially after a ten-year stretch at Dannemora. Even his rivals, although ecstatic at his predicament, scoffed at the notion that Bumpy had turned junk-dealer. But the Feds had a witness, Freddie "Flash" Walker, a two-bit hood Bumpy had befriended and hired as a numbers runner. Bumpy was headed back to prison, this time for another ten years. At the hearing, Assistant U.S. District Attorney Mortimer O'Brien hailed the verdict, adding, "Thank God we're putting away the most vicious and dangerous criminal in Harlem." Bumpy's lawyers appealed the decision.

While free on appeal in June of 1952, Bumpy was riddled with four bullets, three in the belly and one in the chest. He had been shot by Robert "The Hawk" Hawkins, a dangerous young black man whom Bumpy had ordered to stop using dirty language in front of a group of young women seated at Bumpy's table in the Vet's Club, an after-hours joint on Lenox Avenue. Hawkins, who was embarrassed by the admonishment, quietly left the nightclub, only to return within a few moments brandishing a pistol. Bumpy, who was unarmed, tried to walk slowly away from the confrontation but was shot point-blank.

At Sydenham Hospital, where a few years before he had beaten the hell out of "Red" Dillard Morrison, doctors struggled to keep him alive—and succeeded.

In November 1953, the U.S. Supreme Court refused to hear his case. Bumpy, now fully recovered from his gunshot wounds, was first dispatched to the federal penitentiary at Leavenworth, and then transferred to Alcatraz—which he preferred, since there at least he had a cell to himself. Bumpy would serve ten years in the cold, infamous island prison. On Alcatraz, the other inmates showered him with all the respect and courtesies due a veteran criminal of Bumpy's stature. The word was that Bumpy still had powerful contacts on the outside who kept him informed of events in the Mafia world. And it was rumored that Bumpy was so powerful that he could have a man killed in another prison just by giving the word. Charlie Hopkins, who was a good friend of Bumpy's on Alcatraz, recalled, "Bumpy was a sensible guy and well read. He liked to beat the system and he had the brains to do it." Bumpy became an expert in chess, the only game he ever played. The only inmate who could match him in chess was Joe Carnes.

*   *   *

While Bumpy Johnson and Joe Carnes sat peacefully in the warm autumn sunshine of the Alcatraz recreation yard, leaning pensively over their chess board, Carnes couldn't concentrate. Allen West's words of the day before still ran through his brain. *Escape. A way out.* Exhilarating as the thought was, there was still a piece missing. Joe Carnes knew that previous escape attempts had all focused on getting out of the cellhouse—get to the water, get free of the bars, the walls, the guards, leave Alcatraz behind. But then what? Swim to San Francisco? Even if you made it you would emerge from the water like a half-drowned rat, exhausted, cold, and confused.

What chance did a con have walking up Market Street in his dripping prison denims? Steal a car? Take a hostage? Most of the inmates of Alcatraz had clearly demonstrated their deficiencies when it came to making it on the lam. Many, including West, had escaped from prisons before, but none had managed to evade capture; their presence on Alcatraz proved that. It was one thing to plan a clever escape from the island, quite another to organize a clean getaway once ashore.

What was needed was a contact, an outsider, who could arrange a disappearing act once they were free from The Rock. Carnes knew that most inmates had little chance of arranging anything that sophisticated. Some had a few friends on the outside, usually men they hadn't seen in years. But it was all but impossible to contact them from the inside. Family? Few had family members with the wherewithal to execute a getaway. It took money, coordination, and planning—and most inmates came from poverty-ridden families. Maybe the others in the plot with West had contacts on the outside. Maybe that was why they had been chosen to participate. Just like Joe Carnes had been invited along because of his inside knowledge, maybe some other con had been invited because of his outside contacts. Joe didn't know of anybody with that kind of connections. Now he was anxious to know who the other men involved were.

Joe Carnes mulled over such thoughts as he watched Bumpy ponder his next move. He looked at Bumpy. Bumpy was the only man he knew with powerful friends on the outside, and the only man he trusted. Was he the key? He wondered if Bumpy knew about the plot. He generally knew about everything that went on inside The Rock. Bumpy's absolute power was in Harlem, but his organization and influence were broad. He had once remarked to Joe, "I've got investments in Seattle, Frisco, and L.A."

He wanted to ask Bumpy if he knew about West's plan but knew he could not, just as he could not ask West who the other participants were. He looked across the yard to see if he could find West. Maybe West would inadvertently reveal the identity of the others. West was sitting below him with Frank Morris on the lower steps near the handball courts. Morris had taken off his shirt and the two appeared to be in casual conversation. Was Frank Morris in on it? His cell was next to West's on B-Block. He was a logical choice. One could act as lookout while the other dug. And Morris had escaped from every jail he had ever been in—so far.

"Joe," Bumpy said, "it's been your move for at least a minute. You just keep sitting there staring at the yard."

Bumpy's words startled him. "Sorry. I was thinking."

"Yeah, I know. And I have a pretty good idea what you were thinking about. Maybe we should just cancel this until this afternoon. Maybe by then things will be resolved."

Carnes agreed. He wasn't sure if Bumpy was referring to the rumor circulating that a black inmate who had "ratted" on another man was marked for death or if he knew about West's escape plan. Bumpy soon made it clear.

"I had a talk with West yesterday," he said. "He has problems to work out, like stashing stuff. I suggested he talk with you. I could tell by the way he reacted he'd already been around to see you. So, I know the score and you know the score. Just wanted you to know I know because there's a little twist in this thing to come around at the end that West doesn't know about yet."

Joe Carnes was ready to recall these words a thousand times in the days, months, and years after the escape. But, for the moment, he just nodded at Bumpy. Had Bumpy Johnson already agreed to make contact with the outside? Arrange for a boat? Was he going along too? After a moment Joe said, "What do you mean about a 'little twist'?"

"I think you know what I mean, Joe. I suspect you're in this thing up to your neck. So this was something I wanted you to know."

Bumpy got up and the game was over. So was the conversation. Joe Carnes looked down the steps to where West still sat with Frank Morris. They had been joined by the Anglin brothers, John and Clarence.

The Anglin brothers? Could these two be involved? That didn't make sense. They were nobodies.

4

J. W. and Clarence

"Far more crime occurs in the human soul than in the external world. The soul of the criminal, as manifested in his deeds, often affords an insight into the deepest psychological processes of humanity in general."

C. G. Jung

John William Anglin and Clarence Anglin were not well known on Alcatraz. They were relative newcomers. John had arrived from Leavenworth on October 24, 1960, and brother Clarence on January 16, 1961, from the same institution. They were not the hardened criminals one usually thinks of when Alcatraz comes to mind. As so many before them, they had "earned" their tickets to Alcatraz by attempted escapes from other federal prisons.

Clarence and J. W., as John was called by his family and friends, were two of fourteen children, seven boys and seven girls, born to George Robert and Rachel Anglin of rural Donaldsonville, Georgia. George Anglin was a semiliterate farmer who had served in the Army during World War I. He and his wife were honest, hardworking simple folk who struggled during the Depression to raise their large family. One son died in infancy, but the rest were strong, healthy children who helped with farm chores as soon as they were able. The kids attended school in Donaldsonville and went to the Baptist church regularly, but the grinding widespread poverty of the region in the 1930s took its toll. One by one, the Anglin children dropped out of school and went to work to help provide food, clothing, and shelter. The family followed the crops in spring and summer as migrant farm workers as far north as Michigan.

During World War II, the family moved to Ruskin, Florida, a "wide spot in the road" about twenty miles south of Tampa that consisted of a café, a store or two, and a few houses. They settled on a small truck farm a mile east of Ruskin, in a modest but comfortable farmhouse. The older children went to work and the younger ones attended school. The three boys in the middle—Alfred, fifteen; J. W., thirteen; and Clarence, twelve—became an inseparable trio, with Alfred as their leader. Their older brother Rufus remembers that "the boys seemed to have a code. They could communicate with each other in ways nobody could understand." J. W. and Clarence were particularly intuitive and could sense what the other was thinking. The boys were high-spirited, filled with youthful energy, and adventurous. Clarence was the first to let his willfulness lead him astray. He began to play hooky from school and run with another boy, who committed daring but foolhardy acts of petty larceny. On one occasion, the boy stole money from his mother's purse and went to Tampa, along with Clarence, to buy new clothes. When Clarence returned with his new trousers, his mother noticed them but didn't press him about it. "It wasn't long before he came across with the truth," she recalled. He readily confessed and was punished by his father. Because of his early misdeeds, Clarence was often blamed whenever anything went wrong or was missing. But he was a good-natured boy and took his often undeserved punishment in stride. Clarence's mother hoped he would straighten out when the family went north to pick cherries. Robert and Rachel Anglin took their brood to Traverse City, Michigan, every May.

Young Clarence and J. W. always made the most of the family's migrations, finding fun and adventure at every opportunity. They loved to swim and were always the first of the Anglin kids to tackle Lake Michigan when they arrived each season. Frequently in May, the weather was cold and sometimes there was still icy slush from the previous winter in the lake, but that didn't deter Clarence and J. W. Their brother Robert recalls how they would swim straight out into the lake, side by side, until their heads appeared as little dark dots on the surface. Nobody worried about the boys, however; they had demonstrated their swimming ability at an early age. All the Anglin kids were good swimmers, and enjoyed summertime swimming holes, as all kids do. J. W., in particular, liked to show off by diving from highway bridges into shallow mudholes along Dry Creek near their home or by catching alligators in the Little Manatee River and dragging them out of the water. The boys made boats too, out of scrap wood and anything that would float. They practiced their navigational skills along the beaches of Tampa Bay and in the Little Manatee, which ran through Ruskin. J. W. became such an expert swimmer that one summer, when he was about fourteen, he got a job as a lifeguard at a public pool near Ruskin. In school, he won boxing and swimming medals. Once, at Lake Michigan, J. W. found a way to make some extra cash. A man lost the outboard motor of his boat near the dock and offered fifteen dollars to anybody who could retrieve it. Nobody wanted to take on the deep water but somebody did run to get J. W. He hurried to the scene and dove in the murky waters and found the motor on the first dive. He came up and said he thought he could find it for twenty dollars. The man agreed and J. W. dove back down and attached a rope to the motor, which was then dragged out. On another occasion J. W. and Clarence pulled a boy from the cold water, the son of a policeman, who got muscle cramps and couldn't make it back to shore.

The boys grew tall and strong and quite handsome, according to the girls around Ruskin. Clarence was the taller of the two boys, standing just under six feet; he weighed about 170 pounds. J. W. was about an inch shorter than Clarence and twenty pounds lighter. Both were easy-going and friendly, quick to smile. Each had a stubbornly independent streak, too, which sometimes got them into trouble.

When he was older, Clarence told his sisters a story about his and J. W.'s troubles picking fruit up north one season. They had been so poor they had survived on beans and one ham bone. When they headed south in the fall, they stashed the bone in the wall of their cabin so they could make soup with it the following season. But it was gone when they returned. J. W. told about how they had tried to get by just eating cherries as they picked. But they had gotten sick and tried to counter the effect of the cherries by eating peanut butter. That hadn't worked either.

When the family returned to Florida in 1945, Alfred went to work for the Del Monte fruit packing plant. J. W. and Clarence were caught in the middle—too young to earn money, too old to ignore the benefits of quick cash when it came to impressing girls. Frustrated by the poverty that surrounded them, they longed for fancy clothes and money to spend for movies and dates. Their childhood mischief and pranks, such as swiping watermelons and stealing tractor batteries, became teenage misdemeanors. Fourteen-year-old Clarence was caught by the police breaking into a service station one night. He was sent to the State Industrial School for Boys at Marianna, Florida. It was here, Clarence claimed later, he was taught to pick locks as part of the work program. He was released to the custody of his mother a year later.

Despite the lessons of his first serious offense, Clarence was soon in trouble again. This time he and J. W. were arrested after they burglarized a store in South Tampa. They pleaded guilty and both were sent to the state industrial school for a year.

When he got out, Clarence got into one jam after another. His parents were at a loss to explain Clarence's behavior. His mother insisted he and J. W. were good boys and that Clarence's troubles with the law began "after he started going to motion picture shows with girls." Alfred and J. W. were soon getting into as much trouble as Clarence. All three boys became experts at slipping locks and hot-wiring cars. They would steal cars to use in a burglary, or just for joy-riding. They never went in for strong-arm robbery, or assault, and they never possessed or carried guns. Their brother Robert insists they never intended to hurt anybody. They just wanted easy money for a good time, and the adventure of stealing it was half the fun. But the lure of quick money took control of their lives and headed them inexorably toward Alcatraz. But in the meantime, the boys were preoccupied with girls. J. W. became engaged three times, each time to one of three sisters, starting with the eldest.

The boys were flashy dressers. They loved fine clothes and were determined to have them. A continual succession of girlfriends stretched their meager income from the fruit-packing plant to the breaking point. No matter how hard they worked—and, by all accounts, they were both good workers when they set their minds to it—they always seemed to be broke. J. W. kept gasoline in his car for his numerous dates by falling back on the "Georgia Credit Card"—a siphon hose. The boys became expert at late-night raids of service stations. They would pop open a window, let themselves into the darkened station, and help themselves to batteries, tires, inner tubes, and other auto parts that could be quickly turned into cash. They never wanted confrontation; they had an aversion to violence and the possibility of hurting somebody. But once a local business closed up for the night, it was fair game.

As slick as they were at breaking and entering, they were amateurs when it came to getting away with their crimes. Clarence almost always got caught, and he always owned up to his guilt when he did. All three boys clearly knew what they were doing was wrong, yet never vocalized any remorse or offered excuses for their acts. They just accepted their punishment and paid the price. It seemed to their brothers and sisters that J. W. and Clarence thought only of immediate gratification. Get some money—spend it. Clarence routinely borrowed money from brother Robert, with the promise to repay the debt. He always paid, too, as soon as he came into some cash.

By 1950, the boys had outgrown their "juvenile offender" status. They were adults and treated as such by the authorities. In 1951, Clarence and Alfred were caught after a burglary in Manatee County, Florida, and sentenced to four years in the state penitentiary at Raiford. Maybe what they had done finally hit home. The thought of being a convict behind bars for years on end was unbearable. Six months later, Clarence and Alfred escaped from a road camp where they had been assigned. A new pattern began. Over the next six years, Alfred and Clarence escaped from jails and road camps with almost monotonous regularity. Their brother Robert recalled, "They were always looking for a hole to get out of."

When the boys were at large, the Anglin family knew they wouldn't try to come home; they wanted "to protect the family." Sometimes, though, Clarence would appear at the door in the dead of night for a quick change of clothes. He wouldn't say where he was headed, nor would he mention who the other men waiting in the car were. Just a brief stop, a few words: "Don't worry, we're all right," and then he was gone. Days or weeks later, the family would read that he had been captured and returned to prison—with an even longer sentence.

Alfred was particularly clever at escaping and often planned the brothers' escapades. When asked about the dangers of sloshing through swamps and ponds filled with alligators and poisonous snakes, Alfred said, "Snakes won't bite convicts."

Clarence's last escape, his fourth, was from a road camp at Fort Myers, Florida, in 1957. Alfred made his last Florida escape in 1953, and he remained at large for the next five years. J. W. was released from Raiford in 1953 and returned to Ruskin, where he attempted to lead a straight life.

On January 17, 1958, the boys reunited for a "big time" robbery. Nobody knows for sure why they did it. Alfred had been a fugitive since 1953 and Clarence for almost a year. The boys met at the small cabin outside of Tampa where J. W. lived and planned a way to get money, more money than they had ever had. J. W. was deeply in love with a Tampa woman who had three young children. He wanted to support her and the kids and knew he could never earn enough. Alfred had married a fifteen-year-old girl who was his constant companion. Clarence's girlfriend was the sister of J. W.'s paramour. All three boys needed money and were determined to get it. This time the robbery would not be a lark. No more hot-wired convertibles with a trunk full of new tires. This time they would try a daylight robbery—a bank. Their target was the Bank of Columbia in Columbia, Alabama. John drove to the bank and waited outside while Clarence and Alfred went inside, Clarence with a toy pistol. They mistakenly thought that, if they were caught, maybe the toy pistol would mitigate their sentence. In any case, they didn't want anybody to get hurt, unless it was one of them. Clarence pointed the toy pistol at the bank president, one of three employees in the bank at the time, and demanded money.

The small town bank was a pushover: It hadn't been robbed in over one hundred years. The trio roared off in John's Ford Thunderbird and raced back to Tampa, where they hid out in J. W.'s cabin. Their loot consisted of $18,911 in cash and $4,570 in travelers' checks, which they split three ways. The next day they headed for Ohio, where their girlfriends and Alfred's wife awaited them. This time, they had stirred up a hornets' nest. The bank was federally insured, so unknowingly they had committed a federal offense. The FBI and U.S. Marshal's Office joined in an intensive manhunt. Just five days later, FBI agents broke into a house in Hamilton, Ohio, and arrested Clarence, J. W., and Alfred and recovered most of the money. They found the toy gun but tossed it away. Since the bank employees had seen a gun, toy or not, the Anglins were charged with armed robbery although no firearms were found in their possession.

All three pleaded guilty in Federal Court in Montgomery, Alabama, to the charges of bank robbery. They made no statements in their behalf before sentencing. Alfred and Clarence drew fifteen years apiece, and J. W. drew ten, all in the federal penitentiary. Immediately the boys were transferred to state court to stand trial on the state charges for the same crime. To their shock and surprise, they were informed they could face the death penalty under Alabama law, given their previous convictions and escapes. The prosecutor was fed up with the Anglin boys and asked for the maximum penalty. But they were lucky. They each received a sentence of twenty-five years. Thus for their first armed robbery, the brothers were hit with combined sentences of 115 years in prison. J. W.'s former girlfriend recalls, "They weren't bad guys, they were just dirt poor."

Verna, the Anglin family's oldest daughter, adds, "Alfred, Clarence, and J. W. worked long and hard in the fields, and all the money they made they immediately turned over to Momma to keep the rest of the family from starving. I'm convinced in my heart that they robbed that bank to give money to Momma and Poppa, who were old and sick at the time. The FBI agent told me that the three of them were so unprofessional in robbing and escaping that they left a trail a mile wide. One of the first things they did with the money was to buy some fancy clothes." Verna also feels that "the Alabama state prosecutor wanted to throw the book at the boys because they were from Florida. Never once did it come out that Alfred and Clarence had used a toy pistol. Even the police wanted to make our family look bad. The press in that area said the boys had web-feet since they were from Ruskin, a town where everyone was supposed to have a boat in his backyard. No one ever mentioned that the bank got all its money back except for a few hundred dollars, that the FBI took J. W.'s new Thunderbird, which was entirely paid for, and that the prosecutor demanded that the jury give all three the death penalty. In fact, when they robbed that bank, nobody identified J. W. as being involved, since he sat in the car and didn't go in—yet he, too, got thirty-five years. Since we had no money to hire an attorney, a lawyer was appointed. He didn't care and he didn't want to really defend them since in that area robbing a bank was more serious than killing a man. So this so-called attorney told the boys to plead guilty and they would get a light sentence. Well, you can imagine the shock we all had when the judge sentenced them to thirty-five years each. I just heard on television that a savings-and-loan banker got ten years for stealing $35 million."

Verna recalls how several political science classes from the local high school were invited to witness the trial, adding to the family's humiliation. "Momma got so sick that she had to leave and wait in the car. When the bank's lawyer and prosecutor shouted, 'Electrocute them! Electrocute them!' even J. W. got sick and threw up. 'They come from down there in Florida to rob us good people. . . . We should just kill 'em to teach all from that way to stay out of our state.' " Apparently, the elder brother of the Anglin brothers' father, "Uncle Charlie," had savings of $10,000 in the bank and he was quoted by the press as saying, "Give them life imprisonment."

The three brothers were sent to Atlanta Federal Penitentiary to begin their federal sentences. Clarence and Alfred were held in "close custody" because of their escape record and length of sentences. Although Clarence got along reasonably well as an orderly in prison, he was judged by prison officials to be an escape risk and potential trouble-maker. In reference to the brothers, a report reads, "Clarence

Anglin is the larger man physically, appears to be much rougher than the others, and is likely the leader." It was noted that Clarence and Alfred had served time together and had escaped together previously. Officials decided to transfer Clarence to Leavenworth, Kansas. "The Classification Committee felt by all means they [Clarence and Alfred] should be in separate institutions as they are both definite escape risks and quite capable of planning and executing several kinds of overt acts. In separate institutions they should be able to make better adjustments . . . and would not be able to plan anything together."

Before long, it was decided that Alfred was a bad influence on J. W. in Atlanta, so J. W. was also transferred to Leavenworth. It wasn't long before Clarence and J. W. devised a plan to escape. Clarence worked in the prison bakery and had noticed that the boxes used to ship the bread out of the prison to an outside prison farm camp were almost large enough to hold a man. He and J. W. cut the top off one box and the bottom off another. After J. W. wedged himself inside the two stacked boxes, Clarence covered him with loaves of fresh-baked bread and closed the lid. The escape was foiled when a food supervisor saw two men struggling to lift the boxes onto a truck. He opened the top box and dug into the loaves of bread. There was J. W. looking up at him with a grin.

As a result of that escape attempt in August 1960, J. W. was transferred to Alcatraz and Clarence was put in isolation. Two months later Clarence was caught attempting to smuggle a letter to another inmate in segregation, so the following January, he also found himself on a train bound for Alcatraz. He was assigned to a cell next to J. W. in the hopes they would have a beneficial effect on each other. Since Alcatraz was a maximum security prison, there was little worry about escape plots the Anglin brothers might cook up.

*   *   *

Once he gave the matter some thought, Joe Carnes could see the wisdom of including the Anglin brothers in the escape. Their cells were strategically located close to those of West and Morris. Like all inmates on Alcatraz, they undoubtedly had their own plans of escape and maybe they were able to contribute some valuable ideas. Years later he reflected on the impossibility of knowing who contributed what to the plan. He learned from West that the Anglins had considerable knowledge about swimming and navigating in swift currents and in building rafts and boats. They were fearless when it came to cold water and had a good record of escapes through swamps and across rivers and difficult terrain.

As little as Joe Carnes knew about the Anglin brothers, he knew even less about Frank Lee Morris. Morris had arrived at Alcatraz in January 1960 from Atlanta. He was a southern boy, same as the Anglins, about four years older than Clarence Anglin, and in for bank robbery. He was skilled at escape, too—eleven times before he had gotten to The Rock. In fact, he had escaped from every institution he had been in. His cumulative sentence for burglary, auto theft, and bank robbery made him eligible for parole in 1966, but he was an impatient man.

West told Joe Carnes that Morris had met John Anglin at Atlanta and assured him that both the Anglins and Morris were trustworthy. For a short time after Morris's arrival at Alcatraz, he had assisted Joe Carnes in the library. Joe could see at a glance that Morris was clever and bright and curious about books. He helped Joe pass out books and magazines and saw that he was particularly interested in science and technical magazines. Morris was eventually transferred to the glove shop, but he kept up his reading and he did work with drafting tools in his cell. Joe thought that by the time Morris asked to be assigned to the shops, he probably already had a good idea of the materials he needed for an escape.

If Frank Morris was like the Anglin brothers with respect to his criminal background, he was different in many ways. Physically, he was smaller, more compact, about five-feet-eight inches tall and 140 pounds. Unlike the Anglins, he was an only child, born to a sixteen-year-old girl and a thirty-year-old man in Washington, D.C. His father was a fugitive at the time and his mother had come from a troubled background and had spent time in the National Training School for Girls in Washington. By the time Frank was born his father was long gone. Young Frank and his mother moved in with a man who eventually married his mother, but abandoned her soon after because of her promiscuous nature. Frank was shuttled from foster home to foster home and, as soon as he was old enough to try, he ran away. He soon was caught for petty thefts and sent to a juvenile institution. He literally grew up in schools for juvenile delinquents, where he learned the necessary lessons of survival. His native intelligence made him a skillful deceiver: He knew when to turn on the charm and when to cut and run.

Along the way, between juvenile detention, escapes, and petty crimes, Frank learned mechanical drafting and developed a skill for making things by hand and in prison machine shops. His I.Q. was recorded on prison records as 130 to 140. He used his intelligence in cunning ways. Considered by prison officials to be a psychopath, Frank Morris was a loner. He kept his thoughts to himself, revealing only enough to move his plans ahead. He could mix in team sports, but preferred playing chess against himself and reading, solitary activities.

Frank Morris's criminal career was similar to that of Clarence Anglin. From petty larceny and burglary, Morris had graduated to prison escape and finally to armed robbery. He had decided to make one try for big money and then go to Mexico and on to South America and start a new life. In November 1955, Morris and two accomplices broke into a bank in Slidell, Louisiana. They used an acetylene torch to try to cut into the vault and were surprised when the torch set off a tear gas system inside the vault. They managed to make off with $6,000, but they were captured soon after. Morris was sentenced to fourteen years for his efforts.

In Atlanta Federal Penitentiary, Morris joined with another inmate in an escape plan. But the attempt was poorly organized and the guards caught on to it. Morris's cell was shaken down and several lock picks were found. He was sent to isolation. After a few weeks in isolation and "administrative segregation," he was returned to population, where he quickly got involved in another plot. This time he was more careful. He and his companions fashioned bar-spreaders and set up a system of look-outs. They waited until the cell doors were opened during a recreation period. One man slipped to a cellhouse window and began spreading the bars. He managed to get through the window, and Morris was ready to follow him. But they had weakened the window frame and, as Morris was climbing out, the window came loose and crashed to the cellhouse floor. The guards rushed to the scene in time to see Frank Morris running along the corridor back to his cell.

In the hearing that followed, Morris tried to bluff his way out of the obvious. He denied that he was trying to escape and said that he was not running back to his cell.

"Why were you puffing so when the officer passed you, as if you were out of breath?"

"I was not puffing. I don't know how they got that idea."

"You deny being on the south side of the cellhouse at all?"

"Yes. I was in my cell, lying on my bed reading."

"Why do you think the officer said he saw you running down the south side of the cellhouse if it was not you?"

"It was just because I was handy. I was standing in front of my cell when he passed by."

It didn't work. Three months later, Frank Lee Morris was on the train for Alcatraz.

The more Joe Carnes thought about the Anglins and Frank Morris, the more convinced he became that West had made good choices for teammates—and the more doubts he had about the likelihood of himself being included. Frank Morris and the Anglins were new to the Alcatraz guards, and they were clean. Joe knew he was not.

5

Escape: Phase One

"Should they have tried to escape? Even if all the time spent would almost certainly fail? Yes, because they could use the experience to equip themselves to be better citizens later on."

Clarence "Joe" Carnes

The next day, Joe Carnes waited impatiently in the library. He went about his normal routine, chatted with the library workers, and waited. West was bound to show sooner or later. Carnes was worried about West's meeting the day before in the yard with Morris and the Anglin brothers—he knew that no doubt *he* had been the topic of conversation. They must have discussed the wisdom of including a man with so much heat on him. He knew West had talked to Bumpy. It bothered him that West was checking up on him now, after he had invited him to participate. It showed a lack of thoroughness on West's part.

But it was a conversation West had had with an inmate named Vernon that was particularly troublesome to Joe. Vernon knew something about Joe Carnes that wasn't common knowledge. Four years earlier, Vernon had been the inmate projectionist for the weekly movie the cons were allowed to see. Vernon had considered the job to be a plum because it broke the routine. After a while, though, it bored him. One day as he sat in the little projection booth during a movie, he noticed a locked door to a small storeroom. Vernon had often wondered what was inside, so he decided to pick the lock and find out. While the inmates watched the movie, Vernon got into the storeroom and rummaged through the old file cabinets inside. In one cabinet he found a file folder marked "714—CARNES." Joe Carnes was a friend, so the file attracted his curiosity. It contained photographs of odd objects laid on a table—wire, razor blades, rubber tubing, pieces of oilcloth.

The next day Vernon asked Joe about it. Joe was surprised; he hadn't thought of his old escape plan for years. Vernon had discovered the photographic record of Carnes's attempt to escape from the lock-up on D-Block.

"What the hell was that stuff?" Vernon asked. "It didn't look like escape stuff."

"Nobody else could figure it out either, not even the hacks," Joe laughed. "I don't talk much about it. The only guy who knew the full score was Beef Stew. He stored the material for me and helped me get it into D-Block. And he's gone now."

Vernon waited for more, hoping Joe would trust him with the details.

"It was going to be a torch. An oxygen cutting torch."

Vernon stared at him in disbelief.

"You could take all the stuff on that table and make a torch that would cut through a bar in about eight seconds."

"You must be dreaming," Vernon said.

"It's true. Take it or leave it."

"Then why the hell haven't you escaped?"

Joe Carnes shrugged. "It takes more than just cutting a bar or two. Besides, I never have been able to get the material all together at one time." Carnes knew Vernon was dying to know how the junk in the photograph could be assembled into a cutting torch, so he explained.

"We have DC current here, so I didn't have to worry about building a rectifier for AC current. Follow me so far?"

Vernon nodded.

"By running the current through a solution of salt water, you'll see bubbles coming off the electrode. The current is decomposing the water. One electrode gives off oxygen bubbles, the other one hydrogen. One part oxygen by volume, two parts hydrogen—H_2O.

"Then you catch the oxygen and store it. That's where the raincoat material comes in. You allow the hydrogen to escape; you don't need it. But you have to have the oxygen under pressure. So you use the principle of the autombile tire. If an inner tube is inflated to thirty pounds pressure, it will burst. But put the reinforcement of the tire around the tube and it will withstand even more than thirty pounds.

"So you wrap several layers of cloth around the bag made of raincoat stuff—I used seven layers of bed sheet cut into strips. You stitch it up with strong cord and it reinforces the bag.

"Then you have to pump the oxygen into the bag under pressure, so you make another little bag with valves in it made from pieces of tubing. And now you squeeze the oxygen from the big bag to the little bag and you can calculate how much you're putting in because you know the volume of the bag."

Vernon listened in amazement. It sounded plausible. "What was that thing made of paper?" he asked.

"That was an apparatus made of magazine pages, oiled to make them waterproof. It had seven cells in it to hold the salt solution. The holes in it were the places I hooked up the cells to my oxygen bag to catch the gas coming off each cell. I figured I needed only seven cells—more than that and I lost too much voltage to do any good.

"It worked on the same principle as an oxyacetylene cutting torch. The difference is, instead of having continuous heat from the acetylene, you just start the thing cutting and the reaction of the cutting generates enough heat to continue cutting. Any oxygen lance works the same way. Usually you start cutting just by heating up a bolt or something until it's red hot, and then you turn a stream of oxygen on it. Two things happen. The thing being cut starts to burn and the oxygen lance starts to burn. So you have enough heat from two sources to keep the cutting going."

"So how would you start the thing cutting?" asked Vernon.

"I would strike an arc from the wires where the cutting was to start, and go from there. The arc would start cutting and I would apply the oxygen and it would take off on its own heat.

"I don't know for certain if it would work on a bar, but I tried it on a bolt and it cut right through. A bar might carry off the heat too fast, so I was going to devise a blowtorch to furnish enough heat to finish the job."

"How in hell were you going to get out of D-Block with it?"

"Cut through the back of the cell—it's steel. Then climb up to the top, cut through the steel enclosure, and cut through the roof vent."

"What happened? Somebody rat on you?"

"No. Just bad luck. They found the stuff in a shakedown."

Vernon was one of the few people Joe Carnes trusted enough to tell about the cutting torch. The idea might still come in handy someday; the fewer cons who knew about it, the better.

He told Vernon that he had tried several times after that to gather the materials again. But each time the shakedown crew had found it in his cell. The officials thought he was trying to make water-wings out of the raincoat material and tubing. Lieutenant Phil Bergen had once remarked to him after a shakedown, "When are you going to give up, Joe? You've been fooling around with this stuff for years." Joe hadn't replied.

Now he wondered if Vernon had told West about the torch and the guards keeping the heat on Joe Carnes because of it. In fairness to Vernon, Joe thought, Vernon had never promised not to tell others about the torch. Joe knew that whatever Vernon said, he believed that it was the right thing.

*   *   *

West appeared outside the heavy steel mesh and bars of the library and motioned for Joe to come over. West leaned against the bars and gripped the bars with his hands. Joe could see the letters tattooed on the backs of West's fingers. The letters spelled out "H-A-R-D L-U-C-K."

"Joe, we talked about the heat being on you. You brought it up, remember? That was the fair thing to do. We respect you for it."

"You sound like a judge about to give me a life sentence."

"I hope you don't take it that way, Joe. Because that's what it amounts to."

Carnes looked West in the eye. "I get the message. I'll make it easy on you. You guys found out I was telling the truth about the heat on me. Right?"

"Yeah," West answered. "I don't understand how I didn't know. I thought I knew everything about everybody."

"That's the way it is. These hack bastards never let their guard down for a moment. Not where security is concerned."

So Joe Carnes was out. He was calm. He felt almost indifferent.

"I thought you'd be more upset about it, about us changing our minds," West said.

Joe Carnes had known inside that they would come to that decision. Maybe that was why he had toyed with West for three days, savoring the promise of freedom he knew wouldn't last. In his youth he would have insisted on going with them at any risk. But not now. Alcatraz had done this to him: He was older, and he was beaten. He realized his future depended not on escape, but on parole. In his heart he knew escape was a losing game. Sure, you could break out, but they would get you sooner or later. Hardly anybody really made it; only a handful out of thousands who had made it out of federal prisons remained at large after two or three years. And he had to admit he was reluctant to try anything that would disturb his life, including trying to escape.

Joe Carnes's partner in crime back in Oklahoma had played the game straight. He had been sentenced with Joe and had "done his own time" back in Leavenworth. He had made parole several years before and was now free. Joe Carnes had tried to beat the odds in Leavenworth and had wound up in Alcatraz. Again he had tried it in 1946 and had ended up with an additional life sentence. Perhaps inside of himself he was relieved that West had taken him out of the game for one more try.

"What are you thinking, Joe?" West asked.

Joe looked at him. Could this little guy be the one to beat Alcatraz? Allen West? And the Anglins and Frank Morris?

"I was thinking of the odds against you, West. I sure hope you make it."

"I was hoping you'd say that."

"What the hell did you expect me to say? I hope you get caught?"

"No. I didn't mean it that way. I mean we still need your help."

"You bastard, West," Joe said, pretending anger. "You kick me in the ass, send me packing, break my heart, and still have the gall to ask me for help." He paused. "Okay, what is it?"

"Nothing much. Just hide some stuff for us. Here—in the library."

"Let me think about it. Come back in an hour," Joe said. He needed to think it through—the risks, the odds of getting caught. Anything linking him to an unsuccessful escape, or a successful one, for that matter, would mean the hole. And, more important, it would mean his chances for a transfer and eventual parole would be gone. Joe Carnes had a lot riding on his decision. But in the end, he *had* to help. As Charlie Hopkins said years later, "Anybody would have helped if they thought it would work. Anything to see them make it. Anything to help close the place down."

Joe Carnes enlisted the help of one of the library workers. He approached "Denny," a young man who kept to himself and who had never been in any trouble, with a simple proposition.

"How would you like to lose your good time and add a few months on to your sentence—and maybe spend some time in the hole?" Denny thought Joe was joking—but when he found out there was an escape in the works, he readily accepted the challenge. He knew he wasn't going out, but he was willing to help on the chance that a successful escape might close down Alcatraz. Denny told Carnes he had already guessed something was up, having seen him meet with West twice in as many days for lengthy talks. That startled Joe. If Denny had sensed it that easily, maybe the hacks already knew, too. But it was too late to worry about that. He would just have to be more careful. He told Denny just enough to make him useful.

It turned out to be easier to enlist Denny than it was to persuade West that Denny could be trusted. West didn't like Denny because he didn't mingle with other cons. Denny could be a rat, someone who would trade information for a transfer out of Alcatraz. Joe explained Denny's behavior: He was young and "pretty." He was afraid of the "wolves," aggressive homosexuals. West, who was homosexual, could understand that. He accepted Joe's word that Denny could be trusted, but he still didn't like it.

Denny was a first-timer, not violent by nature, just a kid who had stolen a car and taken it across a state line—a federal rap. He had never said how he had gotten to Alcatraz from Leavenworth, but the story was that some guy in Leavenworth had made advances on him and Denny had hit him with a table leg. Just because he was a loner now, Joe reasoned, didn't mean he was a potential rat. He had reasons to be afraid.

Joe didn't like the way the term "rat" was used so loosely. Every time a con was caught with contraband in his cell, he would say, "Somebody ratted on me." In the old days on Alcatraz, a man labeled another a rat with the knowledge that it could cost the man his life. It was a serious rap, backed up with solid evidence; it was never a hollow accusation. The accused might even kill the accuser just to protect his reputation.

Nowadays, Joe noticed, the type of petty criminals coming into Alcatraz didn't know the underworld meaning of "rat." They would call someone a rat just because they didn't like him or had some small grievance. The older cons didn't like this new attitude. To them, a rat was the worst thing in creation, and to use the term lightly was a violation of the old-timers' code. They had been in a criminal environment all their lives and the code of behavior was vital to survival. Men had died rather than rat on another con. They had been tortured, hanged, beaten to death, and electrocuted—and still not ratted. The younger inmates didn't believe there were men like that on Alcatraz. They believed the thing that kept men from ratting was fear, not principle. Newer cons underestimated the importance of "rats" in the prison scheme of things.

There was another meaning of the word "rat." In the old days, fighting among inmates had always been one on one. Two or more men hadn't ganged up on another man in Alcatraz. There had been no "rat gangs" there. Now, individuals tended to enlist support for a planned attack on another inmate. By 1962, it was rare to see a "one-on-one" fight. Usually, it was two or three on one.

In the days after Joe Carnes talked to West, Denny had a few brief conversations with West. Denny seemed to enjoy his inside knowledge immensely. And Joe was pleased that Denny didn't reveal anything to him. He kept his mouth shut. Joe suspected Denny got pleasure from keeping Joe in the dark as revenge for not giving him the plot details after he had agreed to become involved. Now Denny probably knew more than Joe. And that was just as well to Joe. After all, he didn't need to know more; he was more of a "technical advisor" from here on.

West approached him one day a week later with a problem. "Do you know how I could get the star drills up from the industries?"

"Star drills? I thought you said you had them."

"I meant *we* have them. Not quite the same thing, but *we* do have them. But not in the cellhouse."

"Then *you* don't really 'have' them."

"Okay, goddammit! If you want to get technical. Now, do you know how to get the damn things up to the cellhouse or not?"

Joe suggested he ask Larry Trumblay and Teddy Green, two inmates who, several years before, had managed to smuggle all kinds of tools, including an electric drill, from the industries building into the cellhouse. Their escape plan had been discovered before they could use the tools, but they must have had a system that worked in getting the tools out of the industries building. The next day Joe saw West talking earnestly to the two men in the exercise yard and he smiled to himself.

The very next day, Larry Trumblay found Joe Carnes. "How come you put that idiot West on me?" Trumblay said.

"I figured you could help him. That's why I suggested you."

Trumblay pretended to be angry, but Joe knew he wasn't. They were friends, and Trumblay knew Joe wouldn't betray their friendship. Anyway, Joe was eager to learn how they had smuggled tools out of the industries building, and he hoped that Trumblay would tell him, now that he had told West. But it was improper for him to ask. Trumblay saw that Joe wasn't going to ask and was dying to know. "It wasn't easy," he volunteered.

Trumblay explained how Red Winhoven, who had worked in the carpentry shop in those days, had helped him. Trumblay had broken the legs on two of the little wood folding chairs used by inmates in the exercise yard and then complained to the guards that they ought to be fixed. The guards had sent the chairs down to the shop to be repaired. Winhoven had made new legs and bored a hole in each one. He had put drill bits and other small tools in the hollow legs and packed the holes with wood filler so they wouldn't rattle. When the guards had brought the chairs with the dummy legs back to the yard through the snitch box, the alarm had rung. They had ignored it because the chairs had metal bolts in them and the guards assumed that was what had set off the alarm. The tools had remained in the chairs for days while Trumblay had pondered a way to get them into the cellhouse. He could not simply carry them through the snitch box and back to his cell.

Then a stroke of luck had come his way. Workers had needed to get an air hammer into the shower room, which was adjacent to the exercise yard. So they had knocked a small pane from a window in the shower room and run the air hose over the wall by the yard and through the window. "Some other stuff went through that window, too," Trumblay told Joe.

Then had come the problem of getting the tools from the shower room into the cellhouse. That had been even easier. Joe already knew that trick. Trumblay had simply put the tools in his clean sheets as he picked them up in the clothing room and just carried them to his cell. Inmates knew that the guards never bothered to shake down clean sheets from the clothing room. It was a remarkable security oversight on Alcatraz. For many years the clothing room provided a contraband highway to the cellhouse. No inmate ever snitched to the guards about it, and no guard ever discovered it.

And the Anglin brothers now worked in the clothing room! Even so, there were difficulties to be overcome. For one thing, there was now an X-ray metal detector that screened everything coming from the laundry to the clothing room. Rumor had it that it was even better than a snitch box—it had a screen so the guards could see everything in a clothing hamper, metal or otherwise. And, of course, the window pane to the shower room had been replaced long ago. So, even if the "hollow chair leg" trick worked again, it would be hard to get tools from the yard. Even if they managed to get contraband past the snitch box between the yard and the cellhouse, there was a portable snitch box on rollers that could be moved anywhere. It might be waiting inside the cellhouse.

At night in his cell, Joe Carnes often thought about the magnitude of the undertaking, the myriad problems and small details that had to be resolved to perfection if the four men were to have any chance at all. Getting the tools into the cells was one problem, but using them presented many more. There was noise, for one thing. The sound of star drills pounding through concrete would wake the dead. There was the problem of masking the holes as work progressed, and disposing of the concrete dust and rubble.

In any case, the problems were in West's hands. And he had Frank Morris to help him. Joe knew that Morris was bright, probably the smartest man on Alcatraz. And the Anglins were clever boys. And Denny was dedicated to the cause, determined to see Alcatraz fall. So Joe Carnes could rest easy. The responsibility was not his.

Weeks passed into months. Christmas came, as did the new year, 1962. Joe sensed little progress had been made. West, Morris, and the Anglin brothers still showed up each morning in the mess hall along with the other inmates, their faces devoid of any clue as to their frustrations or progress. Surely by now they were well on their way, with well-disguised exits in their cells. Maybe they were even at work on the roof vent.

One day in February, West stopped Joe in the yard and wanted to talk. He needs advice, Joe thought. West said he had a problem with the drills. Joe Carnes's heart sank. Three months and more had passed and they hadn't even gotten started!

"No," West said. "We got the drills, but it was tougher than we had thought."

West said they had tried to get the drill up to the laundry by way of the men on the loading dock. But none of the six who worked there had been completely trustworthy. And there had been the new X-ray scanner. It would surely spot any object in the laundry hamper. Since the installation of the new machine, every bundle of laundry went through the scanner before being placed on the truck. The only way to stash the drills in the laundry would have been to divert the hacks' attention for an instant. And that would have been too great a risk. The drills were crucial to the plan and could not be risked on such a long shot.

The only alternative had been via the yard: Get them from the industries building to the yard and then smuggle them into the cellhouse somehow. Two chairs had been deliberately broken and sent down to the shop. There the star drills had been hidden in new hollow legs and the chairs returned to the yard. Since that part of the plan had worked as well as it had for Trumblay and Green several years before, they thought maybe they could just break a window in the shower room and get the drills in before it was replaced. They had rejected that idea.

They had devised a way to get the drills through the snitch box on the pathway to the cellhouse, but the new portable snitch box was now stationed at the cellhouse entrance, so every con had to pass through two metal detectors. West had enlisted an inmate named Bagget, who had agreed to carry the drills through. Bagget had a long record as a gunman and had lots of bullet holes in him to prove it. In fact, his body contained so many bullet fragments that he set off the alarm every time he passed through a metal detector. So the guards routinely just hand-frisked him and let him walk around the snitch box rather than pass through it. But they made him pass through the new portable metal detector because it was more sensitive and could register how much metal a man carried. The guards always suspected Bagget might be carrying little bits of blade or other metal through the hand-frisk, and this was a way to catch him.

"How did you get him through with the drills?" asked Joe.

West grinned. "He had them stuck up his ass," he said.

"Both of them?" Joe asked in surprise.

"No, stupid. One at a time. He walked like he had a corn cob up his ass. I told him to limp. 'Limp, you stupid son-of-a-bitch, so it won't be so obvious.' "

"How about the portable snitch box?" Joe asked.

"We got lucky."

The portable metal detector had broken down one day and the guards had sent for an inmate named Jim, an electrician. As he had been was working on it in the cellhouse, West had happened by on a painting assignment. He had asked Joe if he could fix the machine so it could pass a piece of metal a little bigger than a shank. Jim could and did. Jim wasn't a friend of West; he didn't even know him well. But he was an old con, and he knew West wouldn't ask for the favor if it wasn't important. So he had done it, no questions asked. When the time had come, Bagget had passed through the metal detector with the star drills without creating undue suspicion.

"You making any progress?" asked Joe. He still didn't know why West needed his help.

"Joe, it's been a hell of a strain. You can't use those drills without making noise. Those black guys across from our cells know what we're doing. They even get down on the floor and peek at us through the vent. Anyday I expect the man to come down on us."

Carnes knew what he meant. Most of the old cons, the old pros from cities all across the nation, distrusted black people. And it was more than simple prejudice. Black inmates in the old days had had a reputation of being "Uncle Toms," eager to curry favor with their white jailers. Often they hadn't subscribed to the same "code of honor" as white inmates, and with good cause. Given the prejudicial way they had been treated by white guards and white inmates, there had been little reason to protect white men. A few old-timers, like Bumpy Johnson, were exceptions. They had grown up in the underworld and understood its rules of conduct. But most black convicts in the old days had been farm boys who had run afoul of the law and brought their fears and hatreds into their cells.

The black convicts likely to find themselves on Alcatraz in the 1960s were different. They tended to be more "seasoned" criminals, who understood the importance of the code. And, on Alcatraz, Bumpy's word was law. And Bumpy had assured West that his men would not betray the escape. But old prejudices die hard, and West was still nervous.

West also told Joe Carnes about the positive side of their efforts. They were drilling holes around the rear cell vents and planned to remove the vents completely and replace them with fake ones. They went to work every night after the 5:30 count and worked until 9:30. The star bits worked well in boring holes in the concrete. At the end of each drilling session, the holes were plugged with toilet paper and soap to hide them. West was able to provide each member of the team with a little jar of cellhouse blue-green paint that matched his cell walls. Thus each night's progress was concealed by day.

West was proud of all the preparations he, Morris, and the Anglins had made, and he was eager to boast about their cleverness. He knew he could trust Joe Carnes completely, so, over time, he explained the plan in minute detail.

The Anglins' cells were side by side, as were Morris's and West's —all on the same side of the lower tier of B-Block. Therefore they worked in teams; each team had one of the star bits. Each team had a set of "jiggering" mirrors, where one man would act as lookout while the other dug. Jiggering mirrors were a common contrivance in Alcatraz, and certainly not unique to that prison. A guard would have to be very sharp-eyed to spot the tiny mirrors sticking through the bars from the far end of the tier. Of course, when the guard came around a corner, the mirrors were quickly withdrawn.

The four inmates had arranged a simple but effective warning system when a guard was approaching. The common method of tapping on the cell wall to alert the occupant of the next cell was rejected. It was too noisy and might be heard by the guard. The Anglins ran twine between their cells and the "digger" attached the string to his light switch. If his brother in the next cell spotted a guard approaching, he would pull the string from his cell and turn off the light in the next cell. His brother then had time to jump into bed and feign sleep.

Joe Carnes marveled at their cleverness. Usually when a con was up to some dirty work, the first thing he did was turn off his light. This was a switch that was certain to fool the hacks.

The team had accumulated an impressive assortment of escape tools and materials. Frank Morris worked in the glove shop and was able to get tape and rubber cement and strong twine. West, on his rounds as a cellhouse painter, had managed to pick up bits of wire and metal. He carried a small plastic bag with him, and when he saw something useful, he stuck it in the bag, tied the top, and dropped it in his paint bucket. Other cons helped out too, no questions asked, of course. Joe Carnes had turned over to West his three treasured hacksaw blades. Inside the utility corridors, where West often worked under the uninterested eye of a guard, he found a treasure trove of useful stuff: lengths of wire, electric cord, short pieces of water pipe, bits of tubing, and wood.

Things were not always that easy. West revealed that once he had almost been discovered. It was after the final evening count, when only one cellhouse guard remains to make the hourly counts throughout the night. West heard the guards leave through the front gate, one by one. When he figured it was safe, that only one guard remained for the hourly rounds, he got out his little wrapped bundle of tools from inside his mattress. He was still on his knees in the dark cell when a guard walked by. West knew it was dark, but surely the guard could see the packet of tools he had unrolled on his bunk. He leaned down, trying to block the guard's view, and, as he moved his arm, the star drill rolled off the bunk to the concrete floor. It struck with a sharp metallic clank. West froze. So did the guard, who was, by then, two steps past West's cell. West held his breath, silently cursing his luck. The guard paused for two, maybe three, seconds, and then continued on his way and left the cellhouse. West was dumbfounded. Why hadn't he come back? Frank Morris in the next cell had heard the drill fall, as had the Anglins, and probably everybody else in B-Block. West hurriedly passed his escape kit down a few cells, certain that the guards would return to shake down his cell. They didn't return. West racked his brain for an explanation. The only plausible one was that the guard thought West had dropped his razor handle. Every inmate was allowed a razor (but no blades— a dull blade was passed to inmates, one by one, under supervision) and it might make a sound like the drill had made. West tested the theory. He dropped the drill again and then his razor handle. They sounded alike. The guard must have concluded that West had dropped his razor. There might have been another reason the guard had let the incident pass. He might have been up to something himself and not wanted to call attention to the fact that he was in the cellhouse after the others had gone for the night. Or he might have just been in a hurry to get home and not wanted to start anything. Who knew?

West was discouraged by how slow the drilling and chipping was going. The four men had already determined the exact size of "door" they would need to make in each cell. Using strips of wood, they had made a frame to represent the opening. They would try to squeeze through it naked like a contortionist wriggling through a tennis racket frame. They kept adjusting the size of the frame until they could slide through quickly. Thus they knew the exact dimensions of the hole they needed to make in the cell wall. Nobody wanted to remove an ounce of concrete that wasn't necessary.

West explained how they were drilling holes about an inch apart around the perimeter of the vent opening. The three-eighths-inch diameter star bits worked fine for that. A hole was started by wrapping the drill bit in cloth to muffle noise, placing the bit in the proper position, and then striking the bit with a well-wrapped shoe. After just a few strikes, and by rotating the bit between each blow, a small hole was started. Then it was a slow process of twisting and pressing the bit deeper and deeper, grinding out finely powdered concrete. The plan was to try to break one hole into another, and then break out big pieces of concrete. Joe Carnes, who had studied probably every engineering principle and technique that might be of use to a prison inmate, suggested a way to speed things up.

"Get spoons," he said. "They make excellent wedges." Carnes was always amazed that the mess hall spoons weren't counted after each meal, as the knives were. It would be tricky to get enough spoons out, but it was possible. He described a system of removing concrete without the noisy and laborious necessity of chipping it away. They should drill holes close together, as they were already doing, and three inches deep, the distance at which the steel mesh ventilator grille was imbedded in the concrete wall. Once the holes were completed, the concrete could be removed easily and quietly. Get three spoons and bend the bowl back and forth until it breaks off. Discard the bowl and sharpen the broken end of the handle to the shape of a screw-driver tip—a wedge. Insert three spoon handles into three adjacent holes, Carnes said. Drive them in as deep and tight as you can. Take one of the short steel rails of the bunk frame and hold it flat against the tips of the spoons sticking out of the holes. Give it a sharp rap, and a square chunk of concrete, three inches deep, should pop out. And then the steel grille should be exposed. Just pry it out. It was simple.

Two days later, West stopped by the library. Carnes looked at him and said, "Well?"

"It worked," replied West. He explained how they had smuggled the broken concrete chunks down to men in the industries and how they had casually been tossed into the bay.

Prior to prying out the steel grilles, the men had made fake grilles to put in place. It had taken only a matter of minutes to crack the concrete around the vent to a depth of three inches. That left plenty of time to adjust and fit the new fake vent covers before the hack made his rounds. Once the real vents were pried out, it was a simple matter to hide the tools inside the utility corridor by reaching through the opening. (Up until then, each man hid his materials in his cell as best he could.) And, of course, they had Denny and others hiding material for them elsewhere. They didn't want to cut all the way through the eight-inch-thick wall all at once, because their work could be seen from inside the utility corridor. The corridors were randomly inspected and workers went in, from time to time, to fix old plumbing.

West and Morris had conceived the idea of making false vents that would cover not only the old vent hole but also the enlarged opening that the drilling and chipping made. For this the inmates used cardboard and artists' canvas board. All four men had taken up painting as a recreational hobby. That was common in Alcatraz. Art supplies were permitted in cells: tubes of oil colors, brushes, easels, and canvas boards, which were stiff, hard boards with linen canvas glued to one surface. It was an ideal material for many purposes. The 18-by-24-inch "Blue Boy Brand" panels were issued to inmates as requested. Using a sharp knife, Morris cut fake vent covers that, when painted by West, looked very much like the steel mesh in the cell vents. When the real vents were cut from the concrete, the fake ones, which included a section of simulated wall, could be slid quickly into place.

The next time Carnes had occasion to pass West's cell on his library rounds, he looked closely at the rear vent. He did the same at Morris's and the Anglins' cells. Very well done, he thought. He admired the skill with which they had disguised their work. The fake vents were not only painted, but carefully textured to match the surrounding concrete. Fortunately for them, the old concrete had many coats of paint and many chips and scratches from decades of hard use. West later explained how they had achieved such realism.

"After we stick the fake panel in, we put fresh putty around the seam. We use a floor brush to tap the soft putty and make it look like pitted concrete. Then we blow cigarette ashes on the wet putty. It makes it the same color as the old concrete, and the ashes stick on there after the putty dries. We have a fake panel for the inside of the door too, so when we take the wire mesh off, we can reach through and putty up the inside.

"From inside the corridor it looks real. I just stick a mirror in there and I can see to put the ashes on it."

"Where did you get enough cigarette ashes?"

"I got a whole bucket of ashes from Lawrence. Remember when he was up in the hospital trying to get a transfer by acting nuts? He saved his ashes for almost a year. Part of his nut act. Anyway, after he left, the bucket of ashes was still there. I managed to get it when

I was painting up there."

West also had access to concrete patch, a kind of water-base quick-drying concrete paint that came to the prison in fifty-pound bags. The white powder was mixed with water as needed by the painters and used on small cracks and holes. West had an ample supply stashed in the utility corridor. It could be used with concrete dust from the holes to make a kind of plaster. It looked good, but was crumbly if anybody poked around in it.

Joe Carnes was impressed. Maybe Allen West had thought of everything. Maybe he would be the first to bust out and stay out. Everything seemed to be going smoothly—and he was glad to be a part of it. But he had the nagging feeling that things were *too* smooth.

One of the dangers of an escape plan that takes months to prepare is that the word spreads. Joe remembered the 1946 escape and how by the time it had come off, every con in the joint knew about it. Everybody knew except the Warden. Widespread knowledge of the plan presents several hazards. The obvious one is that someone might rat to the officials or say something inadvertently that might be overheard by a guard. Another problem is that, since the details of the plan are spread by word of mouth, there is a lot of guessing and incorrect information floating around. That means somebody might accidentally blunder into part of the carefully orchestrated plan and jeopardize the whole operation. While almost all the inmates sympathized with an escape attempt, and were willing to help, there were some who would try to take advantage of it—cut themselves in on the deal. And that's exactly what happened.

Two cons on the top tier of B-Block, Gainey and Stevens, heard about the plan and decided they were in a perfect position to get out, too. Their cells were right under the roof vent above B-Block. All they had to do was cut through into the utility corridor and follow West, Morris, and the Anglins right up the vent. When West heard about it, he went into a towering rage. He wanted to kill the two men outright. But he soon calmed down. Joe Carnes got pieces of the story from Denny and West. For a time there was a rumor that the whole deal was off.

Then, to make matters worse, the whisper went around that the Anglins had suggested to Gainey and Stevens that they cut themselves in. This caused a flurry of angry accusations between the Anglin brothers and Morris and West. Joe Carnes thought the whole thing might blow apart. He knew West was homosexual, and the word was that Frank Morris was bisexual. The Anglin brothers were straight. Maybe there was bad blood between them.

By the time this unfounded rumor got straightened out, the big escape was the main topic of conversation in the yard. Joe Carnes knew from experience that the chances of success were quickly going down the drain. He talked it over with West.

"We're bound to be found out now," West said. "It's just a matter of time. But we're going ahead anyway."

"What about the rift between you guys?" Joe asked.

"That's all patched up now. We calmed down and compared notes. Somebody started a rumor just for the hell of it."

"You going to do anything about Gainey and Stevens?"

"Nah. We thought about it. But I persuaded the guys it was best to ignore them and hope Gainey and Stevens don't get busted."

"You going to let them get out behind you?"

"If they do, that's fine with us. I don't care if the whole joint gets away, just so we make it. Besides, they've just got a little file. They don't have the star drills we used. It's going to take a hell of a long time to get through eight inches of concrete with one little file."

Joe got the picture. He got something else, too. West had said, "The star drills we used." Past tense. That must mean Morris and Clarence Anglin were through the back wall.

"Anyway," West said, "we've got more important things to worry about than Gainey and Stevens. We need raincoats."

6

Escape: Phase Two

"For the Anglins especially, Alcatraz was unbearable. Escape was their
only interest from the start. For guys who live for action, there isn't
much doubt what they should do. For the others on The Rock, it
wasn't a matter of risk or fear. They didn't try to escape because of
sheer laziness."

Charlie Hopkins, #1186 AZ

Raincoats had always figured in Alcatraz escape plans. The cons knew
it; the guards knew it. The waterproof material was essential for getting off a rock compeletly surrounded by water. It didn't take the
superior intelligence of a Frank Morris or the cunning of a Joe Carnes
to know you couldn't risk the cold and turbulent waters of San Francisco Bay without some kind of flotation device. Just as everybody
on Alcatraz had his favorite method of escape, each had his preferred
design for "water wings." But whatever the scheme, it all came down
to raincoats, the only source of waterproof material on the island.

Joe Carnes learned that this group of determined escape artists
had bigger plans than mere "water wings." They were going to make
their exit by inflatable boat. Not just one boat, but two boats! The
team concept used in getting out of the cells would extend to getting
off the island: the Anglin brothers in one boat, Morris and West
in the other. They would need a lot of raincoats for their ambitious
plans. By May 1, 1962, they were ready to start work.

There was always a good supply of raincoats in the prison storeroom. It was just a matter of getting them. These were not the cheap
plastic kind that fall apart after a few times in the rain. These were

U.S. Army standard: olive drab rubberized fabric; durable and strong. Almost every one of Alcatraz's 280 inmates had one and often needed it on the bleak, fog-shrouded island. Other cons would gladly have given theirs to one of the four, no questions asked. They could always claim theirs was stolen and request a new one. But a rash of unexplained raincoat "thefts" would look suspicous. West made plans to get raincoats straight from the supply room.

Allen West already had four raincoats, one from each man, but he needed more. He and Frank Morris figured they would need at least three dozen. It took two sleeves, sewn together, to make one "Mae West"–type life jacket. That would take care of the four raincoats they already had. To make pontoons capable of supporting two men in each boat, they needed thirty-two sets of sleeves, sixteen for each boat. The sleeves would be sewn end to end to form a long tube capable of being inflated. Assuming each sleeve averaged twenty-eight inches long and fifteen inches in circumference, the sleeves would make a boat roughly eight feet long and about three feet wide, each with a double row of pontoons on each side. The back and front panels from the raincoats would be used to make strong triple bottoms for the boats. Frank Morris was at work on an inflation device, made from a metal pipe with a steel rod plunger and a leather diaphragm, similar in principle to a bicycle pump.

At first they had decided to make one big boat that would hold all four men. After considering the difficulty of constructing such an unwieldy craft, and getting it through the roof vent, they decided on two boats. Two boats would be stronger than one, anyway. They weren't sure of the design for the boats—maybe they would find scrap wood on the beach that would work as stiffeners, but they couldn't be certain. One couldn't depend on luck. And these men were too thorough in their planning to even consider "lucky" breaks to get them off The Rock.

Then, as fate would have it, the May 21 issue of *Sports Illustrated* arrived on Joe Carnes's desk in the library. He glanced through it and was startled to see a detailed article on various rubber boats with a discussion of the relative merits of different types. He got the magazine to West as soon as possible. The article not only showed the basic construction of a sound inflatable boat (the Voit two-man utility boat was recommended), it contended that simple inflatable boats could indeed support two men safely. The article reminded the eager readers that "most good inflatables now stress safety features such as dual air chambers that are completely independent of each other and which inflate and seal separately. Many seams are double laminated. Valves on some of the better equipment are designed so that they allow air to enter freely but keep it from escaping."

The article also showed several types of hand-operated inflation pumps. The inflator that caught Frank Morris's eye was the "all-purpose Sports-Lung ($1.35)." It was a hand-operated, metal-reinforced, canvas bellows that looked for all the world like a little concertina. It looked easy to make. But why make it? he reasoned. Why not just *buy* one? Alcatraz inmates often joked about buying power drills and other obvious escape paraphernalia from catalogues. Obviously, the authorities would not let an inmate buy an air pump. But a concertina was another matter. Morris already had an accordion and kept it in its bulky case shoved up against the vent at the rear of his cell. It was a perfect prop to hide the "work in progress." So, he reasoned, it would not seem odd for him to want a concertina. He immediately filled out a requisition to purchase a small concertina from a music store in San Francisco. When the instrument arrived a few days later, Morris removed the sound keys so it would act as a bellows, silently pumping air through a single opening. They had their inflator.

This wasn't the first time that magazines had come to the assistance of the plotters. J. W. Anglin had a copy of the November 1960 issue of *Popular Mechanics*, which contained an interesting article on do-it-yourself rubber vulcanizing. The article explained how a resourceful hunter had made inflatable goose decoys from old inner tubes. The idea of setting up a vulcanizing shop inside Alcatraz was an intriguing one, but impractical. It required a hot press that would have been difficult, if not impossible, to obtain or make.

West hit the jackpot with the March 1962 issue of *Popular Mechanics*, which contained a lengthy article entitled "Your Life Preserver

—How Will It Behave When You Need It?" There, plainly illustrated, were various types of flotation devices, with a critique of each. A magazine staff member tested several types, and photos showed how each one behaved in water. West patterned their life vests after the yoke-type, which fit around the neck and down the chest. The magazine showed two such vests. He noted the warning: "While both vests are good, neither is efficient if it isn't worn properly, with all ties fastened and all straps snugly in place." Yoke-type vests made swimming difficult because of the body's face-up floating position. But then West wasn't planning on doing much swimming.

It was a relatively simple matter to get good material for straps and ties from the shops, and tubing to fashion one-way air valves for the life jackets and pontoons. West and John Anglin had sewing needles and heavy thread so they could work in their cells on the life jackets. The biggest problem during the period before the convicts broke through the rear wall of their cells was storing their accumulated gear. They were eager to work on the boats and life jackets but couldn't very well set up a shop in a cell. John Anglin broke through first and, once inside the utility corridor, helped his brother Clarence enlarge the "door" in his cell.

It became obvious at that point that they needed dummies to take their place in bed while they were out of their cells. All work with the raincoats stopped until the matter of dummy heads was resolved. West remembered Joe Carnes's statement that previous escape attempts had failed because no dummies had been made. Since there was a cell count every hour at night, one hour, maybe two, was the best one could hope for his absence not being noticed. So they had to make dummy heads—and good ones. No rolled-up socks in painted pillowcases would do. These had to look real—real enough, at least, in the dim light of a darkened cell. West, who had the best opportunity to do so, consulted with other cons who were good artists. A man in B-Block, according to Charlie Hopkins, was the best sculptor on Alcatraz. Charlie remembered him in Leavenworth skillfully carving realistic grasshoppers from bits of wood. On Alcatraz, he had no carving tools, of course, but he had knowledge of clay and clay substitutes, like soap. Other inmates who were skilled artists could have helped with hints on mixing flesh tones with oil paint.

J. W. and Clarence Anglin made the first attempt at a dummy head. It wasn't a whole head, just the top of one side of a face, made from a tightly rolled pad of bed sheeting and tape, covered with a layer of West's "cement," and facial features, including a realistic ear, made of soap. Clarence Anglin, who worked in the barber shop, collected tufts of hair from his sweepings and secreted them in his blue prison handkerchief. In his cell, he carefully tied the hair with thread into small bundles, miniature ponytails. He then glued the tufts of hair on the head. They painted their creation, using oil paint. It was crude compared with ones made later, but it worked. The brothers named it "Oink." With the half head in J. W. Anglin's bunk, the U.S. Navy wool blanket snugged up to it and rolled clothing lumped up beneath the blanket to resemble a sleeping man, John was able to work inside the utility corridor in relative safety.

J. W. Anglin made a dummy back and positioned it in front of his ventilator hole, so from inside the utility corridor nothing looked out of place. Clarence did the same after he had broken through into the corridor. By that time, Clarence Anglin and Frank Morris had broken through and the Anglins made a second dummy head, dubbed "Oscar," and gave it to Morris. Oscar was a fuller face, with human-hair eyebrows and a mop of dark curly hair on top. It was decided that Morris and Clarence Anglin would work on top of the cell block to remove the roof ventilator bars.

Allen West decided that he could do more good inside his cell, sewing raincoat sleeves and sealing seams. He didn't break through his cell wall into the corridor. He removed the steel mesh grille and replaced it with a fake so he could stash his raincoat and sewing stuff inside the corridor. But he left a two-inch thickness of concrete undisturbed at the rear of his "door." When the time came he could kick through it and make his way to the roof. J. W. Anglin carefully patched all signs of digging at the rear of West's cell with West's "cement" mixture.

Frank Morris and Clarence Anglin reconnoitered the top of the cell block. The climb to the top from inside the utility corridor was relatively easy. Wooden scaffolding on the second- and third-floor levels had been installed to make it easier for plumbers and electricians. The maze of sewer and water pipes created a ladder that could be quietly scaled in darkness. After the 1946 escape attempt, there had been a recommendation to install steel barriers on each floor so escaping convicts could not reach the top of the cell block. But the plan was too costly and nothing had been done. Morris and Anglin saw the obvious problem when they reached the exposed top of the cell block. Anybody up there could easily be seen by the guard in the gun gallery. How would they be able to remove the roof vent and drag their rafts and other gear up to the roof without being seen?

"You know, we have a major problem," West reported to Joe Carnes. "The hack can see us up there. One glance and we're busted."

"I don't see what you can do about it. That's just one of the risks."

"Maybe. But I've got an idea," West said.

The next day, West suggested to the cellhouse officer, Mr. Rooks, that the top of the cellhouse needed cleaning. West had been up there to do some painting recently and said it looked pretty dirty (he had also used the opportunity to get a good look at the roof ventilator). Officer Rooks agreed and West was sent up a ladder from the third cell tier to the top of the cell block with a broom, dustpan, and stiff bristle brush. He deliberately ran the brush across the bars of the cell block roof cage and a cascade of paint flakes and dirt fell down the face of the cells. Soon Lieutenant Wade made his inspection rounds on the top tier of B-Block and saw the accumulating pile of debris on the walkway outside the cells. Something had to be done. Cleanliness was the order of the day.

West agreed. Something had to be done. He suggested to Rooks that he hang old blankets over the bars to prevent dust from falling over the side. Rooks immediately called the laundry and asked the foreman if they had any old blankets down there. Apparently they did, because Rooks said, "Send some up." West was delighted.

West knew that Rooks would be off for two days starting the next day. He cornered the laundry foreman in the mess hall that noon and said, "Stall sending the blankets until tomorrow. And when you send them, send all you've got."

The next morning two big hampers of blankets arrived in the cellhouse. West explained to the relief officer that Rooks had authorized it. The officer called Lieutenant Wade and, sure enough, he had told Rooks to do something about the dust. So, within the hour, West had hung eighty blankets over the bars atop the end of B-Block —he had created a virtual tent. The view from below was completely obscured. There was a chance that a guard on the top level of the gun gallery could see what West was up to, but the guard seldom came up to the top level since nobody was ever on top of the cell block. The cons in their cells had a hard time believing West could get away with something as brazen as that. Anglin and Morris couldn't believe it either; they decided to wait and see if it lasted before they began work on the roof vent.

Two days later Rooks returned. He walked into the cellhouse, saw the blankets, and asked West, "You really need all those blankets?"

"Well, that's what they sent up. I thought you ordered that many, so I hung 'em up."

About that time, Lieutenant Head, who was in charge of the industries building, happened by the cellhouse. He took one look at the tent West had erected and bellowed, "Who put those blankets up there?"

"West did," said Officer Rooks. "I approved it." West was surprised that Rooks took the heat and didn't lay it off on Wade, who really had authorized it. Maybe he was worried that the breach of security would reach the Warden and he would be seen as a snitch.

"Take them down immediately," yelled Lieutenant Head as he stormed out of the cellhouse. Rooks ordered West to take down the blankets—and West, who had overheard the conversation, gave it one last try, a desperate ploy to save his cell-block tent.

"Who is Lieutenant Head that he can countermand an order by Lieutenant Wade? Head isn't even supposed to be in the cellhouse," West argued. "He pulls no more rank than Lieutenant Wade. Who in hell is he to tell Lieutenant Wade what to do?"

Rooks thought for a moment and then turned away to find Lieutenant Wade, obviously to dump the problem back in his lap. West didn't know what went on in the meeting between Rooks and Wade. Maybe something West had said had struck home. Maybe the two lieutenants had had conflicts before. At any rate, Wade simply said, "Leave the blankets up there."

That night Clarence Anglin and Frank Morris tested the set-up. Immediately after the 9:30 cell count, at which all inmates had to stand at the front of their cells, they removed the fake rear panels to their cells and retrieved their dummy heads from the utility corridor. They carefully placed the dummies in their bunks, squeezed through their escape-holes, and climbed to the top of the cell block. All was silent. The gun gallery guard was on the lower level. They carefully inspected the roof vent to determine what would be needed to remove it and how long it would take. After more than an hour had passed with no commotion from below, Anglin and Morris knew their dummy heads had fooled the guard who had completed his first hourly cell check. They returned to their cells without incident. The system worked.

Now the immediate problem at hand was the roof ventilator. They knew West couldn't stall the guards forever, sweeping and pretending to sweep on top of the cell block. West invented all kinds of excuses to avoid finishing the job, but sooner or later the blankets would come down. Clarence Anglin and Frank Morris went to work immediately on the ventilator grille, made of steel mesh and fastened to the vent shaft by screws. After they removed it, they devised simple clamps to hold it in place and made dummy screw-heads so they could stick the grille back on and remove it easily. While they worked on the vent, Allen West worked nights in his cell sewing raincoat sleeves and securing the unions with friction tape and rubber cement. The boats would have to be prefabricated and the final assembly done on top of the cell block. It was the only work space large enough. At the end of each nightly work session the raincoats were stashed in the roof vent, a safe and handy hiding place. J. W. Anglin, meanwhile, was occupied making two more dummy heads for use on the night of the escape.

West told Joe Carnes they were having trouble with the roof vent. There were more bars than they had expected. And hardened-steel ones too. Carnes recalled having told West about new bars put in after 1933, but he let the matter pass. West said Anglin and Morris had no difficulty removing the lower vent-cover and that they could see up inside the twenty-inch-diameter ventilator shaft. The original soft iron bars were set near the bottom of the shaft. Morris had found a steel pipe in the utility corridor that would work as a lever to pry the bars apart and make a gap big enough for the men to squeeze through. But before they could get out, they had to get past the new bars, set like spokes in a wagon wheel, an impenetrable forest of hard steel.

They tried everything. West had managed to steal an electric hair-clipper from the barber shop, and Morris had skillfully converted it to an electric drill. He and Clarence Anglin had rigged an electric circuit from their cell to the top of the utility corridor using wire they had found in the corridor. The drill was too weak to cut into the steel. West went after a bigger motor. He discovered by accident that the industrial vacuum sweeper that was used in the cellhouse had two motors. It malfunctioned one day and he saw an inmate electrician working on it. He persuaded the electrician to remove one of the motors for him. West arranged a diversion in the kitchen area; one inmate hit another over the head. During the disturbance, West was able to smuggle the motor to his cell. He gave it to Clarence Anglin and he took it that night to the top of the cell block, where he and Morris converted it to a drill. It proved to be too powerful—or at least too noisy—to use. They tried muffling it with a metal cover and rags, but it still sounded like a vacuum cleaner when they switched it on. They would have to remove the bars by hand.

There was little Joe Carnes could do to help West and the others. He thought about revealing his method of making a cutting torch to West, but he knew there would be insufficient time even if they somehow managed to assemble all the necesssary parts.

The plan seemed doomed. Then Frank Morris inspected the web of steel bars more closely. In the darkness of the vent shaft, illuminated only by a crude homemade flashlight, he went over the problem one more time. He noticed that the bars were welded securely to the steel support ring, but the ring itself was fastened to the inside of the ventilator shaft by a number of bolts. The bolts ran into new concrete that would be impossible to remove since there was no room to work inside the shaft. Then he discovered an oversight on the part of whoever had installed the new bars. The six bolts holding the ring in place were made of soft metal. They could easily be cut with a file. Once through the bolts, the entire ring, bars and all, could be shoved out the top of the shaft. With luck the big sheet-metal rainhood over the vent could be popped off at the same time and they would have a clear path to the roof. He informed the others that the time was drawing near.

J. W. Anglin began to assemble a list of names, contacts on the outside. He bundled up his and Clarence's family snapshots and mementos and wrapped them snugly in polyethelene plastic. Each man had to make his own paddle in those final days before the break. Each used a piece of plywood shelving from his cell, painted the characteristic "Alcatraz green." West got some small bolts and nuts and the furniture shop provided wooden handles. Clarence Anglin took the paddles to the top of the cell block and stored them in the vent.

Joe Carnes felt the tension. In the yard each day, men shot quick glances at other men, each trying to figure out what the other knew. Some men avoided others. The Anglin brothers seldom spoke to West in the yard in those final days. Frank Morris spent an unusual amount of time in the northeast corner of the yard where the black inmates usually congregated to play dominoes and talk. Joe wondered why Morris was suddenly so interested in talking with black inmates. Then it dawned on him: That was the only part of the yard where you could get a good look at the north wall of the prison building and the flue that rose from the bakery on the basement level to the top of the building. That was the best way to get down from the roof, and Morris was casing it.

By now, so many inmates knew at least part of the escape plan, and had participated in some small way, Joe thought it was a miracle the hacks hadn't sensed something. If they did know something was up, they didn't show it. Life in the yard appeared normal.

One day in early June, Joe stood with Allen West, talking casually, when Bumpy Johnson passed by. Bumpy looked up, his face tight and unscrutable as usual, and said, "Hi, Joe." Carnes returned the greeting as Bumpy walked on. Bumpy hadn't spoken to West. Joe couldn't remember a time Bumpy had passed by another man without acknowledging him. It was unlike Bumpy Johnson. Was he trying to distance himself from West? Did he have the jitters? Not likely for a man like Bumpy Johnson. Joe wondered if Bumpy had sprung his "little twist." If he had, what was it?

West said nothing. He ignored Bumpy and the snub. Now Joe was positive Bumpy had a hand in things. Had he made contact with someone on the outside? Was there a boat waiting?

On Monday, June 11, 1962, Joe Carnes went to his desk in the library as usual. West passed by the library and greeted Carnes and the others, but kept on walking. A few minutes later, he passed by again, and again he didn't stop. It was getting on Joe's nerves. West was grinning. Joe saw him pass by again and couldn't stand it.

"West!" he called out.

West came over to the library bars as he had done many times before. "What's up?" Joe asked him.

"Nothing much. Nothing at all, Joe."

Joe could see the excitement in West's face. He waited for an answer. Finally West could no longer contain himself.

"Oh, yeah. I forgot one little item."

"Yeah? What's that?" Joe knew West was about to burst.

West looked Joe in the eye and, in a serious, vibrant tone, whispered, "Joe, tonight—we see the moon."

Joe felt dizzy. Tonight! Tonight they would pop the vent. They wouldn't wait. It was tonight or never. Make it or die! Joe was elated. He wanted to shout. West saw how he felt. It had all come to this. They were standing not twenty feet from where West had first approached Joe Carnes about the escape plan months before. All the planning, all the danger, the work, four hours every night, grinding, chipping, twisting, all had come down to a final thrust, and now the moment had arrived. Joe envied West and was excited for him and the others. No man had ever done what they were about to do.

Joe Carnes looked at West and thought how much he had grown to like him in these past months. The time had come. There was nothing more to be said. West turned to leave. "Well, good luck to you, Joe. Hope you make it out someday."

"Same to you, Little Man. Good luck."

Joe watched him go. This was probably the last time he would ever talk with his friend, he thought. Unless they ran into some bad luck. There was still time for something to go wrong.

That evening at dinner in the mess hall, Joe Carnes watched Bumpy Johnson enter the room. He put very little on his tray, sat down, and only pecked at what he had taken. His eyes shifted from time to time to where West sat, but there was no eye contact between them. Anybody who tried to strike up a conversation with Bumpy got only a word or two out of him. It was clear to Joe Carnes that Bumpy must have a lot riding on the escape attempt. He wouldn't be so nervous over the fate of three cons, white guys at that, unless he had committed himself and his reputation to something.

Back in his cell, Joe lay on his bunk listening to the background murmur of the cellhouse. Through the years this sound had soothed him. He couldn't stand absolute quiet. Every now and then, for some unaccountable reason, the cellhouse would fall silent. Not a voice, not a rattle. For a frightening moment he would feel all alone in the prison. He would get up and call to someone just to start a conversation. On this night things were normal, and the cellhouse was filled with low voices, the bangs and rattles of ordinary life in a concrete-and-steel cage.

He smiled to himself, recalling West's frantic search for a dime the previous week. West had asked him if he had a dime so they could make a phone call once they had gotten ashore. Joe didn't have one, nor did anybody else. Finally West found somebody who had given him a dime. Money on Alcatraz was hard to come by. Besides, Joe thought, it didn't make sense. They would need a lot more than a dime if they made it to the mainland. And if Bumpy had arranged for a boat, they wouldn't need to call anybody, anyway. Did West really know what he was doing? Joe had some doubts.

If others felt as tense as Joe Carnes, he could not sense it. He knew West and Morris and the Anglins must be about to explode with excitement. There was nothing to do but wait.

Details of the plan raced through West's mind as he lay on his bunk, waiting for the evening count. Each man would prepare his cell. The dummies had to look right, as much like sleeping men as possible. With luck, the dummies wouldn't be discovered until the morning count, ten hours later. Clarence Anglin and Frank Morris would go out first, climb to the top of the cell block, retrieve the dummy heads hidden there, and return to the bottom of the utility corridor. Then West would break through the remaining thin layer of concrete at the rear of his cell and, for the first time, squeeze through the "door." On top of the cell block they would distribute the load: the tightly rolled deflated boats, the paddles, the hundred feet of heavy wire that they would use to lower their gear from the roof of the building. Then they would make a last-minute check of the tools: the homemade wire-cutter to snip the barbed wire atop the ten-foot-high fence they would have to scale, the reflector, and the homemade flashlight. (Why a flashlight? Certainly not to illuminate their path under the nose of the guard in the watchtower. To signal a boat, perhaps?) Then Morris would squeeze into the vent shaft and stick his clever handmade periscope out the top to see if, by some bizarre chance, a guard was on the roof. Morris was particularly proud of the periscope. It was made in two sections, from canvas board and friction tape, and was about four feet long. He had placed jiggering mirrors inside at the proper angles to reflect an image along the length of it.

The 7:30 P.M. count came: All the inmates stood obediently at the front of their cells as the guard passed along the tier. All present and accounted for. Then came the wait for the mail to be delivered. That was just one of the many small details the four men had taken into consideration. If, by some horrible coincidence, one of the men got a letter, the guard would insist on handing it to him personally. A dummy in the bunk would be discovered.

West was deep in thought and tormented by worry as the guard with the mail passed by his cell. He lay in his bunk in the same position as the dummy would be. He deliberately rolled his head as the guard passed by—a subtle message to the guard—this is a live man in here.

Moments later he heard a scraping sound, almost imperceptible. He knew the sound; he had heard it many times in the past week. It was Frank Morris crawling out of his cell next door. It was followed by sounds rising up the utility corridor. West became increasingly tense. He didn't dare break through his cell wall until he knew for certain the roof vent was open and clear. If anything went wrong up there, and they had to postpone their escape, West knew he wouldn't be able to patch the rear of his cell "door" in time for the morning count. It seemed to Allen West that hours passed. He checked the time. It was 10:30 P.M. His heart leaped as he heard a loud, hollow bang echo through the cellhouse.

A noise like that wasn't unusual. The wind could cause it. Or a sonic boom. But West knew exactly what it was. Anglin and Morris had pushed the ring up and forced the sheet-metal rain hood off the roof vent. It had fallen onto the roof. The vent was open!

Officer Albert Young heard the sound too. He was working the 4 P.M.-to-midnight shift in the west gun gallery. It sounded to him like a man striking a fifty-gallon oil drum with the heel of his hand. It came, he thought, from upstairs, in the vicinity of the prison hospital. He called Lieutenant Weir, who was in the Control Center and was in charge of the shift. While he was on the phone, he heard a second sound, much like the first. Then a third. The last bang sounded like it came from the dining room "cage," a guard-post located outside the dining room wall over an alleyway leading from the cellhouse to the recreation yard.

Lieutenant Weir immediately turned on the paging system when he got Officer Young's call. The paging system in the building served as a listening device and would help to pinpoint the source of the sounds. To Weir, the sounds were coming from the hospital area. He summoned Officer Gronzo and let him into the cellhouse. Gronzo

walked through the cellhouse and hospital for about forty-five minutes and found everything apparently normal. He heard no new sounds,
so he returned to the Control Center and reported to Lieutenant Weir.

"West!" Allen West heard his name whispered and dropped to
his knees and put his face to the small vent at the rear of his cell.
Frank Morris was on the other side. "You got it off?" West whispered, his voice trembling with excitement.

"Yeah. We can see the moon," Morris said. "Hurry, kick the
hole out and let's go."

Without another word, West sat back and put both feet against
a thin concrete separating him from freedom, and kicked. A large
chunk of concrete bounced into the utility corridor. But one side
of the thin wall held. West kicked again. Still it did not yield.

"What in hell!" he muttered. It should have given way on the
first kick. He kicked again. And again—as hard as he could. And
. . . *nothing*. The hole was still too small for him to squeeze through.
He leaned forward and looked at the concrete more closely. Then
he saw it. A steel reinforcing bar imbedded in the wall. For a moment everything went black. Panic flooded over him. A bar! Inside
that thin, last section of wall. Why there, of all places?

"What the hell's wrong?" Morris whispered hoarsely from the
other side.

"Frank, I can't move it. There's a bar I didn't see."

"Son-of-a-bitch!" moaned Frank. He was silent for a moment
as both men thought fast. "Can't you do anything with it?"

"I'm trying, dammit!" West said angrily. "Pull from that side."

Frank Morris pulled and tugged. He cursed under his breath and
strained at the thin section of concrete. He spoke to West: "We're
making a lot of racket. The guys on this side are down on their vents
watching us." He paused again, then said, "Tell you what. I'll go get
J. W. and Clarence and we'll see what we can do."

In a flash he was gone. And West felt a cold knot in the pit
of his stomach. He knew Frank would not be back. They would leave
without him. They wouldn't make the same mistake Doc Barker had
made. Barker had tried to be generous, and it had gotten him killed.

This time, if you couldn't pull your weight, you were on your own. That was the deal they all had agreed to, and West knew it. It had been his responsibility to see that his "door" was ready when the time came. The failure was his alone. If it had been one of the others, West would have been the first to say, "Let him stay. Let's go."

On top of the cell block Frank Morris gave the news to the Anglins. They wanted to go back for West. Frank reminded them of the deal. They had already been lucky once—all that noise when the roof rain hood had toppled off and no alarm had been sounded. Still, J. W. and Clarence knew the agony West must have been feeling—all that planning and work down the drain. Maybe he would get out on his own. It was just a single soft iron bar, after all. The trio came to a quick decision, one that altered everything, including their own chances of survival. Clarence Anglin made one more trip down the utility corridor and left "Oink," one of the dummy heads, in the utility corridor behind West's cell. He tried to help West break the concrete-imbedded bar, but to no avail.

By the time he got back to the top of the cell block, J. W. Anglin and Morris had partially dismantled one of the boats. They had decided three men couldn't make it on one boat, so they couldn't leave one behind on the chance that West would make it out of his cell. But if they reinforced one boat by adding a third pontoon from the second boat, the three of them might make it. That would leave one pontoon behind for West. Maybe, if he got to the beach, he could fasten it to some wood scraps, inflate it with his mouth, and still make it away. It was a long shot, but it was all they had to give him.

After they pushed their gear up the vent shaft onto the roof, they climbed up themselves. The last man up pulled the remaining pontoon, some extra wire, and West's paddle into the vent and left it stashed there. They made their way across the roof and down the bakery flue at the north end of the prison building in full view of the guard tower. The exterior prison lights illuminated the side of the building and the pipe—but there was no other choice; they just had to take their chances that, as usual, the tower was unoccupied. They knew the tower was manned only when the kitchen door was open to receive supplies. But they had never been at that end of the prison building at night and didn't know exactly what to expect.

Once on the ground, again they had to take a chance. Would they be seen by the roving lieutenant, who spent most of his time outside the building? On that point, the odds were in their favor, since the perimeter of the building was so large. After they scaled the ten-foot fence and made their way down the steep, brush-covered embankment to the narrow beach, they were out of sight as far as the guards were concerned. If they hadn't been discovered by that time, they were relatively safe until the 7:15 morning count, after which only one worry remained: drowning in the Bay.

Allen West, meanwhile, struggled, determined to escape from the snare he had set for himself. He still had one star drill hidden in his cell, in a slot gouged in the concrete where the wall joined the floor. He dug it out and chipped away at the concrete that held the iron reinforcing bar. *Too slow,* he decided. In desperation, he pulled at the bar with his hands. Bits of concrete crumbled off it. *Break it!* That was the solution. Break it by the simple principle of metal fatigue. Bend it slightly one way and then another, back and forth, back and forth, as long as it takes until it snaps.

He set to work immediately. His hands became raw and bloody. As he worked, he had to be constantly alert for the footsteps of the cellhouse hack. Those fools, Morris and the Anglins. Didn't they realize that by leaving him behind they had greatly increased their chances of getting caught? If the guards caught him breaking out of his cell, they would quickly find the dummies in the other cells. The Anglins and Morris would be shot in the water. If they had all come back to help him, they could have taken turns and snapped the bar in no time. But he didn't blame them for his predicament. It just seemed to him that they could have played their hand a little smarter.

By 1:00 A.M. West was inside the utility corridor at last. The others had been gone for over three hours. He found the dummy head that Clarance Anglin had left for him and quickly arranged the dummy in his bunk. In minutes he was atop the cell block. The lower vent grille was laying clear of the vent shaft. He reached up and found the pontoon and paddle they had stashed for him. He was touched by their concern. It was their last message: "We hope you make it."

He pulled himself up the vent shaft, squeezed past the remaining bent bars, and, for the first time, stuck his head into fresh air. In the moonlight the prison roof looked serene and quiet. He saw a neatly folded life jacket lying beside the toppled vent rain-cap—one last afterthought.

He scrambled to the end of the building where the others had climbed down the bakery flue pipe. There was no sign they had ever passed this way. He strained to see their boat somewhere in the darkness of the Bay waters. Nothing. When he reached the edge of the building he was stunned to see a guard standing in the catwalk on the water tower.

The noise had done it, he was certain. The strange noises had been enough to arouse suspicion and the lieutenant had placed a man in the tower. He was trapped. There was no way down but under the nose of the guard. Nothing to do but wait. Maybe the guard would be taken off the tower after a while.

So he waited. He waited for hours, until the sun appeared over the East Bay hills and the seagulls screamed at him for being on their rooftop so early in the morning. As he saw the sun rise, he felt his hopes sink. The guard never once left the tower. West made his way back across the roof, down the vent, down the gloomy utility corridor, and back through the wretched hole in the back of his cell. He stuffed the dummy head in the corridor, and climbed into bed. He didn't bother to replace the fake vent cover. He was weary and numb and his spirit was crushed. But he could not cry. His only consolation was that soon all hell would break loose.

Joe Carnes had lain awake all night. After the strange noises on the roof hours before, most of the men in the cell block had settled down for a normal night's sleep. But not Joe Carnes. He knew they had gone. He didn't know about West's disappointment yet, but he knew that, since the alarm hadn't sounded after the noise on the roof, they had made it—maybe. He wondered where they were now—in a comfortable boat somewhere watching the sunrise, sipping fine whiskey and chatting with Bumpy Johnson's buddies? Or were they on the run, wet and tired, trying to steal a car? Or were they cold corpses drifting slowly with the tide under the Golden Gate Bridge?

There was even the possibility that they hadn't gone at all. Maybe the noise had scared them. Maybe they hadn't gotten the roof vent loose. Maybe they were crouched, cold and shivering, in one of the many caves along the Alcatraz shoreline. Time would tell. Joe chuckled to himself at the thought of the hack's face when the dummies were turned.

At 7:15 A.M. the morning standup count began. The inmates of Alcatraz climbed out of bed and shuffled to the fronts of their cells to be counted. Joe Carnes was already there, waiting impatiently to see what would happen. He heard the guards calling off the number of those present on each tier. Suddenly, there was the recount signal for the entire cellhouse! Sometimes a guard would miscount a single tier and there would be a recount—but never for the whole cellhouse. They were gone! He knew it.

Officer Bartlett saw the problem. Two men were not answering the call. The Anglin brothers. They were still in their bunks. He reached in between the bars of J. W. Anglin's cell and patted the pillow. No response. He hurried to the desk of acting Lieutenant Bill Long and said, "We either have a dead man or a dummy in the cell block. I can't wake him up." Long accompanied Bartlett back to Anglin's cell. He reached in and tapped him on the head as he lay in his bunk. No response. He tapped again and felt his fingers sink into Anglin's head. He slapped the head and was stunned to see it roll off the bunk to the floor.

"It's a dummy!" he shouted as he yanked at the blanket, exposing the rolled blankets and clothing that formed the body. He stepped to the next cell, that of Clarence Anglin, and yanked the blanket off. Another dummy! He raced along the lower outside tier of B-Block and saw another still form in Frank Morris's cell. Another dummy! Long immediately sounded the escape alarm.

Officer Waldron, who had given the signal to the Control Center for the 7:15 standup count as his first duty of the day, started for the commotion on B-Block and, as he passed Allen West's cell, heard West call to him from his cell. 'You may as well lock me up," West said calmly. "I planned the entire escape." West held up the fake vent cover he had made. "No shakedown could ever discover this," he declared with pride.

Waldron climbed to the second tier of the cell block and from there could see the open roof vent—the inmates had gone up through the roof vent! Within minutes, the entire escape route to the water's edge had been traced. Associate Warden Arthur M. Dollison was alerted and efforts were made to reach Warden Olin Blackwell, who was on vacation at Lake Berryessa in Napa County.

Lieutenant Mahan, who had rushed to the cellhouse from his apartment after he heard the escape alarm, took four men to the roof. They found the toppled rain hood and the steel "wagon-wheel" ring of bars that had been forced up out of the vent shaft. They searched the entire roof and found the long wire near the bakery flue on the north end of the building. From the scrape marks and the bent support bar on the flue, they knew that this was the escape route to the ground. Meanwhile, Weir and Howell hurried to the north end of the building and found the barbed wire atop the cyclone fence sagging from the weight of the men who had climbed over it. A strand on the outside yard wall had been cut. Weir could plainly see the grass matted down near the water tower. He and Officer Howell followed the trail down to the seawall, where they found another coiled length of heavy wire.

Although the possibility remained that the men were still on the island, there was a strong likelihood that they had indeed escaped. At 7:55 A.M. Officer Mills telephoned the San Francisco office of the FBI and spoke to Special Agent Phillip Bowser. He informed him that at 7:15 that morning, when the prisoner count had been made, three inmates were found missing in Cell Block B. The missing inmates were Frank Lee Morris, John William Anglin, and Clarence Anglin. Three inmates had escaped from Alcatraz and were at large. The alarm was flashed to police agencies, the California Highway Patrol, the U.S. Navy and Coast Guard, and all sheriffs' offices in the Bay Area.

By the time FBI special agents arrived on the island, more discoveries had been made. On top of B-Block officers found West's unused life jacket and, in the vent shaft where he had left it, the uninflated pontoon. It was described by FBI agents as a "partially completed rubber raft approximately six feet by two feet with a wooden valve." They also found a foot-long file, its handle wrapped with rags, a five-by-six-inch mirror, a homemade wrench, a stapler, and a bottle of "Rem-Weld" liquid plastic used for book repair—used at the last minute to create a makeshift boat for West.

A more thorough search of the roof turned up West's paddle where he had tossed it aside, and a five-foot-long piece of rope tied to the ventilator grille adjacent to the vent opening. Agents scoured the rooftop and reported every scrap of material that might be linked to the escape: a one-and-one-half-inch piece of yellow electrical insulation, a piece of razor blade, and an electrical terminal box with two outlet sockets. Allen West's paint bucket, a five-gallon can, was still on top of the cell block, the cement paint in it solidified. When the cement was cracked open, officers found a plastic bag that contained the vacuum-cleaner motor, a homemade flashlight, three spoon handles, and a length of electric cord.

The escapees' cells were stripped and searched. The three men had not bothered to reposition their fake vent covers after leaving their cells. They knew the guard wouldn't see the open vents in the darkness, and by morning it wouldn't matter. In addition to the dummy heads and fake vent covers in each cell, they discovered an array of escape-related objects. In Morris's cell, agents found the issues of *Sports Illustrated* and *Popular Mechanics* magazines containing the articles about boats and life jackets; they also turned up assorted nuts and bolts, a fingernail clipper, and a five-inch file. In J. W. Anglin's cell they found his *Popular Mechanics* magazine describing a vulcanizing machine, a bottle of blue-green paint, a role of adhesive tape, and assorted art supplies.

In Clarence Anglin's cell, beneath his bunk was a bundled handkerchief containing little knots of human hair left over from the dummy heads, a bottle of blue-green paint, and the length of twine that stretched into J. W.'s cell. While Allen West was being interrogated in the warden's office, his cell was searched. The most interesting find was a *Rand McNally Road Atlas* of the United States, Canada, and Mexico; several pages were missing, the ones of Mexico. They also found his tool kit, which contained Joe Carnes's three hacksaw blades, a chisel, and the three spoons and metal strip used to crack the concrete.

The two star drill bits were not found (nor did West reveal their existence in his statement). West later told Joe Carnes that he had broken them and flushed the pieces down the toilet. More likely, West had hidden them in the utility corridor so that future escapees might make use of them.

Allen West was "interviewed" by the FBI in the presence of prison officials. Neither threats nor promises were made to him. He was advised of his right to counsel and that his statements could be used against him. West declined counsel and spoke freely of how he had planned the escape. He said it had begun when he had gotten out of the Treatment Unit in D-Block in May 1961 and decided to break out of Alcatraz. While painting atop the cell block he had noticed the vent and mentioned it to the Anglin brothers as a possible escape route. He said Frank Morris had joined them later, around December, and had become West's partner. They had made a big rubber raft and four paddles and intended to paddle their way to Angel Island and then across Raccoon Straits to Marin County.

If Joe Carnes had any fear of West ratting, it was unfounded. He said nothing about Joe Carnes, Bumpy Johnson, or any other inmate, and gave only enough details of the plan to make it sound convincing. When asked what they had intended to do if they made land, West said they had planned to steal guns, clothes, and a car, and then leave the area and split up. The Anglins would go one way, Morris and himself another. The only weapons they could possibly have were a sharpened screwdriver or a kitchen knife. West not only claimed credit for most of the planning, he took the blame, excluding Denny and all the others who had contributed their efforts. He was the one, he said, who had stolen the raincoats, the spoons, and the tools; he had made the dummy heads, the life jackets.

He said a curious thing, too: that Frank Morris had accompanied one of the Anglins to the top of the cell block each night while they were at work because he, West, hadn't trusted the Anglins and hadn't wanted the two of them up there alone together. After all the four men had been through together, this statement seemed out of place. Perhaps West was attempting to distance himself from the others if they were caught.

All the cells on all three tiers of the outside of B-Block were inspected to see if anybody else had planned to go out with the Anglins and Morris. Officers uncovered a few holes near the ventilator grille in the area of June Heywood Stevens's third-tier cell, and eight holes in the same location in the third-tier cell of Woodrow Wilson Gainey.

When questioned, Gainey and Stevens denied having knowledge of the escape. Gainey admitted he knew West and the others, and Stevens admitted knowing Clarence Anglin. A few days later, Gainey requested a private interview with Warden Blackwell, which was granted. Gainey admitted he and Stevens had originally been in on the escape. They had used sharpened spoon handles to grind holes in their cell walls but had stopped digging holes when West told them they might be discovered. Gainey then abandoned the project. Stevens, who worked as a plumber and had an assignment in the utility corridor in B-Block, stopped, too, when West became afraid some of the other plumbers might discover their work. West had never told Stevens to resume digging, so he had not done so.

The Anglins had kept Gainey and Stevens informed of the progress, he said. The Anglins had told him they were going to make two rubber rafts from raincoats. They had talked of wearing dyed-black long underwear under their prison denims and discarding their prison clothes on the beach before taking to the boats. Gainey thought they planned to go to Angel Island, but said J. W. Anglin had told him they might try for San Francisco because the distance was shorter. The Anglins also had told him they planned to steal a helicopter because Frank Morris had read a book about how to fly one and was sure he could do it. They would fly into the desert somewhere and hide out until the heat was off. Maybe they would steal a "big rig," a big truck and trailer, and bury it in the ground as a hideout. When it was safe, they would dig out and go their separate ways. They also talked about getting together in the future and robbing banks.

According to Gainey, none of the four mentioned any contacts on the outside who might help them. The Anglins said they might try to "bust out" their brother Al, who was in the Atlanta Penitentiary.

Stevens, when interviewed a second time, said he knew nothing, had heard nothing, and could furnish no useful information. The night of the escape he had heard nothing unusual in the utility corridor. He had not dug any holes in his cell and didn't know how they had gotten there. Besides, he had lost his "good time" because of the holes and he didn't care to discuss anything about the escape with the FBI.

Allen West was asked again about Gainey and Stevens. He said only four men had been in on the escape at any time: himself, the Anglins, and Frank Morris. He had not discussed the escape with Gainey or Stevens. He admitted some other inmates may have learned something was going on, but if any did, he didn't know about it.

It appeared there were more than four dummies in Alcatraz.

*   *   *

The search for the three escapees began within minutes of the alarm on the morning of June 12. The cellhouse was searched from top to bottom, including locked rooms, the old dungeon below the cellhouse, the storerooms, the industries building and shops, anywhere three men might hide. Teams climbed over the island from end to end, scouring through shrubbery, looking in caves. The Coast Guard began an immediate water search and an aerial scan of the surrounding islands and peninsula. The police in San Francisco and other cities were alerted. Officials became painfully aware that, if the trio had made it off the island successfully, they might have had as much as a nine-hour head start. If they had survived their ordeal in the water, they could be anywhere. The escape could not be handled as an internal matter. The public had to be informed.

7

Freedom?

"Ha. Ha. We made it."

Frank
John
Clarence

from a postcard to Alcatraz Warden Blackwell
postmarked "San Francisco, June 16, 1962, 8:30 P.M."

Rarely since the end of World War II had there been a story as
meaty as this one. The banner headline of the *San Francisco Chronicle*
the morning after the escape blared "OUT OF ALCATRAZ—BY
A SPOON." It had all the elements of great Hollywood drama: escaped and dangerous convicts with a nine-hour head start; outrageous
conditions on The Rock that would allow three men to dig out of
their cells with *spoons*, dummies in their bunks; a brilliant plan that
had avoided detection. The story made international headlines and
focused worldwide attention on the little island in the middle of San
Francisco Bay. That wasn't the way the Bureau of Prisons wanted
it, but there it was. Prison officials and government officials from
the FBI to the Congress were flooded with telephone calls, requests
for interviews, demands for full disclosure. What was going on within
the walls of Alcatraz, the "escape-proof" prison?

While prison officials revealed to the press the basic story, certain details were withheld for obvious reasons. Besides, they had other
business that needed attention. During the week after the escape, the
search intensified. Inspector Ken Manley, Chief of the Fugitive Detail

of the San Francisco Police Department, coordinated all information received by the police with FBI Special Agent Ray M. Andress. Manley prepared and distributed more than five hundred bulletins containing descriptions and photographs of the escapees to the nine precinct stations of the San Francisco Police Department within hours of the alarm on June 12. By 2:00 P.M. that day, he had dispatched an All Points Bulletin to all California law enforcement agencies as well as to surrounding state police and intelligence units in Kansas City, New Orleans, Mobile, Tampa, and Milwaukee.

Manley and Andress daily pursued all crime reports in the immediate Bay Area in hopes of picking up the trail. No leads were uncovered. The net spread over the entire western United States, including Idaho, Montana, and Utah. Each state's highway patrol chased down all suspicious vehicles, conducted innumerable searches, and established roadblocks. The results were negative.

Meanwhile, Captain B. P. Clark of the U.S. Coast Guard, who was also Captain of the Port of San Francisco, supervised the around-the-clock search of the Bay. Two forty-foot patrol boats combed the waters around San Francisco's piers and yacht harbor, the beaches, rocks, and caves off Alcatraz, and the shores of Angel Island and the Marin coastline from Belvedere to the Golden Gate Bridge. The FBI employed eight small power cruisers to search along the shoreline from Point Belvedere to the Golden Gate and along the Berkeley shore. Clark also arranged for a Coast Guard helicopter to carry FBI agents along the ocean beaches and cliffs as far north as Fort Ross and south to Half Moon Bay. For ten days the chopper hovered over coves, ravines, and shoreline caves as agents searched for even the smallest fragment that might reveal the fate of the three convicts. Observation aircraft with FBI agents aboard scrutinized the rolling coastal hills from San Pablo Bay and Point Richmond to the grassy slopes of the Marin Headlands.

Then, on June 13, a curious thing happened. A man calling himself "John Anglin" made a phone call. The receptionist at the San Francisco law offices of Leslie MacGowan and his wife, Eugenia MacGowan, answered the phone about 10:30 that morning. A man said he wanted to speak to Mr. MacGowan. When the receptionist told him Mr. MacGowan was in court, he asked who was there that he might speak to. She replied that Mrs. MacGowan was there and asked him his hame. "I'll tell *her*," the voice said. Mrs. MacGowan took the call and the man on the line said he was John Anglin. He wanted her to call the United States Marshal and tell him that he would surrender to her [Mrs. MacGowan], that he wanted his "day in court." Mrs. MacGowan was perplexed. The name John Anglin meant nothing to her. She told him she didn't know who he was. He replied, "Read your newspaper," and hung up. She checked with her secretary and the receptionist. Neither had heard of a John Anglin. So she bought a newspaper and was stunned to see a front page story about the escape.

She told the FBI agents sent to investigate that she handled only domestic-relations cases; it was her husband who handled the criminal cases. On one occasion, when he had been a clerk for Judge Walter Pope, since retired, he had worked on a brief for an Alcatraz inmate. As a result, the inmate had been released. His name had spread among inmates and, on several occasions thereafter, he had been asked to assist several individuals. Possibly the escapees had gotten his name from one of these inmates—although he had not worked with an Alcatraz inmate in two years.

The man on the phone had had a low voice and sounded serious. Mrs. MacGowan said he hadn't seemed to have a "good command of the English language." He had made no reference to the other two escapees. Special Agents Rauch and Collopy spent the remainder of the day in the offices of the MacGowans in case the caller tried again.

Was it J. W., or a prank? The man never called back, nor, to anybody's knowledge, was any other attorney in San Francisco contacted. Mrs. MacGowan said she hadn't detected an accent during her brief conversation. Both J. W. and Clarence spoke with the rich accent of Southern Georgia. Frank Morris, for that matter, also spoke with a distinct southern accent.

A report was relayed to FBI headquarters that a seaman aboard a freighter heading out of the Golden Gate claimed he had seen the floating body of a man dressed in blue denim the day after the escape. Apparently nobody else on board had seen it. When the seaman was interviewed, his sighting had grown to *three* bodies dressed in blue denim. Reports came in from up and down California and from Oregon and Washington: Three men and a boy had been seen in a car at a service station near Seattle; two men who answered the description of the Anglin brothers had been seen at a lunch counter; strange men and a woman had been spotted in a car with no license plate. Sometimes the sightings were picked up by the press and played for all they were worth. On the day after the escape, two San Rafael residents, an eleven-year-old boy and a housewife, saw three men on a raft near a pair of tiny islands in San Pablo Bay. Both witnesses said there had been three men aboard, two sitting, one standing. The raft had disappeared behind the larger of the two islands. A few minutes later, according to Mrs. Fred Hill, who had observed the men through her picture window, a small speedboat with another three men aboard had landed on one of the islands. Later it had left. A helicopter was immediately dispatched to the scene and the two islands were searched by Sheriff's officers, police, and the FBI. Nothing was found to indicate the escapees had been there.

The FBI carried on, exploring every possibility the escapees might have used. Agents questioned every boat owner from Sausalito to Berkeley and workers who had been on the shoreline on the night of June 11. They interviewed homeowners in Sausalito and Tiburon who had Bay views, hoping to turn up a clue. Only one boatowner in all the Bay Area marinas had a link to Alcatraz. A woman who owned an eighteen-foot outboard-motor cabin-cruiser in Sausalito was a regular visitor of an Alcatraz inmate. Upon investigation, agents confirmed that her boat had been inoperable during the time of the escape and had not left the yacht harbor for several months. The inmate was not linked to the escape plot.

On the night of June 14, the water search paid off. At 10:15 P.M., as a Coast Guard cutter ran slowly off Angel Island, halfway between Point Stewart and Point Knox, about two hundred yards offshore, Lieutenant Mike Bryan saw a small object caught in the cutter's searchlight beam as it skimmed across the dark water. He reached in and pulled out a home-made paddle about three feet long. It consisted of a piece of blue-green painted plywood with a pine handle bolted to it. Examination of the paddle confirmed that it was similar in materials and construction to the one left behind on the prison roof. Did the paddle mean that the trio had tried for Angel Island rather than San Francisco?

More evidence surfaced the same day. A U.S. Army Corps of Engineers "debris boat," which routinely skimmed the Bay for flotsam and jetsam that might be hazardous to navigation, recovered a suspicious-looking package. Since the escape, the crews of the debris boats paid close attention to everything caught in their nets. Captain Edward Thompson, Jr., of the debris boat *Coyote*, followed a rip tide on his assigned search pattern off Angel Island. He knew that these debris-laden currents would be the most likely spot for something— even a body—to turn up. A crewman spotted what appeared to be a dark, plastic-wrapped package about two or three feet below the surface. He went down into the net to retrieve it and saw immediately that an attempt to seal the packet had been made, but water had gotten inside. Inside the plastic was a second wrapped packet, a plastic wallet. It contained scraps of paper with names and addresses and photographs, snapshots of men and women, several of a pretty brunette. Captain Thompson found a receipt made out to Rachel Anglin for ten dollars deposited in Clarence Anglin's Alcatraz account. He knew he had something and radioed his headquarters.

The *Coyote* went to Fort Mason, where the contents of the packet were spread out in the sun to dry. Within minutes, two FBI agents were there to collect the first tangible evidence since the escape. Warden Blackwell and other federal authorities immediately claimed the packet's recovery bolstered their theory that "the three convicts perished in the chill water without reaching Angel Island." They admitted, however, that if the three were ingenious enough to escape from Alcatraz, they would be clever enough to discard such solid evidence —on purpose—to suggest they had drowned. James V. Bennett, director of the Federal Bureau of Prisons, conceded that the packet could be a ruse. "But," he said, "the list of names and addresses are so crucial for later contacts that they would not toss them into the Bay unless they were drowning."

Did J. W. Anglin accidentally lose the packet in the darkness as he boarded a boat? Was it a ruse? If he really had wanted to keep it, wouldn't he have tied it to his body? When asked about the importance of the family mementos, brother Rufus Anglin said, "Shoot, those boys would throw out anything to save their lives. They could always get more pictures."

As the FBI investigated the names and addresses found in the packet, the air and sea search continued. In the ten days following the escape, Warden Blackwell had his guards search the entire island, including the prison. He was determined to find every shred of evidence. There was also the possibility the three men, or their corpses, were still on Alcatraz. Every building, apartment, and home of prison employees was searched. One family reported that someone had entered their apartment through a kitchen window but had taken nothing of importance. Officials decided it had been a kid looking for some candy. Prison guards patrolled the shore, beaches, and caves, around the clock. Divers with scuba gear probed the underwater grottos below the shoreline. Using telescopes, prison officers scanned the debris-laden rip tide that routinely formed off the island.

Then on June 21, a wad of rubberized raincoat material was picked up on the beach at Fort Cronkhite just outside the Golden Gate. It was a homemade life jacket like the one found on top of the cell block. The next day, another life jacket was pulled from the water just fifty yards off Alcatraz by Officer McCracken aboard the prison launch U.S. *Johnson*. That left only one life jacket unaccounted for and provided the best evidence yet that the men had drowned. The life jacket found in the water was deflated. Apparently, the seams had not held. But had it been lost as a drowning man slipped beneath the surface, or had it been discarded by a man as he climbed aboard a boat? The search went on.

Private citizens got in on the search too. The newspapers were filled with stories of the escape, and the Bay shoreline and ocean beaches were dotted with beachcombers looking for clues. About a week after the plastic-wrapped wallet was found, two teenage boys, Wynn and George Carvill, found a water-logged plastic bag in the shallows near Fort Point. The FBI investigated the find, as they did every piece of flotsam turned in during that period. The bag, about sixteen-by-sixteen inches, was filled with cotton batting commonly used as mattress stuffing. Was it a crude flotation device? The bag appeared large and buoyant enough (when it dried out) to support the weight of at least one man. The FBI made no comment other than to say the plastic wrapping was the same material used to wrap the wallet recovered near Angel Island. No sooner had the FBI agents made the find public than false rumors began to circulate that the "float bag" was bloodstained and matted with human hair.

In the days that followed, the hunt for the Anglin brothers and Frank Morris turned into a waiting game. The water and air search continued until June 22. For prison officials like Blackwell, the game was a grisly one, waiting for the bodies to surface somewhere in San Francisco Bay. For FBI agents, who felt the ingenious trio had in fact made it ashore, the game was one of waiting for one of the three to make a mistake that would reveal their whereabouts. If they had made it safely to shore, had they separated? Had they met contacts who provided them with the means of leaving the area, the state, or the country? Were they hiding nearby? "No comment" was the only statement made by the FBI.

San Francisco FBI Chief Frank Price did venture a comment when asked if the investigation included the Florida haunts of the Anglin brothers and if it was likely the brothers would go there. "That is pure speculation," Price said. "But naturally we are not overlooking any possibilities." Price then discounted rumors circulating among reporters that nine other convicts had been involved in the escape plot, but that six had backed out before the break. Another rumor, which Price tried to deflate: The Anglin brothers had ganged up on Morris and tossed him off the raft.

With each passing day, officials at Alcatraz were more convinced the escapees had not made it ashore alive. However, after the life jackets, no new physical evidence was found to support their theory. Fred Wilkinson, Assistant Director of the Bureau of Prisons, who had taken up residence on Alcatraz, said, "Almost without exception, the pattern of prison escapes has been that we will get reports on the escapees' activities by the third or fourth day. It has been twelve days and nothing has turned up. All we can do is wait on their doorsteps for them to come home—or, what is more likely, to watch for their bodies to turn up. From our past experience, the bodies can surface at almost any moment." He didn't mention what experience his office had in waiting for bodies to pop to the surface of the cold Bay waters.

He also didn't mention that his office had been instrumental in dispatching thousands of additional "wanted" flyers of the three escapees throughout the nation, especially in the Deep South, or that the effort was unnecessary if the Bureau of Prisons was truly convinced the men had drowned. Did the FBI have evidence that the escapees had reached shore or been picked up by a boat? None has come to light.

On June 18, Warden Blackwell received a postcard postmarked "San Francisco June 16, 1962, 8:30 p.m." On it was a scrawled message: "Ha ha we made it," signed "Frank, John, Clarence." Blackwell gave it to the FBI with the comment that it was probably phony since it had been addressed to "Warden, Alcatraz Prison, Alcatraz Island, San Francisco Bay, California." All inmates knew, he said, that the proper address for mail to Alcatraz was "Box 1476, Alcatraz, California." Nonetheless, the FBI checked the handwriting with the Identification Division in Washington, D.C. There was not sufficient examples on file of the three convicts' handwriting to draw absolute conclusions, but the signatures "Frank" and "John" were not similar to those of Frank Lee Morris and John William Anglin. In the weeks that followed, numerous crank letters and postcards arrived with wild claims purporting to be from one or more of the escapees.

As the wait continued and theories abounded, Warden Blackwell and federal prison authorities weighed measures to tighten security on Alcatraz. They still had hundreds of desperate men to deal with, some of whom were convinced the Anglins and Morris had made it. If *they* had made it, why not others? The thirty-year reputation of Alcatraz as an "escape-proof" prison had been tarnished. That reputation was largely the work of publicists and colorful newspaper stories, but Alcatraz officials had gone along with it. They knew that no prison was truly escape-proof and that the security of Alcatraz had been penetrated often enough. But the natural moat and rumors of man-eating sharks in the Bay were enough to dissuade all but the most determined. As Lieutenant Phil Bergen recalled, "We never said it was *impossible* to escape from Alcatraz, only that it would be *very difficult* to escape from Alcatraz."

The officers responsible for security considered, among other things, rotating cell assignments and increasing the frequency of cell inspections. The plan to rotate inmates from cell to cell at unannounced, irregular intervals would disrupt any escape timetable if the planned escape involved digging through cell walls.

* * *

Just as some were convinced with the passage of time that the escapees had surely drowned, others were convinced they had surely made good their escape. If one believed the latter, as many FBI agents did—they would say so, however, off the record only—each passing day lent credence to the theory that the trio had been picked up by a boat. No unexplained local car thefts or burglaries were reported. No one had seen the fugitives or found evidence of their passing. They had simply vanished. If they had been picked up by a boat and taken to San Francisco, Marin, or the East Bay, there would have been time to leave the area by prearranged car or airplane well before the dummies were discovered in their cells. If that was the scenario, they could be anywhere. One inmate later remarked, "Those guys could have been sittin' in Mexico sippin' tequila before the guards even knew they were missing."

Proponents of the drowning theory used the same absence of

clues ashore to support their conclusion. Warden Blackwell and others insisted the equipment and personal effects found in the water added to the theory that the bodies had been swept out to sea and would never be found.

Critics of the drowning theory claimed that prison officials had myths to protect and could not concede the possibility that the three men were smarter than officials had thought. They argued that anyone patient and clever enough to dig his way out of Alcatraz with a spoon would not have left anything to chance. The men had had months to consider, plan, and rehearse what would happen once they hit the water. They knew about the tides, the temperature. They knew the risks. True, the unforeseen could have happened. The boat could have disintegrated. They could have become disoriented and lost in the darkness. But they also knew that their "dummy system" worked, that guards were fooled night after night by the dummies in their bunks. They were convinced that if they made it to the island's edge undetected, their absence would not be discovered until the next morning. Theirs was not a frantic dash to the water, a desperate plunge in headlong flight. They had time, time to look for, and answer, a signal from a small boat safely out of the Alcatraz "restricted zone," a boat the guards would have ignored. They had time to paddle slowly along the tidal drift, not fighting it. There was time for a boat to wait patiently for the trio to nudge their crude craft out just two hundred yards from Alcatraz. There was time for a boat to maneuver into a position blocked from the view of guards on Alcatraz, to pull the escapees from the water. And there was also time to jettison evidence of their choosing: the paddles, the raft, the wallet, perhaps other artifacts that were never found, such as clothing, all in an effort to convince their pursuers that they had drowned.

The FBI considered this theory, even if prison officials did not, and thus agents went to work. They investigated recent visitors to the prison, noting every name on the visitor log for the past six months. Repeat visitors were scrutinized first. Known acquaintances of the three men in the Bay Area were located and questioned. This included questioning all the members of the "Lost Colony," a group of seventy-five or more persons in the Bay Area who had been drawn to Alcatraz because they had a husband, sweetheart, or family member on The Rock. The Anglins had one relative in the Bay Area—sister Patsy, who lived with her husband in Hollister—but interviews with her turned up nothing. (Morris had no local relatives.) In fact, none of the three had received a visitor during their relatively short stay on Alcatraz. Still, the FBI figured there must have been some "buddy system" between the escapees and other inmates, a grapevine that led to the outside world. While the FBI was busy inside the prison walls, they kept up their liaison with police agencies and neighborhood investigations.

June passed, the first two weeks of July came and went. No new physical evidence was uncovered that the three inmates had successfully reached land. Prison authorities reiterated their belief that the strong currents of the week of June 11 had carried the three bodies to the open sea and the chances of recovery were remote. At the same time, they were becoming the butt of jokes about crumbling walls, about dummy heads, about spoons. Wilkinson amended his original statement that the three had probed, scraped, and dug through eight inches of concrete with teaspoons to reach the utility corridor. He now said they had used table knives and metal strips off their bunks and scrap pipe found in the utility tunnel. But Wilkinson held fast to his conviction that the three had tried to swim for it and had drowned.

While prison officials issued press releases and defended the public image of the Bureau of Prisons, the FBI continued to dig. Agents were particularly troubled by the absence of bodies. Even the discovery of one of the three might solve the mystery. What would happen to a drowned man randomly tossed off Alcatraz? Would he sink or float? Where and when would he likely surface? The FBI was determined to find out.

The tide charts for June 11 and 12, 1962, indicate that for the six-hour period prior to 3:00 A.M., the tide in the Bay would flow toward the Golden Gate in a westerly direction. After 3:00 A.M., the tide would flow in an easterly direction toward Berkeley and Richmond. After a review with the Army Engineers in Sausalito of their elaborate model of the entire Bay system, the FBI found that at 10:00 P.M. on the night of the escape there was a "slack tide," which meant that water had been moving in neither direction. Indeed, after 10:00 P.M., the water had started to flow out of the Bay, reaching its peak velocity at midnight. The flow had then diminished until slack tide had been reached at 3:00 A.M. The speed at midnight had been approximately 2.7 knots, while from 10:30 to 11:00 P.M., the speed had been only about 2 knots.

Edward A. Schultz, Chief Engineer of the U.S. Army Engineers office, felt that a free-floating object entering the water after 10:00 P.M. would have ridden the flow right out under the Golden Gate Bridge to the open ocean. It would have been difficult but not impossible, in his opinion, to reach Angel Island on a small raft. Schultz said that if the trio had swum or paddled halfway to Angel Island, riding the flow in a northerly direction, cutting across the outgoing tide, they could have made it all the way before the tide reached peak velocity. And if a boat met them offshore, the feat would have been a piece of cake.

Captain B. P. Clark of the U.S. Coast Guard and Captain of the Port of San Francisco reported to the FBI that the tides for the pertinent period had reached their maximum velocities as follows: maximum ebb current, 2.7 knots at 11:46 on June 11; maximum flood current, 1.8 knots at 6:44 A.M. on June 12. Clark added that the approximate water temperature of San Francisco Bay that night had been 50 degrees; the wind had varied between 5 and 8 knots from the southwest from 11:00 P.M. to 2:00 A.M..

But what about the bodies? FBI Special Agent Robert L. Hamilton consulted Henry W. Turkel, M.D., Coroner for the City and County of San Francisco. Turkel told him there were so many variables that affect the ultimate flotation and travel of a drowned human body that no one can accurately predict what will happen. His experience showed that the majority of bodies recovered had been in the water from one to fourteen days, but there had been occasions when bodies hand not been sighted for three weeks. In some instances, he said, the corpses had risen to the surface a long time before they had been sighted. He recalled that in the last escape attempt from Alcatraz the body had not been recovered until approximately the thirteenth day.

Agent Hamilton learned that there are two basic principles when it comes to drowned bodies. The first revolves around water temperature, that is, coldness and how it tends to retard formation of body gases and thus inhibit buoyancy. The second principle: Body gases are dependent upon the amount of food inside the victim and its bacterial content. Further complicating the equation, Turkel said, marine life—crabs, for example—can attack the corpse and puncture the body cavity, thus greatly increasing the time required for "body flotation" to occur. He also recalled instances where Golden Gate Bridge suicide leapers hit the water in such positions and with such force that their body cavities were ruptured. In those rare instances the corpses would likely be carried into the Pacific without ever surfacing.

Cecil C. Wiseman, Alameda County Deputy Coroner, concurred with his colleague. He had found it impossible to predict when, where, or if a drowned person might be expected to surface in the Bay. There were underwater snags, debris, and rock outcroppings that could hinder natural flotation and hold a submerged body for an indefinite period.

To gather more information concerning the retrieval of drowned bodies, Agent Hamilton met with Paul Jensen, San Mateo County Coroner; Captain B. P. Clark of the Coast Guard; Frank J. Keaton, Marin County Coroner; and Captain T. F. Parnow of the California Highway Patrol. Jensen had no opinion, since during his ten years in office only two "floaters" had been found in his jurisdiction along the San Mateo coastline. Clark said his department recovered two to four bodies per month in the immediate Bay Area; he knew of instances when bodies had been carried on the tide for considerable distances. Keaton noted that, up until three or four years prior, corpses had usually washed up on the beaches of Angel Island. Recently, he said, no bodies had been found there—probably due to a change in the Bay's tides and currents. Now, it seemed, most bodies recovered inside the Golden Gate were found along the Sausalito and Tiburon shores.

Captain Parnow of the Highway Patrol had a number of interesting observations. He noted that between January 1960 and the escape, there had been thirty-five known suicides off the Golden Gate Bridge. Five had hit the rocks beneath the bridge, and their bodies had been easily recovered. Seventeen bodies had been recovered from the water, some immediately, some within a few days, and some within a few weeks. Thirteen bodies had been unaccounted for. In addition, there had been twelve "probable" suicides during the period; none of those bodies had been found. (A "probable" suicide is one in which only a single witness claims a person has jumped and no corpse is recovered. If three or four independent witnesses see a jump, it's considered a "known suicide.") Since the Coast Guard boats are only about fifteen minutes from the bridge and a marker is dropped off the bridge to help locate the jumper, there is usually a good chance of recovery. If a person jumped from the center of the bridge, and during an outgoing tide, however, the odds of recovering the body go way down.

At least one of the three escapees—had they drowned—should have been found. Could sharks have disposed of the bodies inside the Golden Gate? According to one expert, there has never been a known shark attack inside the Golden Gate. The myth of man-eating sharks was allowed to circulate among the prison population, but there was little actual danger to a raft or a swimmer, and little chance that three corpses would be completely consumed by sharks. (Former inmate Charlie Hopkins says a sizable shark was caught off the Alcatraz dock in the late 1950s. He buried it in the garden just south of the recreation yard, where he was permitted to work from time to time.)

*   *   *

Of the more than 1,000 interviews conducted by the FBI between June 12 and October 1, 1962, over 30 percent were with relatives of the escapees, current Alcatraz inmates, their families and acquaintances, and former inmates and their associates. Every Alcatraz officer, from Warden Blackwell to the guards who had been on vacation at the time of the escape, were interviewed.

The first persons interviewed, after those whose names were found in the plastic-wrapped pouch, were those who had either been released or transferred from Alcatraz between January and June 1962. There were five in that category: James F. McKinney (#1233 AZ), released on January 14 to live with his sister in Lexington, Kentucky; Robert Williams (#1275 AZ), transferred to Leavenworth in late January; Angel Reino-Caballero (#1563 AZ), scheduled for deportation but placed temporarily in the State Penal Institution at Atascadero, California; Marshall Edward Nolan (#1364 AZ), released on March 8 to live with his mother in West Sacramento, California; and Joe Albert Boyles (#1338 AZ), who was conditionally released on May 17, 1962, to reside with his cousin in Oakland.

Of the five, only Nolan was seriously considered to be a possible conspirator in the escape, because he had been assigned to B Cell Block, Cell 140, in April 1960 and to Cell 138 in October 1960. In each interview FBI agents stressed the provisions of the "Harboring of Fugitives Statute." Their tone was deadly serious, suggesting that any implication of involvement would return the inmate to prison. Nonetheless, none of the five former Alcatraz inmates revealed any information useful to the FBI, nor was there anything to indicate that they had withheld anything.

Ironically, the two men other than Allen West who knew the most about the escape, Joe Carnes and Bumpy Johnson, were never questioned.

But most of the current inmates were willing to discuss their acquaintance and friendship with Morris and the Anglin brothers. In time, the FBI constructed personality profiles on the trio based on bits of information from inmates who knew them. In addition, agents gleaned insights regarding the escape, life in Alcatraz, and the values and habits of the inmates. But nothing was learned that provided a breakthrough in the case.

Charlie Hopkins, an Alcatraz inmate in the 1950s, once reminded the author, "You have to be careful with anything former inmates tell you. . . . Most of them aren't too objective, and some just plain have trouble with the truth." No doubt FBI agents who interviewed prison inmates were well aware of the possibility they were being told something less than the truth.

Former inmate Joe Boyles told agents there was always talk among the prisoners of escape. He knew all three escapees causally but didn't know them well enough to have their confidence. His cell had been at the opposite end of the third tier from Morris while the Anglins occupied cells on the "flag," or first, tier. Boyles insisted he knew of no one with whom the escapees were particularly friendly, or whom they might try to contact on the outside. This was the extent of information offered by every inmate questioned except for West and Gainey.

Boyles said the theory that the trio took weeks or months to dig through the wall of the cells was erroneous. The rear wall, he said, was in such deteriorated condition from dampness and age that one could break through easily. "Once you break through the outer cement . . . the rest is practically all sand. Hell, if I wanted to I could open up a hole around the vent in three to four hours." He didn't say how he knew this to be true.

Boyles added that any noise caused by chipping and digging could easily have been muffled by other inmates "beating their beds," that is, raising and dropping the bed frames on the floor, a frequent, irritating practice the guards could do nothing about.

Boyles contradicted Warden Blackwell's statement about the frequency and reliability of guard-checks at Alcatraz. On the night of June 11, he said, not one guard came by his cell on routine prisoner count the entire evening. This, of course, was later denied by prison officials. Boyles also disagreed with newspaper accounts that claimed Morris was the brains behind the escape.

"Sure, he may have had an I.Q. of 133 as the papers say. But to me, he was a quiet guy. If the three had a leader, it was the older Anglin brother [John]. He had the brains. He did the planning. And as far as the scarcity of raincoats to make a raft, almost all the inmates had raincoats in their cells and it was simple enough for one man to give another man his raincoat. Hell, all you had to do was ask the guards for another one. They had plenty in stock in the prison storerooms."

In his opinion, Boyles said, none of the three men was in good

Three views of The Rock. The photo on bottom, right, shows Coast Guard boats searching for Frank Morris and the Anglin brothers, Clarence and J. W., the morning following their escape from the Federal Penitentiary on Alcatraz Island on June 11, 1962.

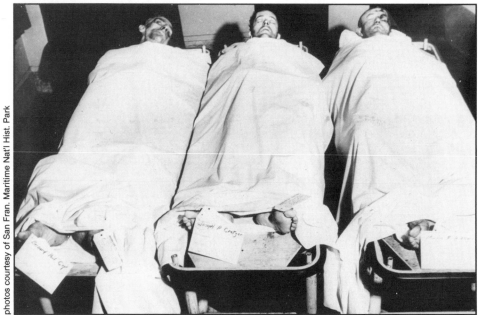

The bloody 1946 escape attempt. *Top:* Outside the main cellblock during the riot. *Bottom:* The corpses of three of the escape-attempt's ringleaders: Paul Bernard Coy, Joseph Paul Cretzer, and Marvin Franklin Hubbard.

Inside Alcatraz. *Top:* Prisoners on their way to the mess hall. The prison provided a varied menu as a way of keeping down inmate disconent. *Left:* A correction officer stands in the open hall of the main cellblock, "Broadway."

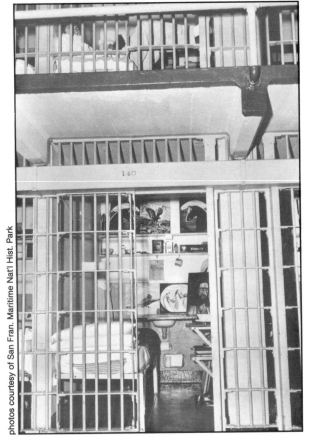

Life in Alcatraz. *Top:* Prisoners congregate within the walls and wires of prison. *Right:* The prison library. *Right bottom:* Two inmates in a photo from the 1950s. Prisoners were often allowed musical instruments in their cells. An accordion-like instrument was used to inflate life-boats in the Morris-Anglins escape. *Left:* An inmate's crowded cell.

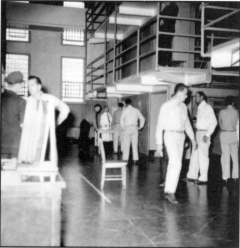

The Routine. *Top left:* A correctional officer on duty on the Alcatraz Guard Tower. *Top right:* Daily "sick call" on "Broadway" in "B" Block. *Bottom left:* Newly arrived inmates, shackled in leg irons, arrive on the island. *Bottom right:* Three correctional officers relaxing around a desk in the inmate visiting area. These photos, never reproduced before, were surreptitiously taken by a correctional officer in 1960.

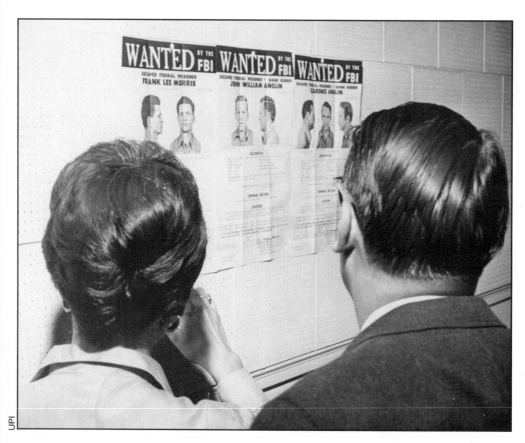

WANTED BY THE FBI! San Fransiscans examine posters of Frank Morris and the Anglin brothers three months after the escape. According to the UPI caption that accompanied the photo at the time, "The search for the three bank robbers from the Deep South . . . is still a top priority with the San Fransisco FBI office. The three may have drowned in their attempt to escape from the fortress-like island prison, but if they didn't they would be the first—and probably the last— to make good an escape from the home of the nation's toughest convicts, soon to be closed."

Army police searched the brush and abandoned buildings on nearby Angel Island the day after the escape. No sign of the three men was found.

The Anglins. *Top left:* J. W. and Clarence Anglin as children. *Top right:* Rachel Anglin, mother of the Anglin brothers, at the time of the escape. *Bottom left:* Clarence Anglin in his mid-20s while hiding out after his escape from a roadcamp at Fort Meyers, Florida. *Bottom right:* J. W. and his girlfriend, Shirley, in 1955.

The Anglin boys liked to look sharp. *Top left:* Alfred and J. W. in June 1955 in Ruskin, Florida. *Top right:* Clarence holding a photograph of a girlfriend just before the big bank robbery. *Bottom left:* J. W. in the federal prison in Lewisburg, Pennsylvania, 1959. *Bottom right:* J. W. in 1955.

AP

Alfred Anglin. *Top:* A dejected Alfred Anglin, then an escapee from the Florida state penitentiary at Raiford, sits handcuffed in a room of the house where he, J. W., Clarence, Jeannette Anglin, a girlfriend of one of his brothers, and the girlfriend's father were arrested in connection with the robbery of $19,000 from a bank in Columbia, Alabama. Jeanette is standing behind him. Much of the stolen money was recovered from one of the trunks shown here. *Right middle:* Alfred and Jeannette Anglin in 1957 in Hanes City, Florida. *Bottom right:* The body of Alfred Anglin. The Anglin family is convinced he was murdered by prison officials when he refused to tell them the whereabouts of his younger brothers after they escaped from Alcatraz. Officially, Alfred was accidentally electrocuted while trying to escape from prison.

courtesy of Robert Anglin

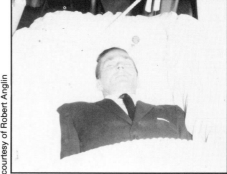

courtesy of Robert Anglin

Time

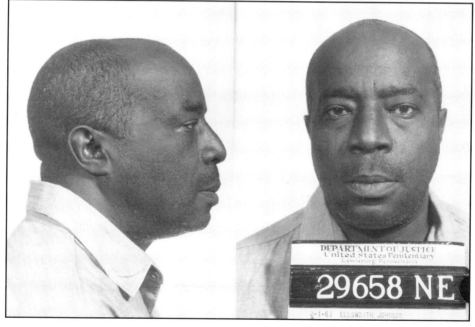

Ellsworth "Bumpy" Johnson, the "Black Capone of Harlem." *Top:* "Bumpy" Johnson in New York City in 1951. Johnson was a notorious racketeer, numbers operator, and dope dealer who was arrested more than two dozen times before being sent to Alcatraz. *Bottom:* Johnson in the United States Penitentiary in Lewisburg, Pennsylvania, 1963, after the closing of Alcatraz, from which he allegedly arranged for a boat to pick up the Anglin brothers and Frank Morris after they escaped from their cells and made it to the cold waters of San Fransisco Bay.

Clarence "Joe" Carnes, who helped the escapees. *Top:* Carnes is led into court, along with Miran Thompson (at left) and Sam Shockley (at right), to face murder charges after the 1946 break-out attempt. Thompson and Shockley were found guilty and executed. Carnes was given a life sentence, receiving leniency for sparing the lives of several guards. *Left:* Carnes in prison. *Below right:* Carnes in 1984, shortly before he died of AIDS.

Charlie Hopkins stands in front of his former cell at Alcatraz in the Fall of 1990. Hopkins, who knew Clarence Anglin and Allan West from reform school in 1946–1947, assisted the author by providing valuable details regarding the life and routine on The Rock.

The escape route . . . .

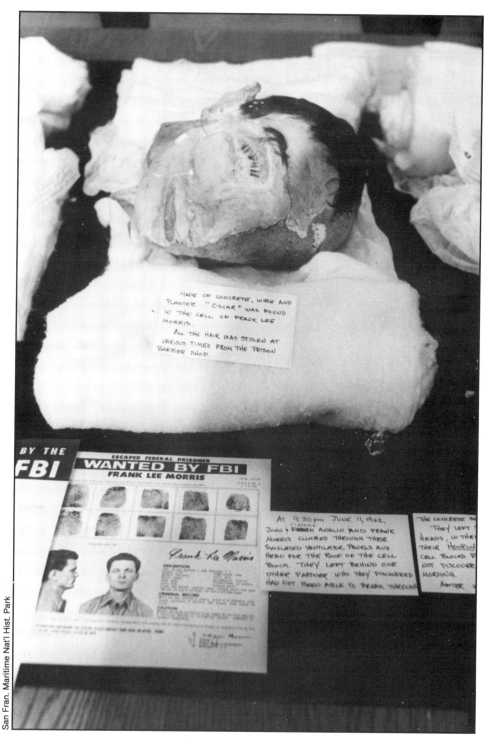

The dummy head, dubbed "Oscar," that Frank Morris used to fool guards. The head was made of concrete, plaster, and wire; the hair was taken from the prison barber shop.

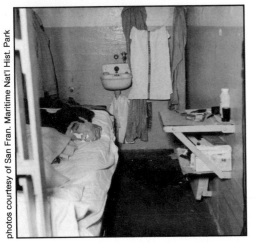

The prisoners' cells. *Top left:* Frank Morris hid his avenue of escape with an accordian case. *Top right:* A correctional officer shows the point of exit. *Bottom left:* The cell of J. W. Anglin, who hid his escape route with hanging garments and towels. His dummy head lies on his bed. *Bottom right:* The cell of Allan West, who broke through the wall too late to catch up with Morris and the Anglins.

The way out. *Top left:* The general avenue of escape: upward through the utility corridor. *Top right:* The roof of the cellhouse: a side view of the vent, grille, and cover used as the escape exit. *Bottom left:* Utility corridor view: An officer holds the removable section of Clarence Anglin's exit cover. *Bottom right:* Through the roof: This photograph shows the prisoners' final exit out of the cellhouse through a vent at the east end of "B" Block.

LIFE JACKET

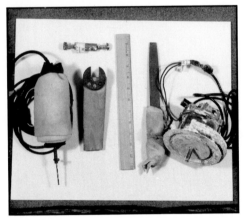

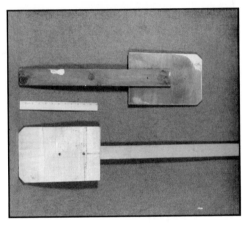

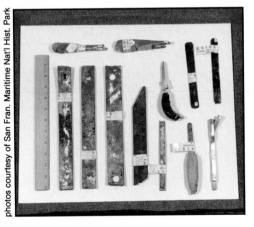

The supplies. *Top left:* Three eight-ounce bottles of blue-green cell-wall paint were used to paint fake ventilator grilles. The small bottle is flesh-colored paint used for the faces on the dummy heads. *Middle left:* Drills used to cut through the bolts in the roof vent. The smaller one was made from electric barber clippers; the larger one is a vacuum-cleaner motor. *Bottom left:* Typical prison-escape tools used for gouging and digging. The escapees collected all sorts of potentially useful tools, including hacksaw blades, whether they used them or not. The wedges, top center, were critical in the escape plan. *Top right:* The unused life-jacket left for Allan West on top of "B" Block. *Bottom right:* Paddles made by the escapees. The longer one was found in San Fransisco Bay; the shorter one was left for Allan West on top of "B" Block.

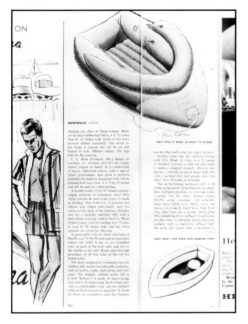

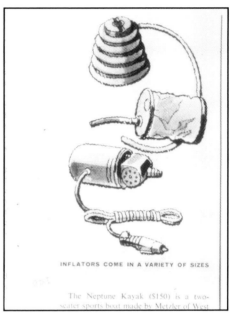

The Neptune Kayak ($150) is a two-seater sports boat made by Metzler of West

The raft. *Top left:* Illustration of the Voit Utility Boat used by the Anglins and Morris as a model for their prison-made escape craft. The illustration was found in "Shoptalk," pages W1–W6, of the May 21, 1962, issue of *Sports Illustrated*. *Top right:* Illustration of the inflators mentioned in the *Sports Illustrated* article. *Right:* How the inmates made two-man boats from raincoats . . .

drawings courtesy of Don DeNevi

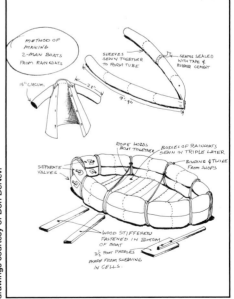

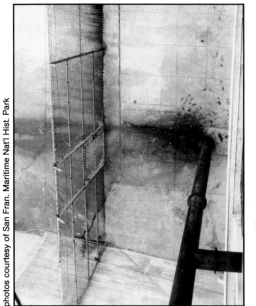

Gone. . . . *Top left:* The escapees broke the barbed wire on the outside of the wall. Note the footprints on the wall. *Bottom left:* The lower portion of the open-vent pipe down which the escapees climbed. *Top right:* A view of the bank leading down to the water's edge. Prison officials believe this is where the escapees launched their homemade craft. *Bottom right:* Area on top of "B" Block where Allan West managed to put up blankets to hide the escape boat and materials. Note the left corner, where West stored his paints. The dark material, center left, is what was left over from the raincoats used to construct the boats.

Four Against the Rock. *Top:* Artist's conception of what Frank Morris might look like today. These and the other drawings were done by Linda Galeener for the U.S. Marshals Service in Tallahassee with the assistance of a local plastic surgeon. *Middle:* J. W. Anglin. *Bottom:* Clarence Anglin. *Right:* Allan Clayton West—the man who couldn't make it.

A FAMILY WAITS . . .

From left to right: Marie Anglin Widner, Robert Anglin, Audrey Bazemore, and Rufus Anglin in November 1990.

Rufus Anglin: "Tell Clarence and J. W. it's time to come home."

Patsy Anglin: "After I get through hugging them, there's going to be nothing left."

Marie Anglin Widner: "When they come home, we're going to have the biggest family reunion ever. And you, Don DeNevi, will sit at the head of the table."

Carson Anglin: "If them boys are out there, and we are hoping they are, you can bet they know everything about the family. They was always that way, caring about their sisters and brothers."

Mearl Anglin Taylor: "As soon as they get here, I'm sending both across the street to pick a branch off a tree and I'm gonna wup 'em."

Audrey Anglin Bazemore: "I know how to get them boys to come home. Just tell them I'm going to bake them a fourteen-layer banana cake."

Robert Anglin, head of the family: "They was really good boys, and it's tragic and sad they spent so much time in jail and running. We sure would love to see them come in."

Internally known trial attorney Melvin M. Belli, Sr., has offered to represent the Anglins and Morris free of charge, assuming the trio have committed no crimes since their escape. On this photo Belli writes, "Clarence and J. W., call me! Melvin Belli." Whoever calls this number will have to prove that he is indeed one of the escapees by answering family-related questions.

enough physical condition to swim any distance. "Sure, some of them did exercises in their cells but not enough to take those waters on. It could be all three of them are still in some cave on Alcatraz. It could be they drowned. And," he added, "it could be a boat was waiting for them."

He concluded the interview by saying, as all the past and present inmates said, "If I hear or get any information about the guys, I'll be sure to call you."

*   *   *

In addition to routine interviews of persons on the FBI list, there were occasional surprises to investigate. Four days after the escape, Warden Blackwell received an unsigned postcard postmarked "San Francisco, June 15, 1962, 9:00 P.M." It read, "Check to see what Jose Lewis [sic] Martinez was up to last Monday night on his boat from Fisherman's Wharf. He wasn't alone—or fishing." Special Agent Norman Frye investigated. He found Jose Luis Martinez working on his twenty-seven-foot cabin-cruiser at Fisherman's Wharf. Martinez, who had arrived from Spain two years before and who spoke poor English, was surprised when he found an FBI man on his boat. When asked about the night of June 12, Martinez explained he had left work at Boicelli and Mercury Company on the Wharf, where he worked as a machinist, had dinner, and then worked on his boat until 8:30. He insisted he had not taken his boat out that night—his boat was not fully equipped and had no lights, and he never took it away from Fisherman's Wharf.

Eugene Trizuto, another mechanic who worked with Martinez, and a close friend of his, told Agent Frye that he specifically remembered working with Martinez that night until about 10:00 P.M., when he had gone home. He vouched that Martinez never had his boat on the Bay. Martinez's employers agreed that Martinez worked on his boat every night and never took it onto the Bay. They added that Martinez was a fine employee, that he attended school on weekends to learn English. There was no hint who might have sent the postcard.

After questioning Martinez, Agent Frye interviewed Officer Bob Checchi, a Mission Station policeman, who remembered that shortly after 1:00 A.M. on the morning of June 12, he had seen a thirty-foot commercial fishing boat that had stopped dead in the water off the St. Francis Yacht Club. The boat had gotten under way shortly after 1:00 A.M. and, with its running lights on, headed west through the Golden Gate. Was this simply another vessel leaving the Bay to reach the fishing grounds before daybreak? Or could it have been the boat Bumpy Johnson allegedly arranged to rendezvous with the Anglins? On any given night there are several dozen small boats, mostly carrying sportsmen or commercial fishermen, on the Bay, coming and going, minding their own business. A boat stopped outside the two hundred–yard "restricted zone" around Alcatraz would attract little attention from prison officers or anybody else. It was impossible to locate or identify every vessel on the Bay that night. And if a boat *had* plucked the three men from the water, its owner would hardly be expected to come forward.

The names in the packet found off Angel Island were regarded as hot leads by the FBI. Upon investigation, however, the names and addresses yielded little valuable information. Agents wasted no time in locating the people linked by circumstance to J. W. and Clarence Anglin. One of the most intriguing names was that of Jack Burnam, an attorney in San Francisco. Most of the names were of relatives and family friends of the Anglins. But an attorney, particularly one who had defended a number of Alcatraz inmates, might provide a link to their pals on the outside. But that was not the case. Burnam could think of no reason why his name was in the Anglins' packet: he had never met or represented them. He was known to several inmates, though, and his name had probably been given to the Anglins by them in case the escapees were caught. Burnam told the FBI he was aware of his duty under the law to inform them should the Anglins or Morris contact him, and that he had no intention of harboring fugitives.

Of the others whose names were found in the Anglins' packet, most, except relatives, denied even knowing the brothers or Frank

Morris. The FBI was stymied at every turn. For example, the water-soaked inscription "Shonda Burns, Cleveland," turned out to be Alex Shondor Burns, who admitted knowing Louie Teller, a convicted bank robber who was on Alcatraz. But Burns claimed he had never heard of the three escapees. "I haven't the faintest idea how my name happened to be among his [J. W. Anglin's] personal effects. Somebody like [Teller] might have given Anglin my name to look up if he got to Cleveland."

Richard Morrell, who had served time with John Anglin in the Lewisburg Penitentiary in Pennsylvania and whose name was in the packet, had been killed in an automobile accident near Canton, Ohio, about a year before the escape. Morrell's stepfather said Richard had been a "lone wolf" who didn't associate with many people; the stepfather had never heard his stepson mention the names Anglin or Morris. Another dead end.

Art Schmidlen of Maumee, Ohio, whose name was in the packet, did know the Anglins. In 1960 the Anglins' mother had vacationed for eight weeks with Schmidlen and his wife. Schmidlen was a "truck farmer" who had hired several of the Anglins to pick tomatoes in season since 1953. He said the Anglin family usually picked cherries at Traverse City, Michigan, each June. J. W. Anglin, he recalled, was the best worker of all; not once, he said, had he caused any trouble. Like the rest, Schmidlen agreed to immediately contact the FBI if he heard anything.

Robert "Bobby" Tickle, when interviewed in Pulaski, Virginia, told agents that he knew who J. W. Anglin was, but he couldn't recall anything particular about him. FBI agents knew Tickle had served time with the Anglins in Lewisburg and were not satisfied with their initial interview, so they returned to question him again. This time he admitted that he knew both brothers well. But the man who knew the brothers best was John Rock, another inmate at Lewisburg. Tickle said the Anglins had planned an escape from Lewisburg and, had they succeeded, would have contacted a man named Manuel Martinez, who had just been released from the Texarkana prison in Texas. The Anglins learned of Martinez, according to Tickle, from two Egyptians incarcerated at Lewisburg for a drug-smuggling conviction.

One of the men on the Anglins' list was currently serving time for grand larceny in the West Virginia Penitentiary at Moundsville, West Virginia. Sure, he admitted, he had lifted weights with J. W. Anglin at Lewisburg. But, he informed the agents, he had no intention of furnishing information to the FBI that might help locate the three fugitives even if he had any. He claimed he knew none of the Anglins' or Morris's associates. "Even if I did, I wouldn't betray him. So you know what you can do with your 'harboring fugitives statute.' "

The Anglin family members who were contacted generally took the position that the two brothers were "black sheep" and ought to be captured and returned to serve their time. All claimed no knowledge of their whereabouts and expressed a willingness to cooperate with the FBI. None had ever visited their brothers in Alcatraz, because they couldn't afford the trip. Agents closely watched the ten Anglin brothers and sisters and their parents for years after the escape.

Several names found in the Anglins' packet turned out to be family visitors of other Alcatraz inmates. When questioned, the visitors said they spoke only of family matters during the hour-long visits to Alcatraz and that the names of the fugitives had never come up. When shown "wanted" flyers by FBI agents, the visitors insisted they had not seen the men and could not help them in any case. "Only at gunpoint," said a friend of inmate Billy Boggs.

*   *   *

Alfred Anglin, who was still in Atlanta Penitentiary when he got the news of his brothers' escape from Alcatraz, came under close scrutiny. Officials doubted that if J. W. and Clarence had survived, they would be brazen enough to attempt to free Alfred, but there was always that possibility. They would perhaps more likely try to send a message to Alfred. Or perhaps Alfred might try to break out to meet his brothers at a prearranged location. Alfred Anglin was transferred to close lockup, and his visitors and correspondents were limited to his immediate family. About a month after the escape, Alfred wrote to his mother assuring her that the boys were all right. He didn't doubt for a minute that they had made it, and he was confident they would find a way to communicate with him. He was determined to make parole—and, despite what prison officials might think, he wasn't going to jeopardize that chance by trying to escape.

Just before Christmas, the Anglin household received a card from "Joe and Jerry." Mrs. Anglin didn't know any "Joe and Jerry." She decided it couldn't be from the boys; it was too obvious. Two young children of J. W.'s girlfriend were named Jon and Jerry; that must have been who sent it. But J. W.'s girlfriend also received a mysterious Christmas card, mailed from Ruskin and signed "J. & J." There were no hidden messages that anybody could decipher, just a simple card. Then Robert noticed the envelopes. Each was addressed in four lines: name, street, city, and state—a common form of address. But in between the name and street, someone had carefully drawn a straight line. Another rule line appeared between the street and city, and another between the city and state. It struck Robert and the family as odd that anybody would go to such trouble. Then Robert remembered something. He went to the big box where his mother kept the many letters J. W. and Clarence had sent them from Alcatraz. The official Alcatraz envelopes each had four fine printed lines; the inmate was supposed to confine his writing within the lines. Were the cards from the boys? The handwriting was unfamiliar—but then it might be if it was from them.

The family pored over the boys' last letters from Alcatraz, as the FBI had done months before. Perhaps there was a clue that had been overlooked. Ten days before the escape, Clarence had written to his mother, "Is anybody going north this year?" Did that mean something? Helen, J. W.'s girlfriend, received a telephone call about a month after the escape, and she was certain it was from J. W. The man spoke little, asked how she was, and said he was O.K. She assumed her phone was tapped, so she said nothing. "It was his voice," she recalls. After she was identified as J. W.'s girlfriend, she received several strange calls, but she discounted them. In time, calls to her and the Anglin family from mysterious persons diminished, although the FBI continued to watch them closely.

In late 1963, Alfred Anglin was certain he would be paroled from Kilby Prison in Montgomery, Alabama, where he had been transferred from Atlanta. About that time he received a package, which, like all his mail, was carefully inspected and X-rayed. It contained a decorative, tooled-leather "horse," a panel of leather about five-by-eight inches, designed to stand like a small easel-type picture frame. A stylized rearing horse decorated the front panel, which was attached to a rear panel with leather stitching. Inspection revealed that nothing was sandwiched in between the two panels—no weapons, notes, or escape tools—so it was delivered to the inmate.

Alfred Anglin immediately recognized Clarence's handiwork. Clarence had made similar "horses" before, and this was typical of his work. At the first opportunity, Alfred cut a small opening in the binding and probed inside. He found a tiny, tightly rolled piece of paper lodged against the inside binding, an object so small it would have gone unnoticed on an X-ray screen. He unrolled the paper and saw that it was blank. Then he remembered the way he, Clarence, and J. W. had sent secret messages when they were kids.

In the privacy of his cell, he held the paper close and held a lighted match beneath it. Just before the paper burst into flame, writing was revealed. The "ink" had been made from a mixture of baking soda, water, and a binder, such as egg white, and allowed to dry. The heat turned the writing brown, and visible.

When Alfred's family visited in December 1963, just before Christmas, Alfred told them his parole was almost at hand, maybe three months away. He sat across a heavy table from his mother, several of his sisters, and brother Robert. He assured them that the "boys," J. W. and Clarence, were "all right." Had he heard from them? Robert Anglin was certain the table was bugged, and Alfred was too smart to reveal anything. He and Robert were allowed to go to the bathroom, where Alfred said it was safe to talk. According to Robert, Alfred told him he had heard from the boys via the leather "horse." He knew where they were and said, "Once I get out, I'll go straight to them."

The family eagerly awaited Alfred's parole, and Robert, who had kept the secret of the "horse" to himself, was especially anxious. Marie Anglin, Alfred's sister, visited him a week before Christmas and he was confident his parole was only a matter of days, maybe weeks, away. Three weeks later, the family had still heard nothing about Alfred's parole. On the night of January 11, 1964, Marie was awakened by pounding at her door during a heavy rainstorm. A neighbor told her she had a long-distance telephone call at his house, which had the only nearby phone. Marie sensed the worst. It was her sister Verna. "I've got bad news," she said. "It's Al. He just got killed."

The Anglin family gathered at the family home in Ruskin and learned the details. Alfred Anglin had been accidentally electrocuted while trying to escape from Kilby Prison. On the night of January 11, Alfred and another inmate had hid in the clothing room of the prison and then sawed the bars and protective screen from a window leading onto the roof at the front of the prison compound. Alfred went out first, wrapped in a dark blanket to hide his white prison clothes. According to prison officials, as he crawled onto the flat roof he touched a high-tension wire and was immediately electrocuted. In his possession at the time were automobile jumper wires and a packet of family snapshots. The acting warden wasn't aware of Alfred's parole status, he said in a letter to the family, and had no reason to believe he would try to escape. "However, we must face facts and the facts are that he did, in fact, try to escape."

Alfred's brothers and sisters were incredulous. What had gone wrong? Why would he try to escape when he was due for parole? Had he gotten another message from the boys? Had he been told he was not going to be paroled? Had he been murdered because he wouldn't tell where his brothers were hiding? Requests by the family for an investigation into Alfred Anglin's death fell on deaf ears. His mother and brother Robert asked the prison chaplain a number of questions concerning the incident. Why, for example, was Alfred's body battered and bruised when it was sent home to Ruskin? The chaplain wrote back to Mrs. Anglin and announced he was resigning from the Prison Ministry and would not be able to help her.

Robert Anglin has speculated that, if the boys are out there, they certainly learned of Alfred's death, and perhaps feel the same fate awaits them if they are caught or surrender to authorities.

8

Aftermath

"I think everybody hopes they made it. After all, everybody's trying to break out of something."

—Anonymous

By the end of 1962, some prison officials had given up hope of ever learning the fate of the three escapees. If they had drowned, their bodies should have been recovered by then. If, somehow, they had not surfaced, there would be little left but bones, resting forever on the bottom of San Francisco Bay. If they had made it to land, surely some clue would have turned up, a sighting, a stolen car, an unexplained burglary. The FBI had not given up, nor had the U.S. Marshals office. The case would remain open indefinitely. Although it might just be wishful thinking on the part of inmates that the trio had made their way to freedom, federal agents operated on the presumption the men were still at large. The intensive search in the Bay Area had ended but, as bits of possible evidence surfaced, they were investigated.

On September 13, 1962, a barnacle-encrusted human skull was brought up from the depths by a fisherman's line a half mile from Alcatraz. Pathologists were immediately summoned by Alcatraz officials to determine how long it had been in the water and whether a hairline crack on the right temple had any significance. Warden Blackwell and other Bureau of Prisons officials had speculated from the beginning that if the trio had found there was insufficient room in the raft, they wouldn't be surprised if the Anglins had ganged up on Morris, killed him, weighted his body, and dumped him overboard.

Could this be the skull of Frank Morris? Or of one of the Anglins?

After a flurry of excitement over the skull, officials were deflated to learn that it had belonged to a man much older than any of the escapees. In addition, even though the lower jaw was missing, the remaining teeth did not match the dental records of the Anglins or Morris. Warden Blackwell considered sending divers down, in spite of that conclusion, to see if a skeleton could be recovered. Then, on September 26, a fisherman recovered a scrap of denim cloth off the western shore of Alcatraz. It was identical, according to Blackwell, to the prison denim worn by the three escapees. He was convinced now that a corpse, or at least bones, rested on the Bay floor near the island. For two days skindivers searched. They found nothing.

*   *   *

Could the three have survived the swim? Businessman Bob Monsen, 44, of San Rafael, California, who routinely swims the Bay waters from the southwestern tip of Alcatraz just below the now demolished guard apartments to Acquatic Cove near San Francisco's Fisherman's Wharf, a distance of 1¼ miles, said recently, "Virtually all the swimmers at the Dolphin Club and the South End Rowing Club, men in their 60's and 70's, feel its a 'walk in the park' to swim from the island to the mainland. Heck, kids as young as ten or twelve do it all the time. For a trained national collegiate swimmer, it takes only twenty minutes. For a good recreational middle-aged swimmer, it takes about forty minutes. For inmates like the Anglin brothers and Frank Morris, the question is whether they had their clothes on. Clothes would make it much more difficult, and swimming without clothes makes you wonder what they would do once they got to Fisherman's Wharf. They couldn't walk around the piers and streets with only their underwear on. So, this leads many of us who swim it all the time to believe that if they made it, whether they were good swimmers or not, a boat had to be waiting for them."

Monsen contends that to swim from Alcatraz to a designated point on the San Francisco mainland is very tricky because of the problems with night navigation. That is, because the tide is either sweeping out through the Golden Gate or driving the waters deeper into the Bay, expert swimmers are going to be severely challenged hitting a particular point. And, certainly, the Anglin brothers would not want to be separated while conducting their swim to the docks, wharves, or cove. Having night navigation assistance would be critical. In fact, it would be easier to swim the distance than to negotiate to a fixed point by raft.

"To us," Monsen said, "it really makes sense to have had a boat waiting somewhere northwest of the island, allowing the outgoing tide to sweep the raft to some general vicinity a few hundred yards of the island. With a raft, you leave your clothes on. The clothes serve as a wet suit against the coldness and bitterness of the Bay waters. But you also have to keep in mind that the coldness factor has often been exaggerated. It's cold, but not *that* cold. Swimming would be a slight problem, but a quiet boat waiting with its running lights on was the best solution among intelligent, well disciplined, determined men.

*　　*　　*

The escape triggered discussions in Washington, D.C., among members of Congress and Bureau of Prison officials about the "escapeproof" prison. Many argued that Alcatraz's days were numbered. Others resisted the idea that the prison had outlived its usefulness. Deputy Attorney General Byron White had inspected the prison in the summer of 1961 and seen the deterioration and verified the rising costs of operation. After congressional hearings on the fate of the prison, U.S. Attorney General Robert F. Kennedy said, "I think we will probably abandon it. It would be a savings to the taxpayers." Congress agreed.

On July 24, 1962, Federal Prison Director James Bennett told San Francisco reporters by telephone, "That's it—that's the end. It's been in the wind, so to speak, for a long time." Both Bennett and Kennedy, however, were quick to deny that the recent escape from the "escape-proof" prison had doomed Alcatraz. Kennedy reiterated what the public had heard all along: It cost thirteen dollars per day to incarcerate an inmate on Alcatraz—compared to five dollars per day in other federal institutions. And the cost to repair the ravages of time and weather to the cellhouse, the industries buildings, and other secure areas would amount to more than $4,500,000. Congress just wasn't interested in spending that kind of money for the rehabilitation of the old prison. A new multimillion-dollar prison in Marion, Illinois, was under construction and scheduled to be completed in the summer of 1963. Unlike the turn-of-the-century fortresslike cell blocks on Alcatraz, the new maximum-security prison would have a series of low-profile buildings made of prestressed, reinforced concrete. The airy, clean lines of the prison would resemble those of a modern electronics plant. Kennedy admitted, however, that another $1,000,000 would have to be spent on the Illinois facility in order to accommodate the 264 Alcatraz inmates: In order to thwart escapes, the prison walls would have to be built twenty feet higher than planned, and the foundation would have to be dug deeper into the ground.

While plans got under way to close the prison on Alcatraz, officials there still had to deal with more than two hundred inmates who had been inspired by the apparent success of the Anglins and Frank Morris. Security was kept tight as the prisoners were transferred in small groups. Then, on December 17, 1962, prison officials' worst fear came true—another escape, one particularly embarrassing to the Bureau of Prisons because one of the escapees actually made it to the mainland, disproving the theory that it was impossible for a convict swimmer to overcome the cold water. Inmates John Paul Scott, 35, serving a fifty-year term for bank robbery, and Daryl Lee Parker, 31, in for thirty years for kidnap and robbery, were kitchen workers who had found a flaw in the prison's security system. In September they had noticed that one of the windows in a kitchen storeroom could not be observed from the nearby guard tower. Over a period of weeks, the pair sawed through a horizontal flat bar covering the window. They used ordinary string moistened with water and dipped in abrasive kitchen cleanser. The window was ten feet above the floor, making it difficult to reach and carry out the slow cutting process. But its inaccessibility also made it difficult for the guards to check for signs of tampering.

Scott and Parker removed their clothes and squeezed through a narrow opening created when the bar was removed. Dragging their clothes and simple water-wings made from inflated surgical gloves, they dropped to the ground. From there, they got dressed and made their way to the water over a fourteen-foot-high cyclone fence topped with four strands of barbed wire. They stuffed the inflated gloves in their sleeves and slid down the embankment into the Bay.

Parker was found clutching the rock outcropping called "Little Alcatraz" just one hundred feet west of the island. He was cold and shivering and surrendered readily. Scott tried for San Francisco but was caught by the outgoing tide and carried toward the Golden Gate. He managed to swim to a little beach hear Fort Point, almost at the mouth of the Gate. Teenagers who spotted Scott lying exhausted on the beach thought he was dead. But he wasn't—quite. He was arrested and taken to nearby Letterman Hospital, where he recovered.

Scott's swim occurred twenty-five years to the day after Ralph Roe and Ted Cole escaped from The Rock and launched themselves into whatever fate was in store for them. Warden Blackwell faced the press the day after Parker and Scott's adventure and reminded them that Scott was lucky. "When men get out, they drown," he said. Referring to Roe and Cole, and the Anglins and Morris, he added, "Remember that many bodies are never recovered from the Bay following boating mishaps or suicides. . . . Some have been found fifteen miles out to sea. All five . . . have drowned in the cold, swift tidal currents. That is still my opinion. I have not changed it, even on the proof yesterday that somebody can swim it." Of course, several swimmers of varying degrees of proficiency had made the swim before. In the years since Alcatraz closed as a prison, hundreds of people—men, women, and children, amateurs and professionals—have braved the cold water and made the swim. Recently an eleven-year-old girl became the youngest person to swim from Alcatraz to San Francisco.

That was the last escape attempt from Alcatraz. The "phase out" of the prison continued. Inmates were shipped to various federal institutions around the country and, on March 21, 1963, the last inmates of Alcatraz Federal Penitentiary boarded a boat and left the island. After three decades of housing some of America's most infamous criminals, the cellhouse was empty. Except for caretakers, the island was deserted.

*   *   *

The controversy over what to do with the island of Alcatraz began soon after the Anglin brothers and Morris made their escape. Now the debate focused on how the island should be transformed, since it no longer housed a prison. San Francisco Mayor George Christopher envisioned "some tremendous monument such as the Statue of Liberty" on the island. He renewed the 1939 drama of a landscaped parklike island with a tribute to liberty in the form of a monumental statuary. A museum of penal history appealed to some, a luxury hotel or gambling casino to others. Some felt the island should be left to nature, given back to the pelicans; a few suggested blasting the island out of the water to ease navigation in the bay.

And one wag suggested Alcatraz would make an excellent prison.

Although ideas were abundant, money was not. The prison buildings lay vacant for the next fifteen years except for the period of Indian occupation. In 1978 they became part of the Golden Gate National Recreation Area.

More than 1,000,000 tourists, some 5,000 each day, now flock to the island to see the concrete walls, the forbidding bars, the cells once occupied by legendary figures and notorious criminals. The names of Clarence and J. W. Anglin and Frank Morris faded from the newspaper pages. Their faces appear on postcard-sized "wanted" posters in the museum gift shop and in displays in the cells they once occupied on B-Block. They squint into the bright lights surrounding the mugshot camera, forever frozen as humorless, dangerous-looking characters, devoid of the energy and imagination that enabled them to do the impossible.

*   *   *

Sixteen years after the escape, the FBI decided enough was enough and brought its active participation in the case to an end. On February 10, 1978, through the cooperative efforts of the FBI, the U.S. Attorney's Office, and the San Francisco branch of the National Park Service, all the physical evidence relating to the escape was turned over to the Golden Gate National Recreation Area to be stored in the archives of the Maritime Museum.

Every now and then, over the years, leads have come into the Federal Marshal's office. Frank Morris was seen in Chicago; the Anglins were rumored to be in South America (as were Cole and Roe, still missing after the 1937 escape); a woman claimed to have married one of the Anglin brothers. As recently as May 1986, some excitement was created when a story ran in the Rawlins, Wyoming, *Daily Times*, which quoted Clarence Anglen, 30, an inmate serving a ten-year sentence for armed robbery at the Wyoming State Penitentiary. Anglen said that his grandfather, who had died in 1980, was Clarence Anglin. He had changed the spelling to Anglen after reaching Iowa following his escape from Alcatraz.

Frank Morris and J. W. Anglin had been eaten by sharks, Anglen claimed, and his grandfather had lost two toes to sharks as well. The younger Anglen talked about his "famous" grandfather. He told how the old man would disappear for days at a time and the kids would be told he was off on a drunk. But he was actually in the hills hiding out, tipped off by relatives that the police were poking around. Young Clarence Anglen said his grandfather had told him about his escape from Alcatraz in 1975, after the young man had been released from the Utah State Penitentiary. "I guess it must run in the family," the old man had said.

According to Dennis Berry of the U.S. Marshal's office, the story was checked out and found to be lacking in substance. "He knew a few things, but not enough to be taken seriously," Berry said. The old man had been born in 1912 and had spent most of his life as a hog farmer in Missouri and Ohio. He was a God-fearing man who broke no laws. The age difference alone between the two "Clarence Anglins" was considerable—eighteen years. But the younger Anglen insists that his grandfather was Clarence Anglin. He said the trio had escaped on a raft made from empty Clorox bottles. His grandfather, the only one to make it to shore, had made his way to a freight-train depot and gotten on a boxcar and awoken to find himself in the Midwest somewhere.

The riddle of The Rock persists. With the passage of time, some of those with first-hand knowledge of the escape have passed from the scene. When Alcatraz was abandoned in the fall of 1963, Bumpy Johnson was transferred to Lewisburg for a short time. Within a few months, he was released on parole. In July 1968 Johnson suffered a massive heart attack and died. If he had participated in some way in the escape from Alcatraz, his secret died with him. Allen West was transferred from Alcatraz to McNeil Island in Washington and from there to Atlanta. He never again talked about his role in the escape. He died in prison in 1978 from natural causes. In early 1963, four months before Alcatraz was closed, Joe Carnes was transferred to the federal medical facility at Springfield and then to Leavenworth.

When I began research for my first book on Alcatraz in 1972, (*Alcatraz '46—The Anatomy of a Classic Prison Tragedy*, Leswing Press, 1973) I tried to locate Carnes, since he was the only surviving participant in the bloody 1946 shoot-out. I was told he had been killed in a fistfight in Leavenworth. In checking prison archives, I learned quite by accident that Carnes was alive. In 1970, he had been released to the McLeod Honor Farm at McAlister, Oklahoma, to serve out his life sentence. I met him there and began a fifteen-year correspondence and friendship, during which Joe Carnes (I knew him as "Clarence") provided valuable insights not only into the 1946 escape attempt but into the 1962 escape as well. He was released on federal parole in December 1973 when he was 46 years old. For the first time in his adult life he tried to fit in as a free man; he encountered prejudice and difficulties he had not imagined. He began a long struggle with alcohol and drugs that led him, in 1988, to the medical facility in Springfield, where he was treated for kidney disease. At age 61 Clarence "Joe" Carnes died from the complications of AIDS, contracted through intravenous drug use.

The only people now who can solve the riddle and fill in the gaps in the story are Frank Morris and J. W. and Clarence Anglin. Assuming they are living (Morris would be 62, J. W. Anglin 60, and Clarence Anglin 59 at this writing) and have adapted themselves to new identities somewhere, there would seem to be little motivation for them to come in voluntarily from the cold. In the preparation of this manuscript, I interviewed all ten siblings of J. W. and Clarence Anglin. Naturally they would love to have their brothers return to the family fold. They are convinced the boys are alive, so much so that they have, in the past, asked for clemency on their behalf from the governors of California, Florida, and Georgia, and President Ronald Reagan. All, except for Governor Deukmajian of California, responded and expressed the opinion there would be little gained from further incarcerating the Anglins should they surrender to authorities. The U.S. Marshal's Office and district office of the FBI are of a similar opinion. Their main interest would be in clearing the books once and for all, not in retribution. After all, if one includes time served in self-imposed exile, each of the three men have spent more than forty years isolated from society.

*   *   *

The riddle of Alcatraz may, someday soon, be resolved. Much of what the reader might conclude must involve some opinions and guesses. But there *are* some hard facts: The Anglin brothers, Frank Morris, and Allen West did plan an elaborate escape that was undetected by prison officers. The Anglins and Frank Morris did escape from their cells undetected. They escaped from the cellhouse undetected. They reached the water undetected. They are missing. Those are the obvious facts.

There are other—perhaps less "hard"—facts about Clarence and J. W. Anglin that lead me to think they made it, facts concerning their behavior prior to, during, and after the escape. For each there is also a counterpoint.

1. They would not try anything suicidal. They were eager to escape, but not desperate. Their parole dates were reasonably close, close enough to dissuade them from making a foolhardy gamble. They knew they could swim well and could work well as a team. They would not have agreed to make the attempt unless they believed it would succeed. They were, however, risk-takers and, as children, they had been foolish. One could argue that their criminal career does not reflect intelligence and cunning. Had they matured to the point where their determination and intelligence worked for them?

2. If they made it, they would never reveal their location to their family, and never try to contact them, except by a coded message. Their early experiences taught them the folly of trying to involve family members, even though their family was a close one. Moreover, they always sought to protect their siblings and not subject them to suffering because of their own misdeeds. So the fact that the family has heard nothing conclusive from J. W. or Clarence does not necessarily lead to the conclusion that they drowned. Clarence, however, *did* contact his mother and brothers after *earlier* escapes from road camps. Would he be able to restrain himself?

3. If they made it, they would never walk into a trap. After repeatedly being captured after escaping earlier in his career, Clarence Anglin had developed a sophisticated means for remaining at large. After his last escape from Raiford, he remained free for almost three years; his brother Alfred was uncaught for five years. Had they not committed a crime that focused a massive manhunt on themselves, perhaps they would never have been found. That leads to my final perception concerning the Anglin brothers.

4. If they have remained at large successfully for twenty-eight years, it is because they have "walked the chalk line," as brother Robert Anglin calls it. They would be very aware that an arrest for even a simple offense might result in a fingerprint check and discovery. Prior to their escape from Alcatraz they seemed unable to stay clean. Clarence, in particular, was determined to get money the easy way. Would their experience in federal prisons and the sobering ef-

fect of a possible death sentence be enough to set the brothers on the straight-and-narrow path, and keep them on it, for all these years?

The likelihood of their successful escape improves considerably if one hypothesizes that Bumpy Johnson did, in fact, arrange for a boat to pick up the escapees. Bumpy was closely allied with the Genovese Mafia family and certainly had connections. One call from someone who had visited Bumpy to "Fat Tony" Salerno would have been sufficient to set the plan in motion. But why would Bumpy do it? Just to see somebody make it? Just to break Alcatraz? Why didn't he cut himself in on the escape? Maybe he thought he was too old, too close to parole.

Would he cash in big I.O.U.s just to help four redneck, small-time nobody bank robbers who could do nothing for him in return? Possibly. Bumpy Johnson was a complex man, motivated by a strong sense of ethics and justice within the framework of violent crime. He prided himself on doing the unexpected. His ability to confound his enemies by unpredictable actions had saved his life more than once. If he did assist the Alcatraz escape, his only personal risk was to his reputation as a man who got things done.

9

The Riddle Continues to Ravel

"Oh, lovely freedom . . . be it ever so slight."

Morton Sobell, #996 AZ

Twenty-nine years after the escape from Alcatraz by Frank Morris and the Anglin brothers, a small but growing number of people—ranging from high-ranking U.S. Department of Justice officials to former Alcatraz inmates like Charlie Hopkins—are hoping the lives the escapees have lived since 1962 will prove to be the *Les Misérables* stories of the twentieth century. But an unsolved bank robbery in the rural panhandle of Northern Florida in 1983, coupled with the claims of "Cathy," an anonymous caller to "Unsolved Mysteries," the popular NBC television series, in February of 1989, are persuading some in law enforcement to conclude that at least Frank Morris and Clarence Anglin are alive, and possibly active in crime.

In an exclusive interview on WJHG-TV Channel 7's 6:00 P.M. news broadcast in Panama City, Florida, just before Thanksgiving in 1990, U.S. Marshal W. L. "Mac" McLendon of the Marshals Service's Tallahassee office startled viewers by announcing, "We now have clues which possibly link Frank Morris and Clarence Anglin, two of the three escapees from Alcatraz Federal Penitentiary in 1962, to a 1983 bank robbery in Greenwood, and maybe another bank robbery in 1963. We also have leads that point to where Morris and Anglin were living in the Marianna, Florida, area." The marshal went on to say that he believed the trio had succeeded in escaping and had eventually returned to the South "because all three, especially the Anglin brothers, had strong ties in the Jackson County area." McLendon pointed out that the three had accomplished a total of fourteen escapes, ranging from Florida institutions such as the Arthur G. Dozier School for Boys to the Raiford State Prison. "Actually," he went on, "they escaped from the same reform school or road gang several times. If anyone could figure a way to get out of a penitentiary, it was those three. Yet they always seemed to return to Jackson County."

Jackson County Sheriff John P. McDaniel followed up by commenting, "With their known mode of criminal activities, there is a *possibility* they could have done it, even though I'm not thoroughly convinced." Later, McDaniel wrote the author, "Anyone—including Morris and the Anglins—could be a suspect until the case is solved."

McLendon continued the newsbrief by asking viewers with tips on the whereabouts of Frank Morris and Clarence Anglin to call his office in Tallahassee. Composite drawings of the two sketched by Gerry Bagget, Sheriff McDaniel's secretary, who also serves as a staff artist in the Jackson County Sheriff's office, were then flashed on the screen. Bagget had worked closely with an anthropologist from Florida State University in creating the composites. (Composites were also prepared by Linda Galeener for the U.S. Marshals Office in Tallahassee. Galeener sketched the drawings with assistance from a Florida plastic surgeon.)

"Remember two things," concluded the marshal. "Number one, if they did escape successfully, and I definitely believe they did, they would be folk heroes. Number two, they would be worth millions of dollars in book and movie rights. After all these years, the maximum time in federal prison they would face would be five to seven years for escaping. After all, justice has to be served. But even that sentence could be cut. And they owe no time in the South. They could come in clear."

The news report was seen by more than half a million Northwestern Florida residents, including Verna, the oldest Anglin sister, who lives with her husband in Graceville, Florida. Verna, who had always doubted that her two younger brothers had survived the frigid waters of San Francisco Bay, immediately called Marie, her sister, who resides in Leesburg, Georgia. In turn, Marie called the author in his

San Rafael, California, home. Although I had been communicating closely with the staff of the U.S. Marshals Office in San Francisco, I had not been told of this development. All three of us were stunned that as late as November of 1990, law enforcement officials were suddenly reactivating their investigations into the two unsolved bank robberies and the search for Frank and Clarence. Although Verna and Marie pooh-poohed the possibility that their brother would risk robbing a bank at the age of 54, they were ecstatic that a U.S. Marshal in Tallahassee believed Clarence was alive. I was disheartened over the possibility that Clarence was involved. In short, my silly prejudice—"once a criminal, always a criminal"—surfaced, and I was uneasy. But with this announcement by McLendon and McDaniel, I knew that before long I would be on my way to Marianna, Florida, via Atlanta. I hoped that Jeanette Anglin Williams, Alfred's widow—who had remarried and later divorced, and who now lives in Douglasville, outside of Atlanta—would pick me up at the airport and that together we would drive down to Florida to learn what we could.

In the days that followed, a few tips trickled into McLendon's Tallahassee office, all of which the U.S. Marshals office dutifully investigated. One woman claimed she was currently working side by side with Clarence on a farm near Malone, Florida; she wanted to know if there was any reward money available. "This piece of low-life had to escape from somewhere," she said. Other callers insisted they recognized the composite drawings of both Morris and Anglin, some claiming the two were well known in the region and that Clarence actually lived in Marianna. One man claimed he had spotted Clarence in Cottonwood the day before.

In addition to this flurry of activity, the NBC affiliate in New York City telephoned Dale Cox, Marianna bureau chief for WJHG-TV in Panama City, for information concerning what was believed to be the imminent arrests of the two escapees. Thereafter, NBC and a WJHG-TV station employee spoke on a regular basis. The decision was made by the WJHG-TV program director to follow up the initial broadcast with a second news item, because there had been insufficient time in the first report to air all of McLendon's pertinent comments. The Alcatraz feature, according to Cox, had been developed as part of an ongoing effort by WJHG-TV to assist law enforcement when possible by asking for public input on unsolved crimes within the coverage area.

McLendon reappeared on WJHG and again asked viewers for information. "All three of those men definitely escaped from Alcatraz and are hiding somewhere in this area. I'm convinced of that. The Anglins come from a large family. Some of the boys and girls were raised in Donaldsonville, Georgia, and Ruskin, Florida.* All the information I have adds up to the fact that Clarence and Frank Morris are possibly here. Those two have known each other since reform school days down here and if they tied up together, they could escape from anyplace, including Alcatraz. I base the fact there is a possibility they robbed the Greenwood bank on the two disappearing so quickly, almost immediately, within minutes, which strongly suggests that they were not outsiders, that they lived in the area. But remember, I don't have one piece of conclusive supporting evidence they are involved."

Why these sudden announcements by McLendon and McDaniel?

On Wednesday, February 2, 1989, NBC aired a one-and-a-half-hour Alcatraz special shown on its "Unsolved Mysteries" series. Coincidentally, a few hours prior to the airing, George Anglin, Clarence's father, died at the age of 92; he was buried in Ruskin, Florida. Because the program reconstructed the 1962 escape attempt and displayed photographs of Morris and the Anglins, as well as a successful swim from Alcatraz to the mainland and an unsuccessful attempt to paddle a raft to shore, hundreds of telephone calls were received in the studio offices in Burbank, California, after the program. One was from a woman who identified herself only as "Cathy." (McLendon later learned that the woman's full name. To protect her privacy, she'll be referred to here as "Cathy MacDonald Ames.") A remarkably intelligent woman who has a master's degree in psychology, Cathy is married to a truck driver, and the two spend most of their time travelling the highways connecting Texas, Alabama, and Ohio.

---

*small farming communities near Marianna and Tampa

Cathy told David Rajter, a staff assistant for Cosgrove/Meurer Productions, Inc., in Burbank, and one of several monitoring the lines for call-ins, that she had just returned to her Houston, Texas, home in time to watch the final minutes of the program and recognized one of the photographs of the escapees. She asked Rajter for further information about the broadcast but was told that "Unsolved Mysteries" has a policy of only receiving, not distributing, information. Rajter believed that this caller was sincere—different from most of the preceding callers, who had insisted that he or she knew one or the other of the trio, was their father, had been married to one, or had spotted all three at a bus stop "yesterday," etc. Because of the searching nature of her voice, and the struggle she was undergoing on the telephone to spontaneously piece together her recollections, Cathy seemed "genuine."

Although Rajter would not share his file with the author (due to company policy), Dale Cox, who neither had any contact with the U.S. Marshals office in San Francisco, nor had read the actual Cosgrove/Meurer file, has nonetheless been privy to the information, along with other leads, which have been accumulating during the past year and a half in the the the U.S. Marshals office in Tallahassee. In addition, he has studied the·Anglin-Morris file in the Jackson County Sheriff's office in Marianna developed by local chief investigator Major John Dennis. In his numerous telephone conversations with the author and in his "Notes On Alcatraz Escape: Greenwood Connection," he reveals that Cathy MacDonald Ames was born in Okaloosa County, Florida, some 100 miles from Marianna, and grew up in and around an area she described as the "Three Corners," the point where the borders of Florida, Georgia, and Alabama merge. Normally, the "Three Corners" area is defined as Jackson County, Florida; Houston County, Alabama; and Seminole County, Georgia. Later, Cathy's parents moved to Jackson County. Today, Cathy would be a woman in her midforties.

Cathy described how her father and uncle had been heavily involved in the Ku Klux Klan during the 1950s and 1960s and claimed that the Klan had had a heavy "influence" upon the local municipal governments in Okaloosa, Walton, and Jackson counties. Both her father and uncle had been involved in the infamous racist Birmingham bombing, she said—an accusation later corroborated by McLendon, who added, however, "If there has ever been an active KKK in this area, it is not known to me." Cathy said that as a little girl she had lived on a farm next door to Clarence's small brick house and that along with her parents she had visited him from time to time. She had liked the man very much, she said, because he was kind. Cathy's father was "a distant cousin of Clarence's father," and Clarence had always been welcomed in her home. She further stated that as a child she had known all three Anglin brothers, Clarence, John, and Alfred. She had lost contact with the three when she left the country to travel in Europe. McLendon noted with interest that Alfred Anglin, *not* referred to in the "Unsolved Mysteries" special, *was* mentioned by Cathy.

But, as far as the Anglin brothers and sisters can recall, there has never been a "Chambliss" relative on either their father's or mother's side of the family. Cathy said that she had a photograph taken of herself in 1986 standing between Clarence and her mother. But later, when the U.S. marshal flew her in to Marianna, she could not produce the photograph—one, by the way, that could be a crucial piece of evidence and which every member of the Anglin family would love to see.

When Cathy returned from Europe, she said that Clarence was back in Jackson County after a long absence. She had learned from her mother, who is now deceased, that Clarence had committed a bank robbery and been arrested, but had completed serving his sentence and was back at work on a rural farm in Jackson County. In fact, during the 1970s and 1980s, she had seen him from time to time out in the fields, or along the dirt roads near their property line, when she visited her parents.

Cathy said Clarence had a daughter named Rachel who had worked as a waitress in the Red Lobster restaurant in Dothan, Alabama; she may have also worked in the Bonfire Club just outside of town. A later investigation by McLendon did not turn up a "Rachel," although employees at the Red Lobster and Bonfire restaurants do remember a Rachel Armani (a psuedonym), who quit suddenly in March of

1989. Dale Cox checked through all the high-school yearbooks for those years Rachel might have attended senior high in the area and could not find a "Rachel Armani." Of the two Armanis in the telephone directory, neither had ever heard of her.

Cathy's telephone conversations with Rajter were held every day over a four-day period. All the inconclusive but intriguing information gathered was forwarded to Tallahassee. Especially intriguing was her account of an alleged escape plot hatched by a former sheriff of Walton County, Florida, and now a preacher. According to Cathy, this man had left DeFuniak Springs, the county seat, shortly before the escape, flew to San Francisco, and made contact with a "friend" in nearby Lafayette.

The then-sheriff and the "friend," who owned a boat, had picked up the Anglins and Morris by a prearranged flashlight signal on the night of the escape. Wilson then supposedly returned to Okaloosa County in a station wagon, which Cathy felt was peculiar since he had flown to San Francisco. However, the woman did emphasize that she had not actually seen the man return to the area. Cathy's allegations about the former sheriff were thoroughly investigated by McLendon and proven to be totally false. He is a man of impeccable character and reputation and Cathy's claims have embarrassed the gentleman.

What puzzled authorities was the fact that Cathy could remember the exact name and address of the "friend." When the author called directory information, he did indeed locate "the friend." I telephoned the man in question only to have him convince me after a half hour's discussion that he had only recently moved into the East Bay community. Neither the man nor his brothers owned, or ever had owned, a boat. This was the very first time anyone had called him to check on the matter. When people in the area, relatives as well as neighbors, were told of Cathy's accusation that one of the Anglin sisters had "influence" over the former sheriff, all laughed heartily, saying it couldn't possibly be true.

Cathy seemed to focus in her conversations with Rajter on the Ku Klux Klan issue. She felt that the Blakely-Donaldsonville area was heavily involved in Klan activities and that the organization had probably played a role in hiding the brothers and Morris upon their return in the summer of 1962. The author has to emphasize, however, that he has not seen, or heard, one single reference in fact or hearsay from either Anglin friends or family reminiscences, or in prison records or law enforcement files, that either Clarence or J. W. were associated with the KKK.

Cathy described Clarence as a tall, quiet, soft-spoken, somewhat religious man who neither drank alcoholic beverages nor swore. His once brown, wavy hair had turned gray. She said that he earns his living from the small profits of the farm his brick house is on, although he has the reputation among neighbors as being an expert in repairing clocks. His most distinguishing personality characteristics are his "gentleness" and the tattoos on his arms—tattoos which, incidentally, matched those listed on the Bureau of Prisons records and FBI files.

When asked by Rajter to describe the exact location of Clarence's brick house, Cathy stated that he should first drive north from Marianna on State Road 71. Her farm, and the adjacent Anglin property, "is located off the highway between Greenwood and Malone. You have to travel along the highway until you see a mail box with only the name Clarence on it. At this mail box, which is on the left side of the road, you turn down a dirt road, although I've forgotten if it leads to the right or to the left. At the end of this road, you come to a one-story brick house, where Clarence lives. Behind the house with the shed attached is a small trailer, or a small shack, where a recluse lives." Cathy suspected that the "recluse" might be Frank Morris. Never once in all her conversations with Rajter did she mention seeing J. W. Anglin.

Then, as abruptly as her conversations with Rajter had begun, they ended. Cathy said that she had talked enough and that the only way she could convince him and McLendon was for them to go to Marianna and see for themselves if this was indeed the Clarence Anglin and Frank Morris the authorities were looking for. She concluded by saying that she had spoken to her dying mother in western Florida in order to refresh her memory only to have her mother demand that she mind her own business. At this point, she hung up.

McLendon, who in the meantime had been doing all the legwork on her claims, was impressed by her knowledge of the county, her descriptions of the back roads near State Road 71, and the claim that she and her mother had actually spent several days with Clarence in his Greenwood house. After a long period of time, the U.S. marshal was able to reestablish contact with Cathy, who said she had been on the road with her husband. Yes, she would be willing to fly down to Marianna and accompany two deputy U.S. marshals—one from Tallahassee, the other from Atlanta—to the site.

The authorities awaited her arrival with anticipation; she knew "things she shouldn't know." But after being picked up and being driven to Greenwood, Cathy became more and more "strange." She was unable to locate the dirt road she had previously described. Moreover, her conversation began to veer off on bizarre tangents. In the car with the deputies, Cathy described how her brother had worked on the moon, how she was being bombarded by moonbeams, and how spacemen from hovering spacecrafts were in the area. McLendon wondered: Had Cathy changed her mind about revealing the whereabouts of the brick house and begun putting on an act? Or was she drifting in and out of reality because of the pressure she was now under? In any case, the closer she got to the "dirt road," the more odd she became. Still, no one could dispute her description of the exact locations and designs of the tattoos on Clarence's arms.

*   *   *

According to Dale Cox, an interesting development occurred between the staff of Cosgrove/Meurer Productions and the U.S. marshal. Rajter had sent via teletype a compilation of Cathy's statements to McLendon in Tallahassee several days following the original February 2, 1989 telecast. The teletype arrived in the marshal's office on a late Friday afternoon, after closing. On the following morning, McLendon received a page on his beeper at home from an individual requesting that he return the call. McLendon called the number, which proved to be in a hotel, and spoke with an unidentified man who said he represented

CM Productions. This fellow asked when the marshal was going to make the arrests of Morris and Anglin. "Mac" responded that he had no knowledge of what he was talking about. The CM man asked if McLendon had received the teletype from his Burbank office. "Mac" replied that he hadn't, but would check. One of his assistants then went into the office and found the teletype in question.

Arrangements were then made for the Cosgrove/Meurer Productions camera crew to accompany McLendon and Cathy to Marianna. Major John Dennis, the special investigator assigned to the case, was notified that the marshal would be arriving in town to look for a fugitive, but was not told of the nature of the arrests. When the carloads of men and their equipment van arrived in Marianna, McLendon told McDaniel that a camera crew from "Unsolved Mysteries" had requested to go along during the search. The search lasted several hours and was called off when the sheriff, Major Dennis, McLendon, and the Cosgrove/Meurer Productions crew could not locate the mail box with the name Clarence on it. The officers confined their search to State Road 71 and the dirt roads extending both east and west from it. In this manner, a two-mile-wide corridor extending between Greenwood and Malone was searched.

Other attempts have been made to locate the house in question. Dale Cox believes the search did go far enough north on State Road 71, but may not have extended far enough to the east or west. In fact, after reviewing county property lines and ownership lists, Cox feels there are many homes in northern Jackson County that could match Cathy's description. When he showed two friends in the area the composites of Morris and Anglin, several indicated they recognized Frank but not Clarence. Neither of these people who recognized the escapee knew who Morris was. John Dennis also investigated houses that resembled Cathy's description, and he came up with a few possible sites. But, according to Sheriff McDaniel, "Almost all the houses in that neck of the woods look like what she described. You just can't go knocking from one door to another. These are backwoods people. And they certainly don't want strangers and television crews searching through their properties." According to Dale, who checked out his own target, new people had moved into the house soon after the initial "Unsolved Mysteries" airing, and right after Rachel quit her job at the Red Lobster. As for Cathy? She has, as of this writing, disappeared again. Hundreds of telephone calls at all hours over a three-month period during weekdays and weekends to her home in Houston have gone unanswered. The phone is not out of order or disconnected. The calls are simply unanswered. The author has called more than three dozen Ameses in the 904 area code, hoping that at least a relative would know her whereabouts. No one has ever heard of Cathy MacDonald Ames.

Meanwhile, the investigation into a possible Marianna link between the 1962 Alcatraz escape and the Greenwood bank robbery continues, even though the five-year federal statue of limitations for bank robbing has run out. An unsolved bank robbery in Marianna in 1963 is being checked, although Sheriff McDaniel feels he is almost certain he knows one of the men who committed that crime; that person is now deceased.

*   *   *

The little town of Greenwood has two major thoroughfares passing through it and lies to the north of Marianna in the heart of Jackson County's farming communities, noted for their prisons, peanuts, and historic homes. In 1983, an unidentified bearded gunman entered the Greenwood branch of the Farmer's Bank of Malone and escaped with approximately $8,500, taken from both the cash drawer and vault. The robber was observed by Harrell Glisson, a Jackson County sheriff's investigator, then off duty. Driving through Greenwood moments before the robbery, Glisson noticed the man, later identified as the suspect, walking along State Road 71. He was wearing dark sunglasses and a baseball cap. Within a few minutes of Glisson's passage through town, the bearded thief entered the bank and robbed it. Allegedly, he then quickly fled on foot. Some witnesses claim he trotted into an adjacent house, but sheriff's investigators believe he was picked up by an accomplice driving a yellow Chevrolet Nova. Tellers immediately sounded the alarm, and Glisson, hearing the report on his car radio, and other deputies descended on the scene. The highways passing through Greenwood were sealed off by sheriff's deputies within two minutes of the robbery. Not one trace of the suspect(s) was ever found, including the Chevrolet Nova. The distance between the Greenwood bank and the "brick house" Cathy described is less than a mile and a half. To this day, the robbery is unsolved.

Also unsolved is the robbery of the Citizens State Bank in Marianna by two armed men in early April of 1963, ten months after the Alcatraz escape. The robbers were seen approaching the bank on foot along Lafayette Street in downtown Marianna. They were wearing coverall-like khaki flying suits with Navy summer flap-jackets and silver-colored helmets. Because construction was underway on the new Jackson County courthouse, the men's garments did not arouse attention, since most of the workers were similarly attired.

Upon entering the bank as it was opening for the day's business, the men approached Mrs. Helen Lloyd, a bank employee. She stated that the taller of the two men seemed apologetic throughout, assuring the women they would be safe. The other man said he would blow Executive Vice President William A. Welch's head off if he did not open the vault. The more stern of the two then demanded that Vice President Bowers Sandusky lead them into the teller's vault, where the robber took some twenty minutes to empty the bank of its cash. Sandusky and the robber then crammed $115,000 into two sacks, which appeared to resemble U.S. Navy duffel bags. The vice president told reporters that he followed the directions of the gunman for fear he would shoot him. He also noted, though, that one of the robbers was especially polite, promising him he would not be hurt in any way.

In addition to wearing coverall-type outfits, the two men were masked behind helmets, dark sunglasses, and gloves; gauze covered their faces. They entered the bank around 8:20 A.M. via a rear door used by employees. When the robbery was complete, the shorter of the two asked for the keys to Sandusky's automobile, telling the banker that he knew he kept them in his pocket and where the car, a 1959 model Chevrolet, was parked. Leaving his accomplice to guard the employees, who had been ordered to lie down on the floor, he walked out, got the banker's car from a nearby parking lot, drove it to the back of the bank, and entered to get his partner and the money. After cutting the telephone wires, the two gunmen ordered the bank employees and customers to remain on the floor for ten minutes following their departure.

Evans Holley, a courthouse employee, saw the two robbers drive by in Sandusky's car, but thought nothing of it until he heard of the robbery a short time later. He described one of the robbers, as did the bank employees, as being about six feet tall and weighing approximately 180 to 185 pounds. The second was thought to be several inches shorter, weighing about 165 pounds. Although the shorter robber asked Sandusky whether his car contained enough fuel for the two to make it south into the interior of Florida, the men and the car were never seen again. Sheriff McDaniel's comment to the author regarding this robbery by the Anglins and Morris was one of skepticism. "I think I know who robbed that bank, but don't have the conclusive proof. Sure, the inmates from Alcatraz could have robbed it, as well as anyone in Greenwood. But, then, so could you or me."

*   *   *

So many thoughts ran through my mind as Jeanette—Alfred's widow, who could hardly have refrained from accompanying me to Marianna and who was present during my interview with Sheriff McDaniel—and I drove back to Atlanta. On that very December 15, 1990, Jeanette and Alfred would have been married thirty-three years. Tears flooded her eyes as she drove and talked of their relationship, leaving the author without a doubt that after all this time she was still very much in love with him.

To that moment, there had not been one confirmed sighting of any of the three escapees, although one of the Anglin girlfriends, Helen, confided that she had often spoken with J. W. since July of 1962. Yet, for all we knew, the bones of the Anglin boys and Frank Morris could be at the bottom of the bay just north of Alcatraz Island.

Jeanette and I were perplexed. Cathy knew too much to be dismissed as a simple "nut case," as she was called by a U.S. marshal in San Francisco. Unnerving was the fact that she didn't remember enough to be convincing. Questions began to haunt me as I watched the landscapes of southern Georgia roll by. Why was J. W. not mentioned either by Cathy, the sheriff, or the U.S. marshal? Surely John would be with Clarence; the two had been inseparable since his birth. Jeanette concluded that J. W. might be dead. Was it *his* corpse the seaman on board the foreign freighter had spotted floating outside the Golden Gate? And how about Cathy mentioning Alfred's name, indicating that she had known all three brothers when she was a little girl? What about her ability to remember whose name was on the tattoo? Would Clarence and Frank risk robbing banks after having successfully returned to Florida? I could understand the escapees not turning themselves in. Why would they risk being returned to a prison, with its much younger, more vicious inmate population, if they had achieved peace and security now? After all, you could never be sure whether some ambitious, publicity-hungry assistant U.S. attorney trying to prove his or her mettle would persuade an equally publicity-hungry federal judge to make an "example" out of them in the name of justice.

In that five-hour drive, Jeanette, who had known Clarence well (he had lived with her and Alfred for almost a year after their marriage), pondered the numerous intangibles. For example, wouldn't it be natural for Clarence to name a daughter "Rachel" after his mother, whom he loved so deeply? In fact, in the late 1960s and early 1970s, Jeanette reminded me, Clarence's mother received flowers each Mother's Day from an anonymous sender. This persisted until Mrs. Anglin passed away in 1973 at the age of 72. And two unknown, heavily dressed and made-up women had attended that funeral, quietly sitting in the back near the FBI agents who had also attended.

Then there was the almost apologetic nature of the taller of the two bank robbers in the 1963 Marianna case. The lone robber in the 1983 Greenwood heist had also been polite. Clarence was taller than either Morris or J. W., and, if J. W. had indeed been a participant in both robberies, he probably would have waited outside with the getaway car, just as he had done in the Columbia, Alabama, bank robbery in 1958. Jeanette recalled that during the 1958 robbery, Alfred deferred the holdup briefly to give a glass of water to an older woman customer who had fainted. "That was typical of all three of those boys. Although they did wrong, they always considered the feelings and safety of the people they were robbing. But I can't speak for Morris."

I asked myself if I would rob a bank after having successfully escaped from an "escape-proof" penitentiary. If I didn't have any money, I might risk the venture once every twenty years or so—especially in an area where I had plenty of friends and relatives and where I could melt into the backwoods within seconds. When Clarence's father, George, died on February 4, 1989, at the age of 92, he left behind thirty-six grandchildren, sixty-one great-grandchildren, and five great-great grandchildren. All these grandchildren, to say nothing of the Anglin brothers and sisters, have friends and relatives, who in turn have relatives and friends. The permutations of these relationships could number over a thousand individuals, many of whom would be willing to hide the fugitives. Furthermore, Clarence liked to dress stylishly. I couldn't get my mind off the fact that two bearded men had visited the deceased George Anglin in the funeral parlor before the formal services; they had been very well dressed. The sum of $115,000 in 1963 plus $8,500 in 1983 could add up to a lot of nice clothes.

Cathy knew the Greenwood and Malone areas of Jackson County intimately. Her comments about Clarence being an expert in fixing clocks sounded authentic. Did Rajter hear "clocks" when she said "locks"? He claims he heard "clocks." Clarence had learned all about dismantling and repairing clocks as part of his industrial training in reform school. To me, it made little difference: clocks, locks, escaping, and robbing banks all required the same type of calm, highly intelligent, and structured thinking patterns.

Then there were all the odd bits and pieces of questions and statements to the author made by Dale Cox, who had access to Sheriff McDaniel's file and solid information from "Mac" McLendon. Questions that were asked by many, but never detailed or fully explained include: "Did you hear about the money order signed by an Anglin sister from a nearby Tri-State Bank that the brothers left in a tree as the signal they escaped successfully and were in the area?" "Do you know if anyone is keeping tabs on a watchmaker named Morris in Greenwood?" "Did you hear about the two men in a yellow car who were run off the road after the 1983 robbery and sheriff's deputies let them go?" Cox, a highly competent reporter working hard at his job as Marianna bureau chief, later pointed out that it is his practice when approached by someone seeking information to ask questions, some based on fact, others not, to ensure the legitimacy of the inquirer. His questions to the author are not to be considered fact and do not reflect any knowledge greater than McDaniel's or McLendon's about the mystery.

When such questions are added to the fact that R. B. Watson, the chaplain at Kilby Prison in Alabama who had befriended Alfred, had disappeared after Alfred's "accidental" death by electrocution, I knew that my next book would focus exclusively on the full and amazing story of the "Anglin Boys." All my attempts to trace Watson have been unsuccessful. Could he tell me whether Alfred had been murdered, as Jeanette and the Anglin family insist, or whether he had died accidentally trying to escape in 1964 (to join his brothers?), as the warden at Kilby had claimed?

One thing was certain. Jeanette and I were pleased that our visit to Marianna had in no way led the authorities to the escapees. We hadn't gone down there to do that. When Sheriff McDaniel asked me point blank if I knew where the Anglins were, I responded, "I most certainly do. They're out there in the trunk of Jeanette's car." The affable sheriff laughed good-naturedly, realizing that we knew no more than he did concerning the whereabouts of the escapees. Jeanette and I hoped that the Anglin brothers and Frank Morris would turn themselves in before someone pointed them out or were discovered by the authorities.

Upon informing Robert, the elder spokesman for the Anglin family, of our visit with McDaniel, he laughed heartily. "Remember what I've told you all along. If my brothers turn up, every bank robbery that has been committed in the South since June 12, 1962, is gonna be laid on their shoulders. So, all this talk doesn't surprise me much because it's only natural. But I feel that if Clarence and J. W. are alive, they are not going to be so foolhardy as to commit a crime and leave their fingerprints around. They know that if their fingerprints come up on an FBI computer, the government is really going to get involved, and those boys wouldn't want that. No, you can be sure my brothers, if they are alive, are living quiet, respectable lives, probably each with his own family."

Jeanette commented on the drive back to the Atlanta airport, "I bet them boys, with their kids fully grown, are probably laughing right now at all the fuss and commotion they've caused."

Upon returning to the Bay Area, I learned from a telephone conversation with "Mac" McLendon that the Florida Department of Law Enforcement analysis of the fingerprints in the 1983 Greenwood robbery demonstrated that they did not match those of Clarence Anglin or Frank Morris. I was greatly relieved. I also learned that "Morris," the clockmaker who had owned a jewelry and watch shop in Marianna, had died a few months before. McDaniel told me he had known the man for more than forty years and that he was a "widely respected citizen."

In talking with McLendon, I was surprised that he did not know the Anglin brothers had used a toy pistol in robbing the Columbia, Alabama, bank in 1958. Nor had he known of Alfred's death in 1964. In turn, I did not realize how far back Clarence and J. W. had known Frank Morris. Not only had the three been associates together in the Raiford State Prison at Starke, Florida, but they had also known each other in various reform schools as teenagers. "Mac" assured me that both Clarence and J. W. did not owe Florida—or, for that matter, Alabama—any time for their previous escapes from road gangs. This would be good news for the Anglin family, since the prevailing belief had been that the "boys will not come in because they owe so much unserved time to Florida, Alabama, and California."

A week after my leaving Marianna, Dale Cox aired on WJHG-TV 6:00 P.M. news a four-minute video clip he had shot of me with Johnny McDaniel in the sheriff's office. After updating viewers on the progress of the investigation, Dale showed the sheriff stating, "I can't rule anything in or out on the Alcatraz trio." After being introduced as an author from California researching the backgrounds of the missing men, I was shown saying that if the three had been successful in getting out of the Alcatraz cellhouse and down to the water, they sure wouldn't have turned to each other and asked, "What do we do now? Drown?" I then urged them to come in because their sisters and brothers were waiting for them. "You should spend your remaining years at home," I said. I also stressed that Clarence and J. W. had never once hurt anyone, that virtually all the money stolen from the Columbia bank had been recovered, and that their only crime was having escaped from Alcatraz, thereby beating the Federal Bureau of Prisons, and later the FBI and the U.S. Marshals Service. I concluded by asking that they come in before Christmas, since it would make a whole lot of people happy.

With that broadcast, several interesting leads developed. The most important was a call from a retired U.S. Department of Agriculture worker who had previously conducted door-to-door farm surveys for Jackson County. An elderly lady claimed that during a recent survey, while going from door to door to hand out leaflets, she had encountered a man who lived in a brick house, which had a shed attached to it, somewhere between Greenwood and Malone. The man was approximately five-foot-eleven, and he weighed about 185 pounds, "and was mostly gray-headed now, with a pronounced stomach, but otherwise thin." He resembled one of the composites shown on the news. After she knocked on the front door, the man stepped out from behind the shed and asked what she wanted. "Are you here to see my green card?" The "green card" in Florida has nothing to do with immigration. It is a card that allows farmers to qualify for lower property taxes. The woman said no, she wanted to discuss the survey with him. The two talked at length. She noted the man, approximately sixty years old, was especially kind and considerate. She was certain she had seen this man with bluish-gray eyes before, in the Ribbons and Wood arts-and-crafts store in Marianna. Now he wore overalls and a blue denim shirt and light blue denim jacket. His hair appeared to have at one time been brown and wavy; she did not notice any tattoos. Clarence had hazel-blue eyes and was five-foot-eleven.

Another woman called and claimed she recognized the composite of Frank Morris as bearing a striking resemblance to a man who worked on a farm near Eufala, Alabama, less than seventy-five miles away. She said that Morris was often seen at a restaurant called Perrymore's on one of the lakes near Eufala with "farmers from Donaldsonville," where the Anglin brothers still have several relatives.

Such tantalizing sightings are certainly not unusual for a search of this magnitude. Since June 12, 1962, the debate concerning whether the fugitives survived has fueled the curiosity of the movie-watching public, as evidenced by the popularity of Clint Eastwood's *Escape From Alcatraz* and the NBC movie "Alcatraz—the Whole Shocking Story." Certainly Johnny McDaniel and "Mac" McLendon would chase down every call. Each has told the author that Clarence Anglin, and possibly Frank Morris, had been in the Marianna area. For how long, no one could be certain. Competent Jackson County investigators such as John Dennis and Claude Widner, who reopened the two unsolved bank robberies, were virtually certain the escapees had had nothing to do with them. Certainly, the men had help in hiding. But both were wise enough not to stay in any one place for very long. As of this writing, each of the wanted men seems to have completely disappeared from the region. Perhaps this is why Robert Anglin was so calm when I informed him of the sightings. When I asked him if he would drive up to Marianna from Ruskin to knock on some doors with me, his smiling, enigmatic comment was, "Well, you know it's an awfully long way up there." Strange for a man who who hasn't heard from a brother presumed drowned for the past twenty-nine years.

*   *   *

On Monday, December 24, 1990, the San Francisco *Daily News*, a tabloid for the legal, judicial, and political worlds of the greater Bay Area, published a front-page article entitled "Escape From Alcatraz— Authorities Trailing Long-Lost Fugitives in Northern Florida." With the dateline "Two Egg, Florida," the copyrighted story by Dale Cox— who, when not serving as Marianna bureau chief for WJHG-TV, is the editor of the *Piney Woods Gazette* in Two Egg—and Dennis Pfaff, a staff reporter for the *Daily News*, was picked up by the Associated Press and caused a minor sensation across the front pages of the nation's newspapers and evening news broadcasts. "Quality" dailies, like the *San Francisco Chronicle*, refused to carry the story, since nothing significant was being reported. Eagle-eyed editors with reputations to maintain were not going to participate in the annual "If I am not Anastasia or Martin Bormann, I'm certainly Jesse James" stories. Anytime the wanted are sought, and their composite drawings are flashed on television screens or splashed on front pages, hundreds of people are going to call in with tips on their whereabouts.

The well-written article summarized the search activities in the northwest area of Florida since February 1989, quoting Richard "Dick" Bippus, chief deputy U.S. marshal for the Northern California district, as saying, "It's like a roller coaster looking for those three. It goes uphill and downhill. We're on an uphill right now. Our interest is more active today, let's say. Contrary to almost everyone else, who believe the inmates drowned, I believe the three are out there. They are probably leading the life of good citizens, or else they would have been picked up by now. A surrender would help everyone. It would be nice if the Anglins turned themselves in and we could get rid of this. And they in turn could stop looking over their shoulders. But, remember, they still owe time. That's why we're out there now." Bippus went on to say that in the past two years, as many as six U.S. marshals and five sheriff's deputies had concentrated on the Two Egg area, some ten miles from Marianna. This, of course, was the same area that Cathy had struggled to locate and the Marianna campaign worker had described.

Four points in the lengthy article caught my eye. One revolved around the point that the three Anglin brothers were identified almost immediately after they robbed the Columbia bank in 1958 only "a few miles from their old home town of Donaldsonville." Dale Cox had forgotten that Alfred, Clarence, and J. W. had left the community for Ruskin, Florida, when they were little boys. No one could recognize them as men in their late twenties and early thirties. And, of course, Dale was not in a position to know that someone who was not related, but who was very, very close to J. W., could have tipped the FBI as to the whereabouts of the robbers.

The second point worth considering was the statement by Ann Diestel, a National Park Service ranger. Several weeks after the 1962 breakout, she said, a body clad in light blue clothes had been found washed up on a Marin County beach. According to Diestel, the corpse had not been identifiable. Nowhere in the classified FBI report spanning the three months following the escape was there any mention of the body. Wouldn't the Bureau of Prisons have thoroughly examined such a corpse in hopes of discovering that it was indeed one of the escapees? Can a corpse in blue denim be that unidentifiable?

Also surprising was the mention that the breakout had led to recriminations among Bureau of Prison personnel, followed by the a cover-up of crucial escape details. Although the author, who reviewed all the known documents on file in the J. Porter Shaw Library in the Golden Gate National Recreation Area archives at Fort Mason in San Francisco, found no hint of official dissatisfaction or unofficial "exiles" of Alcatraz officers, he is not about to say they couldn't have occurred. Phil Bergen would know, and he has never mentioned any reprimands or scapegoating.

The last point was less intriguing. According to Cox and Pfaff, Jolene Babyak, daughter of an Alcatraz associate warden, says that her father learned that a seaman aboard a foreign freighter spotted a body clothed similarly to an Alcatraz inmate floating around in the Pacific outside the Golden Gate about a week after the escape. Because the freighter had no radio to call in the sighting, nothing could be done to make a search for the body worthwhile. As mentioned earlier in the book, this blue-denim-clad corpse was known to the FBI. But this was the first time I had heard of an ocean-going freighter not having a radio to send the U.S. Coast Guard a message!

As of May 1, 1991, law-enforcement officials are as mystified as they were on June 12, 1962. Other than some public "sightings" and a lot of hearsay, no one has come up with conclusive evidence on the whereabouts of the escapees. In spite of all the hullabaloo generated by the Associated Press stories that Clarence, and Frank were "spotted" in the Two Egg community of northern Florida just before Christmas of 1990, not one single new lead has surfaced. Does this substantiate the belief that the trio drowned? Or does it prove that the Anglins and Morris are still outsmarting the entire U.S. Justice Department? U.S. Marshal McLendon commented rather dryly, "About the only thing that came from all that media attention was that my office can no longer comment on anything pertaining to the search. All future inquiries now have to go through the public affairs office in Washington, D.C."

And as for Dale Cox? He continues to receive anonymous phone calls from people who hang up after a few moments. These calls come in about four or five times a week, to the dismay of his young wife, Teresa. His answer: "In my line of investigative work, and because I have a listed number, I get crank calls from relatives of the people I report on. Sometimes they are very aggravated. You can bet, however, that I will continue my job. The information provided by Cathy and others may, or may not, eventually prove accurate. In my opinion, there has not been enough evidence as yet to either confirm or disprove her story. I feel certain that over time I will be able to either prove or disprove Cathy's facts. I believe that the Alcatraz story is sufficiently important to warrant very careful investigation of any leads."

10

Clarence and J. W., Legally

"On Alcatraz we used to say, 'First, there is 'being.' Then 'doing,' and being 'done' to. Now, all we want is 'being' again."

Charlie Hopkins, #1186 AZ

As brilliant and creative as they were, it is surprising that neither Frank Morris nor the Anglin brothers were interested in exiting Alcatraz via the legal route.

There were no filing of habeas corpus petitions in the federal courts, no appeals or motions, no attempts to overturn their convictions—no pending actions of any kind. Legal fights meant reliance on justice, and none of the three believed in miracles. While their fellow convicts were content to allow Alcatraz to dull their senses, resigned to spend their sentences in limbo, Morris and the Anglins knew that in their cases patiently relying on the foibles of lawyers and parole boards was the height of insanity.

Why?

The Anglins would never forget how the court-appointed attorney to defend them in the 1958 Columbia, Alabama, bank robbery urged them to plead guilty as a way of getting leniency from the judge. They trusted him when he didn't introduce the fact that the weapon employed was a toy pistol, that no one was hurt, and that all but $500 of $18,000 had been recovered. So the three gullible brothers were horrified to hear the maximum sentences the judge pronounced in the name of the law. Would Clarence and J. W. ever trust a lawyer again? Did they believe a competent and caring attorney even existed? And, if they did, where would they obtain the money to pay for his or her services? And even if the family did scrape together enough money, would the legal process move fast enough for them? If they ever contemplated resorting to an attorney, all they had to remember was their friend George Ellis, a bank robber and kidnapper. Back at the federal penitentiary in Atlanta, he had attempted to escape through a sewer pipe—not because he desired to be free, but because he wanted to kill his attorney, who he felt had betrayed him.

No. The Anglins and Morris would risk the odds against them rather than rely on legal issues. Let the other cons turn to Alcatraz inmates Courtney Taylor and Henry "Beef Stew" Sanders, the two "legal eagles" of the institution. Let them take on the prison authorities, who also distrusted attorneys, who made it difficult for inmates to file briefs, who subjected them to strict shakedowns, including rectal examinations after their privileged attorney visits. And let them try to prepare their own appeals—the Alcatraz "legal library" was a joke. Located in an A-block locked cell, the material consisted of half a dozen outdated and disintegrating U.S. Legal Codes, two broken-down typewriters, and a small table and chair, hardly the stuff honoring the court's mandate that Alcatraz establish a law library so that inmates unable to afford counsel could do their own research. Free circulation, however, was allowed of the *Federal Reporter* and the *Supreme Court Reporter*, which informed readers of current federal cases.

Today, most retired Alcatraz personnel, including Phil Bergen, the former captain of the guard, feel that Alcatraz was an effective "turntable," not some "dumping ground." Inmates, they believe, had no reason to want to escape. But to many inmates, and to the Anglins especially, this federal prison meant isolation and lifelessness. Descriptions of The Rock as "a living death" was no idle hyperbole. Certainly the brothers and Morris were well-fed, housed, clothed, and medically cared for. Not one of the three charged the institution or its officers with "crimes against humanity." Still, the endless, circumscribed routine, the tedium and boredom, the 145 hours a week locked in a five-by-eight-foot cell with its 75-watt bare electric light bulb probably would have meant an early death for such free-spirited men.

The very nature of their characters would make impossible their participation in the "Alcatraz Experiment." It could only anesthetize their souls against all feeling, and that they would not allow. As they did from every reform school, road gang, and every state and federal prison they had been in, they would escape. Any other course would have meant giving up.

Sure, Alcatraz had seen many changes and innovations since 1934. The "no talking" rule had long since been abolished; two letters a week were allowed to be sent and received; there were twenty-four movies a year; educational correspondence courses could be taken; head-sets were allowed in individual cells, so inmates could listen to music, news, and sports events; and most of the officers no longer believed in using a maximum of counterforce to regain control of an individual or group. Not lost on the Anglins and Morris, however, was the indisputable fact that the "Experiment" continued to exist and that it would be much easier to relocate all the cemeteries of nearby Colma, California, than to win early release dates through the law.

Dostoevsky said that society can be judged by how it treats its criminals. All Clarence, J. W., and Frank had to do was look around in the cellhouse and recreation yard to see the human wreckage of the "turn-table" concept. They knew they would not join those 4 to 6 percent of the inmates from the prison's population who were annually sent to the federal medical and psychological facilities at Springfield, Illinois.

*   *   *

Although it does not have a high priority, nor has it intensified among local police and sheriff's offices, state law enforcement agencies, the FBI, or the U.S. Marshals Service, the escapees are searched for whenever credible leads come in. Only the U.S. Bureau of Prisons clings to the notion that Morris and the Anglins drowned in San Francisco Bay on the night of June 11-12, 1962,* lest three Southern farmboys

---

*When the author requested the FBI files of Clarence and J. W. under the Freedom of Information Act provisions, I was politely informed by an agent in the San Francisco

destroy its myth that Alcatraz was inescapable.

Now, with hints abounding in the family that the Anglin brothers, at least, may be willing to turn themselves in, what can Clarence and J. W. expect in terms of a legal defense by a criminal attorney to prevent them from returning to federal prison?

Virtually every attorney the author consulted, including professors of criminal law at the Stanford University School of Law, the Boalt School of Law at the University of California, and the Hastings Law School in San Francisco, believe that there are two issues involved in the Anglins' surrender: the legal and the political. First of all, the escapees still owe the government prison time. Because precise sentences are involved, there is no statute of limitations for escape from a federal penitentiary. In addition, the escapees face a new charge: unlawful flight from confinement. In essence, the Anglins and Morris must legally resume serving their prison time to the conclusion of their original sentences.

It is difficult for a criminal attorney to construct a defense until all the issues raised by the government are clarified. But a few of the theoretical points likely to be focused upon can be discussed. San Francisco criminal attorney Michael H. Metzger, a well-known former federal and state prosecutor specializing in state and federal criminal practice, said he would begin by asking whether their act of escaping—when no bodily harm or injury was caused to prison officers, other inmates, or the public—was inherently criminal. Certainly it has to be acknowledged that an escape from a federal penitentiary violates the letter of the law. But isn't there a higher law, an unwritten law, involved: the law of survival? Isn't every person entitled, in the absence of using violence, to attempt to secure his

---

office that I had to produce a signed and notarized "release" from each of the brothers, although twenty-nine years had passed since the escape. I answered that if I could obtain a signed and notarized "release" from either or both brothers, I *wouldn't need* the files. Doubly polite, the agent responded, "Because we presume the Anglins are alive, you'll have to appeal our decision to withhold the files to FBI authorities in Washington, D.C." As of this writing, the author has received no response to his appeal.

or her own freedom? From our country's earliest history in the Revolutionary War, American soldiers have had the obligation, if captured, to attempt an escape. Indeed, escape is an honorable duty in military minds. In addition, it's good common sense. A person's basic nature is to prevent physical and psychological injury to him- or herself, if he or she can do so without harming others in the process. Virtually all of us would consider someone insane if he or she chose voluntarily to remain incarcerated in a "box." Why would rational people consider it irrational to try to get out? Any cornered animal, even if tame, seeks release from restriction. If humans consider it admirable for animals to seek freedom, why wouldn't humans praise other humans for escaping from similar confinements?

When the author approached Melvin M. Belli, Sr., at his law offices in the historic Belli Building in the San Francisco financial district to ask what his defense might be should the Anglin brothers suddenly present themselves, the internationally respected trial lawyer laughed, "pro bono, pro bono! I'll defend those boys for nothing, if they've been respectful citizens all these years. Defending them would be for the public good. Just tell them to call me. My number is (415) 981-1849." The irascible 84-year-old barrister, whom *Life* magazine labeled America's King of Torts, has written innumerable legal books and received many distinguished awards and honors during his controversial career. Often maligned for his "flamboyancy" by lesser legal minds ("the only difference between an ambulance and Belli is that the ambulance gets there faster" goes the quip), the astute observors praise his professional work. Belli is one of the founders of the International Academy of Trial Lawyers, the San Francisco Lawyers Association, and a past president of the Association of Trial Lawyers of America, and he might well be the perfect person to handle the legal and political aspects of any Anglin trial.

"With all due respect to the U.S. Justice Department, which has tried for some thirty years to catch the fugitives, the first thing I would do would be to make Clarence and J. W. captains of the U.S. Olympic swimming team. In all seriousness, though, if the two men have kept their noses clean since the escape, there's an excellent chance I could see to it that they would not spend another day in jail. Given the fact that they used a toy pistol in the original crime, that almost all of the money was recovered, that the Anglins never hurt anyone, that in their escape from Alcatraz they caused no injury to the guards, except to their pride, and that today they are utterly and completely rehabilitated, as demonstrated by their noninvolvment in any crimes for the past three decades, I could build a dandy defense around compassion," claimed Belli. "Mercy must always be the major part of justice, and, if the two brothers want to return to the public, a forbearing citizenry will certainly allow that. My God, wasn't compassion one of the founding principles of this nation? Didn't our forefathers, who fled injustices and oppression, come to this nation with a vow that clemency would be an integral part of freedom and democracy?"

Belli continued: "I also know that I could find many lenient people in government who would consider restoring those two to citizenship without giving them any points for making their impossible escape from Alcatraz. Now's the time to return them to society. One of my major arguments would be that Clarence and J. W., and Frank Morris for that matter, actually achieved what 1600 other Alcatraz inmates dreamed of doing since 1934: they made it! They accomplished an amazing feat! But, in looking for government tolerance, I would not give them credit for that. I would argue before the jury that credit be given for their years in exile and while in exile quietly reinstating themselves to society's principles of law and order. We Americans are not a punitive people by nature. I could find some government officials, judicial or otherwise, who would be sympathetic and merciful."

With a sparkle in his eyes, the proud advocate concluded the interview by saying, "You tell Clarence and J. W. to go to a pay phone and call me right away. If they do, I will tell them they can trust me in handling their defense with competence and for free. This goes for Frank Morris, too. It's high time the government, the public, and the escapees themselves bring this issue to closure. Remember this key fact of life, this key to all democracies, the key which I would use as a pivotal point before a jury of good people: 'All man does is live.' "

In San Rafael, California, Attorney Gary T. Ragghianti, of the law offices of Ragghianti, Lusse & Thomas, argue that it hardly seemed appropriate to insist upon retribution after a thirty-year absence should the Anglin brothers come in. The highly respected attorney said, "To bring the full arm of justice down on these men today would be, simply stated, 'magnification of technicality' at the expense of reason; a blind, mechanical, and mindless reaction to a case which demands application of reflection, thought, judgment, and a healthy measure of common sense."

Our system of criminal justice has other and higher priorities to address at this time, Ragghianti felt. Assuming the fugitives weren't criminals during their years at large, he would attempt to persuade the government that the interests of justice in this matter would best be served by a quick plea of guilty to the "ancient" escape, a brief period of probation (or none at all), and no incarceration for the three. "Hopefully, the U.S. Attorney would seriously receive such a proposed disposition. It provides each side some modicum of accommodation and attention to their respective positions in dealing with this very stale criminal act. It would even make sense to drop all the charges immediately, as a way of saving court time and expense— a signal accomplishment in the criminal justice 'business.' On a more personal note, I hope that if the Anglin brothers have been on their good behavior after all these years, they run for judgeships in their Florida communities."

Should the Anglins suddenly show up in the reception offices of Michael Metzger's Sausalito suite, the famed criminal attorney would prepare a defense along several lines. First, he would disinter the court procedures and arguments in the original 1958 trial for the Columbia, Albama, bank robbery in an attempt to invalidate the original convictions. What defects could he discover in terms of modern standards? The resurrection of that trial, in which the prosecutor demanded death sentences for the three brothers, and where an entire senior high school class was ushered into court to witness the humiliation of the bank robbers, might alone result in the Anglins never spending another day in federal prison.

Metzger would also argue the "realpolitik" of the issue: No rational public benefit would result if the government insisted that the brothers and Morris continue their "ancient" sentences. Since the Anglins would be entitled to a jury trial for the escape charge, the attorney would hammer away on the theme that, in practical effect, the two brothers had served out their sentences several times over. During the past thirty years, so many constitutional changes have occurred, including changes in parole statutes, that serving one-third of one's sentence is now common practice. The Anglins' sentences were excessive and cruel, as were their circumstances in Alabama, considering the prejudice of some of the public, who wanted to teach "Florida boys a lesson for coming up into our state and robbing us." The argument would be that Clarence and J. W. needed to escape to avoid being kept in dungeons. They had the duty to escape in order to live.

Another issue would revolve around the old saying, "Dead men tell no tales." Certainly it's common knowledge that the Anglins and Morris escaped from Alcatraz. But how many of those on duty that night of June 11 and 12 are still alive to testify that it was indeed the Anglins and Morris who accomplished the feat? Granted, this is the weaker of the three arguments, but legally it has enormous implications.

Metzger, and virtually all the other attorneys I spoke to, felt that there would be such an overwhelming emotional component to the Anglins' trial, especially if it could be demonstrated that no other crimes had been committed, or citizens harmed, by the three during their twenty-nine years of hiding, that no jury in America would send them back to prison. A jury would acquit them, regardless of the fact that the law was technically violated. A jury could be brought to understand that justice would not be served by a guilty verdict. The essential argument for Metzger and others would center, indeed pivot, on common sense.

11

Conclusion

"Alcatraz . . . hard as a rock . . . you took two of my brothers away
that cold night. . . . I hope and pray they made it because nothing has
ever been found. . . . They did something that no one else ever had . . ."

from a song composed and dedicated to Clarence and
J. W. by 18-year-old Mary Nell Anglin in July of 1962

This book has focused upon one of the greatest riddles in U.S. prison
history. It has also made an attempt to introduce the reader to other
issues, including the enigma of the institution where more than 200
of the most "hardened" criminals were jammed tightly together and
governed by 150 civilian personnel. A true understanding of what
Alcatraz was—what it was intended to do, the successes and failures
of those who served in it, as well as the feelings of those who were
incarcerated in it—has never been fully explored. Over the past fifty-
seven years, myths, legends, and utter nonsense brazenly nurtured by
the media have littered the shelves of the nation's libraries. I hope
that what I have learned from three of my friends—inmates Clarence
"Joe" Carnes and Charlie Hopkins, and former officer Phil Bergen—
and what has been condensed into these pages, is not more of the
same old Alcatraz clichés currently sold to the unsuspecting 5,000
tourists a day who visit the prison's bookstore after first making a
bee-line to the cells of Morris and the Anglin brothers.

In a sense, the reader has to face the same dilemma as the author. On the one hand, Joe Carnes and Charlie Hopkins offered a
gold mine of inmate feelings and insights. On the other, Phil Bergen
questioned my reliance on the "antiestablishment views of inmate

consultants." Joe is no longer available to debate, while Charlie retorts, "A lot of what the former captain says is true. But his opinion of the antiestablishment views of Carnes, Alvin Karpis, me, and the others is based on the fact that we never broke in spirit and were men to the end." (Phil emphatically counters: "Not so! Hopkins does not know what my opinions are, nor on what 'fact,' or 'facts,' they are based.")

Perhaps the debate between the keepers and the kept during the twenty-nine-year life of the penitentiary, the same length of time that Morris and the Anglins have been free, will continue as long as they and others associated with Alcatraz live. Bergen, the most knowledgeable man alive on the history of the prison, and on the thinking and values of the officers who served there, will always be a deeply respected, if sometimes caustic, friend. But so will Joe and Charlie. And, for that matter, so will Morris and the Anglins, if they have never stolen anything or hurt anybody in the years following their escape.

*   *   *

And what of Clarence, J. W., and Frank, who still have $5,000 rewards on their heads?

It would take another volume to do full justice to the complexities of their individual personalities. Were they simply arrogant, cocky, callous braggarts, as one San Francisco writer insisted? Were they the embodiment of the American success story, as much of the public believes? Questions such as these are yet to be answered. But one thing is certain: Each man was incapable of harming another human being. Each was incapable of ruthlessness or treachery.

The Anglin brothers were deep and profound men with warm, disarmingly gentle manners about them. They were certainly mercurial, but, according to those who loved them the most, that slipperiness was balanced by a inner maturity and sensitivity all their own.

Indeed, it is their "slipperiness" that endears them to the millions of Americans who visit Alcatraz and their cells. They are three of the few rare people who live for action; there was never any doubt what they should do if incarcerated. For Alfred, Clarence, and J. W., captivity was unbearable and escape their only interest from the moment they arrived in an institution. Inertia and fear would not dampen their instinct for survival. Neither would the prison's immediate difficulties, perceived by the vast majority of inmates to be insuperable. Every other activity and every other consideration, except to protect their family, was subordinated to escape. So, using their few resources, their endurance, their humor, their luck, and, most important of all, their basic mental strength (some would say their pure "cussedness"), they set about "breaking The Rock." Whatever is thought of them, however they are perceived, their incredible escape from Alcatraz represents an American success story of sorts—accomplishing in the face of seemingly impossible odds what no one has ever achieved before: They single-handedly forced the closing of the infamous island penitentiary.

Phil Bergen argues otherwise. "The disparaging press notices, etc., concerning the Morris-Anglin 'escape' *may* have had *some* effect on the *timing* of the closing. But that is all. The decision to close was made much earlier, prior to the establishment of United States Prison, Marion, Illinois, years earlier, prior to the multimillion-dollar appropriation for U.S.P., Marion, which was designed and authorized as a 'substitute' for Alcatraz." Bergen says there were many contributing factors in the deactivization of the penitentiary: the excessive cost of operation, a sewage disposal problem, and the deterioration of the gigantic I-beams that support B and C cellblocks. "But the real reason, the primary reason, was because Jim Bennet wanted to close it for 29 years, and, in Robert Kennedy, he finally found an attorney general with the guts to defy 'J. Edgar,' the 'father' of Alcatraz!"

And today?

Sheriff John P. McDaniel of Jackson County, Florida comments, "I believe that Morris and the Anglins are out there somewhere. In fact, we know it. I'm not going out there in the backwoods looking for them, because I believe they have left the area. If they should be discovered, or if someone tells me where they are, you can bet I'm going to do my duty and put handcuffs on them. Then I'm going to sit down, offer them a cigarette, relax, and listen to their incredible story. A lot of the folks down here want to believe in them."

So do a lot of other people, including the author of this book.

Virtually all my friends, including a steady date and her son, agree with the U.S. Bureau of Prisons that Morris and the Anglins drowned in the early morning hours of June 12, 1962. My eighty-year-old mother scolds, "Donald, I hope you're not embarrassing our family name with all your nonsense about their being alive."

Why do I believe Morris and the Anglins survived?

First, there are too many unexplained phone calls and postcards, family recollections of mysterious appearances and flower deliveries —to say nothing of the unresolved public sightings. There is the telephone call to San Francisco attorney Eugenia McGowan the morning after the escape, a voice asking for "our day in court." There are the Christmas cards received by family members from the mid-1960s through the late 1960s with the names and addresses underlined in the Alcatraz letter format and signed by "Joe [Jon?] and Jerry," the names of Helen's boys. There is the leather horse and its hidden message to Alfred during the summer of 1962, and Alfred's whispered statement to Robert, Sr., in the Kilby Prison bathroom, "I can go right to those boys today." There is Alfred's escape attempt from Kilby in 1964, probably to join Clarence and J. W. There are the two "heavily made-up women" who sat unnoticed amid FBI agents during mother Rachael's funeral in 1973 and who did not identify themselves by signing the guest registry. There the two unknown, well-dressed, bearded men who arrived prior to father George's funeral in February of 1989 and, after weeping before the open casket, quickly left the funeral parlor without speaking to the funeral director's son or signing the registry. There is a claim Rachael made one morning that, "I saw the boys last night. They came up to the window and spoke softly to me, asking how we all were doing, if me and Dad were all right. Your dad slept through it all. But they were right here at the bedroom window. It was no vision. It happened." There are the flowers Rachael received every Mother's Day with no signed card or return address. There is brother Carson's repeated statement, "You can bet them boys know everything about us, what's going on in our families, right now." There is the fact that the entire family always speaks of Clarence and J. W. in the present tense. There is Cathy's intimate knowledge of the Anglin brothers. There are the sightings by numerous residents in and around the Two Egg community of northern Florida, not far from where the brothers were born. There is the statement of Robert, Sr., that "my brothers were excellent farmhands and they would get a job easy with a farmer or rancher—getting a Social Security card in the early 1960s was pretty easy." And then there are the beliefs of the U.S. Marshals Service that Clarence and J. W. are alive.

Second, of all the circumstantial evidence that abounds, none is more convincing than the testimony of J. W.'s former girlfriend, Helen, who told the author, "After all these years, I guess it's O.K. to talk about Jon, something I always used to refuse to do. I know for a fact that J. W. is alive. He called me a month after the escape. I was so surprised and happy to hear his familiar voice. But he kept the conversation short and sweet. He asked me if I was doing all right, how my two sons were, and told me to keep a low profile because the FBI would be watching me and his family for a hundred years. Then one day about six months later my oldest son came home and said that he had seen J. W. on a Tampa street. 'Momma, I saw J. W. I know it was him. I know his walk and his size. It was definitely him!' he said. John would call me once or twice a year throughout the rest of the 1960s. In those days the FBI was hounding, hounding, hounding me. Once they broke into my house and tore my place apart, searching for God only knows what. Remember that J. W. and I had been planning on getting married. He had wanted money for me and my sons, plus his Mom and Dad, who were elderly and sick and couddn't work anymore. He always said that I was being watched, but that somehow he would check in with me. When I remarried in the 1970s, I would get a call from time to time and the person on the line would not say anything. I would ask, 'J. W., is that you? Is that you? J. W., talk to me. I know it's you,' but there would only be breathing, and after a pause the person would hang up. In my heart I knew it was John and his way of telling me that we were still friends and that he was safe."

As late as May 1991, several mysterious phone calls have been received, as they were throughout all of 1990, by Audrey, the second oldest Anglin sister, and Rufus, the oldest brother, at the original Anglin home in Ruskin, Florida. When each picks up the receiver, no one speaks. There is only breathing. The person generally remains on the line, as if savoring the moments, until Audrey or Rufus hangs up. Other brothers and sisters have received similar phone calls over the years. But as the family grows older, the calls appear to be increasing. Is the FBI or the U.S. Marshals Service harassing the family? Hardly. Is some prankster who knows the family's unlisted numbers playing upon the emotions of the Anglins, who have been considered outcasts by much of the Ruskin community for the past half-century? Perhaps no one understands what is going on, but family members hope Clarence and J. W. are trying to make contact with Robert, who lives off and on with Audrey and Rufus, and who never answers the phone.

Is it possible the boys will speak only to their brother?

Is it possible Clarence and J. W. are ready to come home?

A Personal Word to
Clarence, John, and Frank

From W. L. "Mac" McLendon
U.S. Marshal, N/FL
(904) 681-7676

The NBC "Unsolved Mysteries" program on February 9, 1989, featured your famous "Escape from Alcatraz." Phone-in leads of your whereabouts have been checked by the U.S. Marshals Offices in Tallahassee, Florida, and San Francisco since that time. The program has been rebroadcast three times and numerous leads have been checked throughout America.

Although there are strong differences of opinion among law enforcement professionals, and there are no verified reports of your survival, I, personally, believe your escape was successful and that you probably have lived very respectful lives ever since. Since none of you has been accused of any new crimes over the years, there is very little reason for you to remain in hiding.

The mystery surrounding your sensational escape, and what you three have been doing over these past years, can be solved by turning yourselves in to me, or other proper authorities. The rewards of putting an end to your fugitive status would outweigh any minor punishment that might await you.

An Open Letter to My Brothers

From Robert Anglin
Ruskin, Florida
May 10, 1991

As your older brother who hasn't seen you for thirty-three years, I would like to say to you both, Clarence and J. W., that I hope with all my heart you made it out safe from Alcatraz and are alive. If you read these words, know that many things have happened since you left that place. Alfred is gone; Mom and Dad are gone; and lots of uncles and aunts are gone. Momma and Daddy had lots of fine grandchildren, great-grandchildren, and great-great-grandchildren they had never seen and who, I'm sure, would like to meet both of you. It seems like a lot of people here in Ruskin, and all over the country, are pulling for you fellows to come home. Everybody that we in the family have talked to hopes you made it O.K.

I can speak for all of us here—Rufus, Verna, Audrey, Christine, Carson, Marie, Mearl, Patsy, Nell, and Jeanette—when I say we pray very much to see you again someday. If you happen to see this letter, I ask for both of you to meet me at a certain place—the place where John picked Clarence and two of his friends up when they escaped from the Ft. Meyers Road Camp. The business that was there at that time is not there anymore. But a new business is at that location. I would like to challenge you to meet me there, July 20, 1991, between 11:00 A.M. and 1:00 P.M. I will be in the parking lot waiting on you. There is so much to talk about, the most important being for you to see it's safe to come home. Don, your brothers and sisters, and Jeanette will stand by you as long as it takes to get you free. Then we can be together again as a family, like Momma and Dad asked when they passed away. We all love you, we all believe in you, and we all want you home. I'll be waiting.

"Man"

To: Clarence and J. W.
From: The Author

It's time to come in. Drop me a letter or card indicating (so that I'll know its you two) either Ruthie's last name, your Momma's full maiden name, or the name of the man who always hired you to pick cherries. Indicate how I can get in touch with you. "Man," Marie, and your other brothers and sisters, and Jeanette, say that you can trust me. We will work together for your freedom.

Don DeNevi
555 Atlantic Avenue
Alameda, California 94501

P.S. Audrey says to hurry up because she has a fourteen-layer banana cake waiting for you. Marie says she and the others are going to throw the biggest family reunion the state of Florida has ever seen. Mearl says after you two pick the branches you want, she's "gonna whup you both with them." Patsy says, "There ain't going to be anything left" after she's through hugging you. Verna will ask, "Well, *where* have you two been? Are you back from the dead?"

Appendices

Appendix A

Possible Sequence of Events on the Night of June 11 and Morning of June 12, 1962

Contrary to the official Bureau of Prisons belief that the homemade raft of prison raincoats began dismantling once the three escapees were in it on the Bay waters, resulting in their drowning, the author maintains that the following is probably what happened:

June 11

10:15 A.M.: Allen West whispers to Clarence "Joe" Carnes, "Tonight we see the moon!"

3:30-4:30 P.M.: Anglin brothers and Frank Morris eat their last "chow" in the Alcatraz mess hall.

5:00 P.M.: Final lockup and official evening stand-up count.

5:00-6:00 P.M.: Mail delivery and possible distribution of C-store cigarettes from Navy ship stocks. Usually this occurred on Mondays, Wednesdays, and Fridays, although it was possible the routine could change. Therefore the escapees had to be present in their cells when the lieutenant walked by distributing the free cigarettes.

6:30-7:00 P.M.: The unofficial count begins. As many as three officers participate in the counting of inmates in their cells. This continues throughout the night and early morning hours— but this usually means the counting of "heads" asleep in their bunks.

8:00 P.M.: The Anglins and Morris begin crawling out of their cells.

10:30 P.M.: The escapees strive to push the sheet-metal rainhood off the roof vent; three loud, hollow bangs echo through the cellhouse.

10:50 P.M.: The inmates reach the water and begin the slow process of inflating the rafts.

The breeze is from the southwest—not favorable to reach a boat "downstream" on the tide, but the wind is only five to eight knots.

The plan, as Bumpy told West, who explained it to Morris and the Anglins: A boat would wait for them for a three-night "window," from one hour after sundown until midnight, or until the tide began to flow into the bay. Each night, June 10, June 11, June 12, the commercial fishing boat would position itself about three hundred yards off Alcatraz, due north of the island. When a light signal was received from the beach of Alcatraz, which indicated the men had made it to the water's edge and were ready to go, the boat would slowly ghost on the tide at an angle to intercept the escapee's boat as it rode on the current toward the Golden Gate.

If it was foggy, all bets were off. (In early June there are frequent afternoon fogs on the bay, but by 9:00 P.M., the fog often will dissipate.)

As the escapee's inflated boat approached, the fishing boat maneuvered to block the view from Alcatraz so that anyone on the island would not be able to see the boat stopping to pick up the men.

Bumpy used a code to inform a visitor or a correspondent that he needed a boat for a planned escape on a given date. The men in the boat would know little of the plan. Their orders would be to wait for a signal, pick up the men, and put them ashore at a pre-arranged location.

When Morris and the Anglins reached the water, they knew their dummies were working and that they probably would not be discovered missing until morning. As the Anglins took turns pumping up the boat and their life jackets, Morris set up the signal light, a homemade flashlight like the one found atop the cell block. (That one was a spare, left behind for West.) The tiny light was set in a cardboard box, open on one side. The interior of the box was painted with silver paint and set with a small magnifying shaving mirror. When the box was pointed north, and the light flashed, the box hid the beam from anyone on Alcatraz and directed it toward the open bay. The waiting boat responded by hoisting a small light on a halyard, lowering it, then hoisting it again. That was the signal for the men to launch their boat.

Once the three escapees were hauled out of the water, unobserved by anyone on Alcatraz, the inflatable boat was ripped apart and cast adrift, as were the paddles, life jackets, and waterproof packet carried by J. W. Anglin, all "proof" that the men had drowned. (Remember that, according to the FBI report, an off-duty San Francisco police officer strolling along a beachfront hiking trail near the San Francisco Yacht Club noticed what appeared to be a small fishing vessel or cabin cruiser dead in the water northwest of the island for about fifteen minutes around midnight.) The boat headed at normal speed out of the Golden Gate and due south. The three men were given a change of clothes and $500 each in small bills. They napped below as the fishing boat churned its way south past Pacifica, Half Moon Bay, and on to Moss Landing, a commercial and sports fishing center.

June 12: The three reached Moss Landing at 3:30 A.M. Nothing on the radio had indicated an escape from Alcatraz, so the men knew they were still undetected. They worried about West. Perhaps he had been caught and the police were already searching for them. But they had to stick to the plan. This was no time to panic. They casually walked ashore with their fishing gear, had a quick breakfast in one of the several small diners along the wharf, and waited until a car picked them up. The car, with a single driver who asked no questions, took them south through the Salinas Valley to U.S. 99 near Fresno.

Morris wanted to separate as soon as possible, but the plan was to stay together as long as possible. With luck they would not be missed until the 7:15 A.M. count. The car radio was kept on constantly. By 9:30 the car was south of King City. No announcement came over the radio, but the three men knew the escape had been discovered. They must have had a good chuckle at the thought of the hacks finding the dummy heads.

They stopped in San Luis Obispo, where Morris bought a bus ticket to a certain point. The Anglins decided to stay with the car and driver until the radio reported an escape. They drove on south across the California border and into Arizona where they melted into the Southwest.

By the time the search for them was organized to include border crossings and interstate highways, the three men had a twelve-to-fifteen-hour head start. A lot can happen in that amount of time.

Meanwhile,

1:00 A.M.: West finally breaks through his cell and is in the utility corridor.

5:45 A.M.: West gives up all hope and returns to his cell.

7:15 A.M.: Morning stand-up count and the discovery of the escape.

Appendix B

FBI Bulletin To All
Law Enforcement Agencies
June 12, 1962

Facts as to Dangerousness

Subjects at Large Are All Convicted Bank Robbers and Should Be Considered Extremely Dangerous

Descriptions

RE: FRANK LEE MORRIS

The following description of FRANK LEE MORRIS is set forth as obtained from prison records, as well as various police records:

Race: White
Dates of birth: September 1, 1926; September 1, 1922; September 1, 1928; September 1, 1925
Places of birth: Washington, D.C.; Mobile, Alabama; Elizabeth City, North Carolina; Ednor, Maryland
Height: Approximately 5'7½"
Weight: 135 to 145 pounds

Complexion: Medium fair

Eyes: Hazel-gray

Build: Medium

Teeth: Good, February 1950

Scars and marks: Scar on middle of forehead; cut scar on left forearm, near wrist; scar on left biceps; vaccination scar on upper left arm; scar on left little finger; scar on left elbow; several scars on both shins; 1″ scar on left foot

Tattoos: Devil's head on upper right arm; star on left knee with "7" above and "11" below; star on right knee; star on base or back of left thumb; "13" on base of left index finger; circle between left thumb and index finger; "N.T.S.B." or "N.B." on upper left arm; star on center of forehead (possibly removed); "C" on back of left index finger

Residences: 902 Howard Avenue, New Orleans, Louisiana, September 1956, June 1955, January 1952, January 1950, December 1948; Washington, D. C., September 1956, January 1956; Ednor, Maryland, June 1939

Occupations: Mechanical draftsman; painter; car salesman; laborer; fighter; odd jobs

Identifications: Fingerprint classification is

22 M 9 U I00 12

L 1 U 000.

Signature available in Identification Division, FBI. Dental chart maintained by U. S. Penitentiary, Alcatraz Island, California, and copy available in San Francisco Office file.

Relatives: None listed in files at Alcatraz Penitentiary. When investigated in 1945 and again in 1951 in connection with Selective Service Act violations, MORRIS advised on both occasions that his parents died when he was 11 years of age. He claimed his father's name was FRANK WILLIAM LYONS and believed his mother's name was MARY. In 1945 he claimed his only living relative was EDITH WILSON, an aunt, then purportedly residing in Elizabeth City, North Carolina. Extensive investigation to locate and identify this aunt during Selective Service Act investigations was unsuccessful. In 1955 Vital Statistic Records, Washington, D.C., revealed FRANK MORRIS was born September 1, 1926, Gallinger Hospital, Washington, D.C., father's name EDWARD FRED MORRIS, age 36, a construction engineer, address 1310 D Street, Southeast, Washington, D.C.; mother THELMA MARIE PHILLIPS, age 17, housewife, resided Rockville, Maryland.

RE: JOHN WILLIAM ANGLIN

The following description of ANGLIN is set forth as obtained from the records at the United States Penitentiary, Alcatraz Island, California, as well as police sources:

Race: White
Dates of birth: May 2, 1931; May 2, 1930; May 7, 1930,
Places of birth: Donaldsonville, Georgia, Colquitt, Georgia
Height: Approximately 5'11"
Weight: 140 pounds in February 1958
Complexion: Ruddy
Eyes: Blue
Hair: Blonde
Scars and marks: Scar left side abdomen; scar left cheek; dim cut scar inside left forearm near wrist
Residence: Ruskin, Florida, February 1958, January 1958, October 1951, November 1948, December 1946
Occupations: Farmer; laborer
Identifications: Fingerprint classification is
20 L 29 W I00 17
I 12 W 00I.
Signature of this individual is available in the Identification Division, FBI. The U. S. Penitentiary, Alcatraz Island, California, has a dental chart concerning ANGLIN, a copy of which is maintained in the San Francisco Office file.
Relatives: Parents—GEORGE R. and RACHEL ANGLIN [, Ruskin, Florida]

Brothers—ROBERT JUNIOR ANGLIN, same address;
RUFUS ANGLIN   "   "   ;
CARLTON ANGLIN   "   "   ;
ALFRED RAY ANGLIN, presently incarcerated U. S.
    Penitentiary, Atlanta, serving 15 years on same bank
    robbery JOHN charged; CLARENCE ANGLIN, es-
    caped from Alcatraz with JOHN;
Sisters—VERNA NEWBERRY
AUDREY BAZDEMORE, same address;
MARIE WIDNER   "   "   ;
MEARL SIMS   "   "   ;
MARY NELL ANGLIN   "   "   ;
CHRISTINE GRIFFIS
PATSY LEWIS

RE: CLARENCE ANGLIN

The following description of ANGLIN is being set forth as obtained
from records of the United States Penitentiary, Alcatraz Island, California, and various police sources:

Race: White
Dates of birth: May 11, 1931; April 11, 1931; March 11, 1930;
    May 11, 1932; May 11, 1930
Places of birth: Donaldsonville, Georgia; Colquitt, Georgia
Height: Approximately 5'11"
Weight: 167 pounds, December 1960
Complexion: Ruddy
Eyes: Hazel-blue
Hair: Dark brown
Teeth: Good, June 1951
Scars and marks: Pitted scar between eyes; scar on left side of upper
    lip; cut scar back of third joint of right ring finger; mole on each
    side of stomach; vaccination scar on upper right arm; scar on
    outside edge of right forearm

Tattoos: Scroll and "ZONA" on left wrist, outer or upper forearm; "NITA" on upper right arm

Residences: Ruskin, Florida, December 1960; Ruskin, Florida, February 1958, January 1952, June 1951, May 1951, March 1950, November 1948, December 1946, June 1945; Box 221, Raiford, Florida, January 1958

Occupations: Cabinet maker; laborer; farmer

Identifications: Fingerprint classification is

18 0 27 W 100 21

L 27 W 010.

Signature of this individual is available in the Identification Division of the FBI. U. S. Penitentiary, Alcatraz, Island, California, has a dental chart for ANGLIN, a copy of which is maintained in the San Francisco Office file.

Relatives: Parents—GEORGE R. and RACHEL ANGLIN [, Ruskin, Florida]

Brothers—ROBERT JUNIOR ANGLIN, same address;
RUFUS ANGLIN   〃   〃   ;
CARLTON ANGLIN   〃   〃   ;
ALFRED RAY ANGLIN, presently incarcerated U. S. Penitentiary, Altanta, serving 15 years on same bank robbery CLARENCE charged; JOHN ANGLIN, escaped from Alcatraz with CLARENCE;
Sisters—VERNA NEWBERRY
AUDREY BAZDEMORE, same address;
MARIE WIDNER   〃   〃   ;
MEARL SIMS   〃   〃   ;
MARY NELL ANGLIN   〃   〃   ;
CHRISTINE GRIFFIS, Sebring, Florida;
PATSY LEWIS, c/o General Delivery, Hollister, California

Appendix C

Identification Records of Subjects

Frank Lee Morris

The following identification record for MORRIS, under FBI No. 2 157 606, dated June 13, 1962, is set forth:

Contributor of Fingerprints	Name & Number	Arrested or Received	Charge	Disposition
Sheriff's Office, Clarksburg, West Virginia	FRANK LEE MORRIS, #—	6/8/39	Runaway from Washington	Returned to Washington
National Training School for Boys, Washington, District of Columbia	FRANK MORRIS #10934-N	11/13/40	District of Columbia Juvenile Court	6 yrs. 9 mos. 18 days, 4/9/42, Dist. of Columbia Parole, parole violation 5/2/42, sentenced 1,970 days
U.S. Marshal Miami, Fla.	FRANK LEE MORRIS, #—	not given fingerprinted 4/29/42	parole violation	5/2/42 delivered to Nat'l Training School for Boys, Washington, D.C.
Federal Reformatory Chillicothe, Ohio	FRANK MORRIS #21473	1/22/43 in transfer from Nat'l Training School, Washington, D.C.	6 yrs. 9 mos. 18 days	

Police Department, New Orleans, La.	FRANK WM. LYONS #44500	10/1/45	Article 62 released to simple burglary	Sentenced 3 yrs. Angola Penitentiary, 11/19/45
State Penitentiary, Angola, La.	FRANK LYONS #35584	12/18/45	Simple burglary	3 yrs. 7/12/48 discharged
PD, Miami Beach, Fla.	FRANK LYONS #A-14230	12/16/48	Failure to make criminal registration, vagrancy investigation	12/22/48 1. released to Sheriff's Office; 2. released to SO
SO, Miami, Florida	FRANK LYONS #99564/12/19/48/breaking & entering grand larceny, hold for Miami Beach PD	1/6/49, 4 yrs. State Prison		
State Prison Raiford, Fla.	FRANK LYONS #44399	1/11/49	Unlawfully & feloniously breaking & entering a dwelling house located in Dade County, Florida, with intent to commit a felony: to-wit, grand larceny	4 yrs.
SO. Stuart, Fla.	FRANK LYONS #——	1/26/50	Escaped prisoner	In jail, released to Lee County, Florida Sheriff
State Prison, Raiford, Fla.	FRANK LYONS #46298	2/28/50	Escape (larceny of an automobile)	3 yrs. consecutively with #44399 (2 commitments, 1 for 1 yr. and 1 for 2 yrs. to run consecutively)
Sheriff's Ofc., Sarasota, Fla.	FRANK LYONS #--	11/7/50	Larceny of automobile	12/5/50 sentence withheld on larceny of automobile returned to state

				prison from where he had escaped
PD, New Orleans, La.	FRANK LYONS #44500	1/10/52	Article 64 armed robbery fugitive from justice Article 962 possession of marijuana	5/19/52 10 yrs. Louisiana State Penitentiary to run concurrently on charge armed robbery
State Penitentiary, Angola, La.	FRANK LYONS #42025	6/13/52	Violation "RS" 15:529.1 (habitual) (2) following conviction possession of marijuana & armed robbery	10 & 10 yrs. concurrently Total 10 yrs.
Customs Agency Service, Brownsville,	JOSEPH A. McENTREE #--	7/30/55	Section 545, Title 18, U.S. Code & Marijuana Tax Act	
U.S. Marshal, New Orleans,	FRANK LYONS #2788	1/12/56	Unlawful flight to avoid prosecution Mann Act violation	2/17/56, process dismissed on charge of UFAP—robbery Mann Act indictment dismissed 9/19/56
		1/16/56	bank robbery	14 yrs. count 1; 5 yrs. count 2; to run concurrent 9/19/56
PD, New Orleans, La.	FRANK LYONS #44500	finger-printed 1/23/56	held for Federal authorities in Parish prison	
JSM, New Orleans, La.	FRANK LEE MORRIS #3226	9/13/56	Attempt to escape while awaiting trial under an indictment	Dismissed 9/28/56

SO, Bir- mingham, Alabama	FRANK LEE MORRIS #32835	9/22/56	Federal theft	turned over to USM
U.S. Peniten- tiary, Atlanta, Georgia	FRANK LEE MORRIS #77796	9/23/56	Burglary of Fed- eral Deposit Ins. Corp. bank	14 years
U.S. Peniten- tiary, Alcatraz, Calif.	FRANK LEE MORRIS #1441-AZ	1/18/60	Burglary of FDIC bank	

John William Anglin

The following identification record of JOHN WILLIAM ANGLIN, FBI No. 4 745 119, received June 13, 1962, is set forth:

Contributor of Fingerprints	Name and Number	Arrested or Received	Charge	Disposition
SO, Tampa, Fla.	J.W. ANGLIN #29921	12/4/46	breaking & entering, grand larceny, 2 counts	12/24/46, released to juve- nile authorities
PD, Tamp, Florida	J.W. ANGLIN #35794	12/26/46	investigation B & E	released 12/26/ 46
SO, Tampa, Florida	JOHN W. ANGLIN #29921	11/16/48	Petty larceny	11/23/48 discharged
SO, Tampa, Fla.	JOHN W. ANGLIN #29921	10/15/51	vagrancy investigation	12/11/51, 2 yrs State Prison
State Prison Raiford, Fla.	JOHN W. ANGLIN #49025	12/11/51	Grand larceny	2 yrs., 7/21/53 released by expiration of sentence
USM, Cincin- nati, Ohio	JOHN WIL- LIAM ANGLIN #USM 58-20	1/22/58	robbery of Fed- erally protected bank	

USM, Montgo-mery, Ala.	JOHN WIL-LIAM ANGLIN #8656	2/4/58	bank robbery	2/10/58 sentenced 10 yrs.
U.S. Penitentiary, Atlanta, Ga.	JOHN WIL-LIAM ANGLIN #79624	2/13/58	bank robbery	10 years
U.S. Penitentiary, Lewisburg, PA.	JOHN WIL-LIAM ANGLIN #25034-NE	4/8/58	bank robbery	1/20/60 transferred to U.S. Penitentiary, Leavenworth
U.S. Penitentiary, Leavenworth, Kansas	JOHN WIL-LIAM ANGLIN #77350-L	1/22/60 in transfer from U.S. Penitentiary, Lewisburg, Pennsylvania	bank robbery	

Clarence Anglin

The following identification record for CLARENCE ANGLIN, FBI No. 4 731 702, received June 13, 1962, is set forth:

Contributor of Fingerprints	Name and Number	Arrested or Received	Charge	Disposition
SO, Tampa, Fla.	CLARENCE ANGLIN #242k6	6/2/45	breaking & entering & grand larceny	7/6/45 to Florida Industrial School Marianna, Fla.
Fla. Industrial School for Boys, Marianna, Fla.	CLARENCE ANGLIN #2002	7/6/45	incorrigible breaking & entering grand larceny	until legally discharged 8/26/46 discharged to Mother
SO, Tampa, Fla.	CLARENCE ANGLIN #29919	12/4/46	breaking & entering grand larceny two counts	12/24/46 to Juvenile Court

PD, Tampa, Fla.	CLARENCE ANGLIN #35795	12/26/46	investigation breaking & entering	released 12/26/46
SO, Tampa, Fla.	CLARENCE ANGLIN #29919	3/3/50	breaking and entering	3/3/50 to SO, Seminole County, Georgia
State Board of Corrections Atlanta, Ga.	CLARENCE ANGLIN #-- Thomas County "P.W.C." Thomasville Georgia	3/14/50	burglary	1 to 2 years
PD, Tampa, Fla.	CLARENCE ANGLIN #35795	5/5/51	breaking & entering grand larceny	turned over to County Jail 5/7/51
SO, Bradenton, Fla.	CLARENCE ANGLIN #--	5/28/51	breaking & entering	
State Prison Raiford, Fla.	CLARENCE ANGLIN #48453	6/22/51	burglary	4 years
State Prison Raiford, Fla.	CLARENCE ANGLIN #48454	6/22/51	breaking & entering with intent to commit felony grand larceny	5 years to run consecutively with #48453
SO, Bartow, Fla.	CLARENCE ANGLIN #P-8240	1/9/52	escaped from State Road Camp #36	Released to Taylor County SO, Perry, Fla., 1/10/52
State Prison Raiford, Fla.	CLARENCE ANGLIN #49911	6/13/52	breaking and entering	4 years consecutively with #48454
USM, Cincinnati, Ohio	CLARENCE ANGLIN #58-18	11/22/58	robbery of Federally protected bank	removed to "MDA" Montgomery Alabama 2/4/58
USM, Montgomery, Alabama	CLARENCE ANGLIN #8655	2/4/58	bank robbery	15 years custody Attorney Gen'l 2/10/58

U.S. Peniten-tiary, Atlanta Georgia	CLARENCE ANGLIN #79622	2/13/58	bank robbery	15 years
PD Montgo-mery Alabama	CLARENCE ANGLIN #90510	2/4/58	Suspicion	
U.S. Peniten-tiary, Leaven-worth, Kansas	CLARENCE ANGLIN	#75456	4/11/58 rec'd in transfer from U.S. Peniten-tiary Atlanta, Ga.	not given
USM, Topeka, Kansas	CLARENCE ANGLIN #60–361	12/19/60	attempted escape U.S. Penitentiary Leavenworth	12/19/60 2 years run consecutively
U.S. Peniten-tiary, Alcatraz California	CLARENCE ANGLIN #1485-AZ	1/16/61 transfer from U.S. Peniten-tiary Leaven-worth Kansas	bank robbery & attempt escape	

Allen Clayton West

The following identification record for ALLEN CLAYTON WEST under FBI No. 4 229 558 dated June 20, 1962, is set forth:

Contributor of Fingerprints	Name and Number	Arrested or Received	Charge	Disposition
PD Savannah Ga	ALLEN WEST #14095	8/27/44	Larceny of auto	9/7/44 indet sent to State Farm for Boys
SO Savannah Ga	ALLEN CLAY-TON WEST #45522	Marine Electri-cian advancing worker 1/4/45		
St Dept of Corr Atlanta Ga #M-29081/11468	ALLEN WEST #--St Prison Reidsville Ga	4/27/45	lar of auto	6 mos

PD Savannah Ga	ALLEN CLAY-TON WEST #14-095	9/6/45	Gen Inv	10/1/45 2 to 5 yrs on chg of burg & Larc autos
St Dept of Corr Atlanta Ga #A-17871	ALLEN WEST #--St Prison Reidsville Ga	10/12/45	burg.	2-5 yrs 3 cts conc 8/26/48 cond rel on chg of burg simple larc (2 cts)
Army	ALLAN CLAYTON WEST #RA 14290819	9/17/48 Tampa Fla		
ALLEN C. WEST #18296-Lee	11/18/49 in trans from Ft Hancock	Sodomy AWOL Break Arrest	4 yrs	
USP Lewisburg Pa	ALLEN C. WEST #18276	1/5/50 in trans from Petersburg	sodomy AWOL & breaking arrest	4 yrs 1/17/50 sent reduced from 4 to 3 yrs per Dept of Army Blue Seal Letter new rel dates are: condl rel 10/14/51 expires full term 6/16/52 7/1/50 trans to USP Atlanta Ga
USP Atlanta Ga	ALLEN C. WEST #70385	7/3/50	sodomy AWOL & breaking arrest	3 yrs 10/21/51 cond rel
PD St. Peters-burg Fla	ALLEN CLAY-TON WEST #10708	10/30/51 vol crim reg		rel
PD St. Petersburg	ALLEN CLAY-TON WEST #10708	3/11/52	inv B&E & GL	bound over to Cirt Crt trial not held
SO Clearwater Fla	ALLEN CLAY-TON WEST #5160	3/11/52	B&E 2 chgs	BOT Cirt Ct $5000 bond
Fla St Pr Rai-ford Fla	ALLEN C. WEST #49861	5/30/52	B&E w/i to comm a felony	4 yrs 2 comm of 4 yrs ea to run conc

USM Jackson Miss	ALLEN CLAY-TON WEST #53 38	1/29/53	NMVTA	pend 5/20/53 5 yrs
SO Meridian Texas	ALLEN CLAY-TON WEST #-	2/24/53	burg	
SO Stephenville Texas	PAUL LET-TOW #--	2/24/53	burg	
USP Atlanta Ga	ALLEN C. WEST #73619	5/30/53	NMVTA escape & att to escape for Fed custody	5 yrs
PMGO Wash DC	ALLAN C. WEST #RA 14 290 219	10/21/49	AW 93	4 yrs D/D
USP Alcatraz Calif	ALLEN CLAY-TON WEST #1130-AZ	4/14/54	NMVTA & escape & att escape	5 yrs sent
USP Atlanta Ga	ALLEN CLAY-TON WEST	6/30/56 rec by tran for #1130-AZ Alcatraz Is Calif	NMVTA escape & att escape	
PD Atlanta Ga	ALLEN CLAY-TON WEST #176292	12/20/56	foreign holding for Leon Co Fla	rel to Leon Co Fla Auth 12/24/56
USM Balto Md	ALLAN C. WEST	9/9/57	Escape Act (B/E) Dyer Act	removed to Savannah Ga 10/4/57 on chg of Dyer Act
PD Atlanta Ga	ALLEN CLAY-TON WEST #176292	10/6/57	in transit USP	rel to Fed Auth 10/10/57
USM Atlanta Ga	ALLEN CLAY-TON WEST #021295	10/6/57	in transit from Balt Md to USM Savannah Ga	
USP Atlanta Ga	ALLEN CLAY-TON WEST #79652	2/21/58	transporting stolen MV interstate	10 yrs
USP Alcatraz Calif	ALLEN CLAY-TON WEST #1335-AZ	6/23/58 rec by transfer from USP Atlanta Ga	transporting stolen motor vehicles interstate	

Appendix D

"Alcatraz Rock"
by Mary Nell Anglin

It's kinda like a city floating out there all alone.

I have two brothers John & Clarence that use to live there, but now they are gone.

They must have fled for their lives when they jumped into that shark filled waters that night.

Chorus: Alcatraz, you are hard as a rock, for you took two of my brothers away that cold night. It sure looks dreary & scary out there, but they did something that no one else ever had.

Just imagine the water and how cold it felt and I bet they were wishing they were back there in bed.

But I hope and pray that they made it because nothing has ever been found.

Chorus: Alcatraz, you are hard as a rock for you took two of my brothers away that cold night. It sure looks dreary & scary out there but they did something that no one else ever had.

July 1962

Appendix E

The Mysterious Death
of Alfred Anglin

Feb. 10, 1964

Dear Mr. & Mrs. Anglin:

Your recent letter to Assistant Warden O. F. Wells has been handed to us for reply.

As to your request for a letter of explanation, there is very little to explain. Your son, along with inmate Othis Senn, on the night of January 11, 1964, secluded themselves in the Clothing Room of the Prison and sawed the bars and protective screen from a window leading on to the roof at the front of the Prison Compound, using hacksaw blades secured in handmade frames they had built previously while on their regular job assignment at the Prison Textile Mill. Your son went out of the window first on to the flat roof. At about the time his feet were in the hole, he came in contact with a high tension wire across the roof, causing immediate electrocution. He had in his possession at the time, jumper wires, designed to jump the ignition switch of automobiles, a colored blanket for covering their white clothing and all the pictures that were sent to you by Chaplain Watson, were in a package in his pocket.

I am not familiar with his Parole Status but we feel as you do that there was no reason for his trying to escape. Since arriving at this Institution, he had displayed a good attitude, had been in no trouble what so ever, doing well on his job and getting along well with the Officials and other inmates alike. So we had no reason to believe that he was going to try to escape. However, we must face facts and the facts are that he did, in fact, attempt to escape.

The question about the color of the writing paper is of no particular significance since the paper is printed at Draper Correctional Center using what ever color paper they may have in stock at the time they receive our order. As to his personal clothing, we gathered up all clothing that was known to belong to him. The only personal clothing he would be allowed would be underwear, sox and possibly a white shirt. All other clothing, by policy must be issued.

We are certainly sorry that this happened and sympathize with you in your hour of trouble. If we can be of further service, please call on us.

Yours truly

WILLIAM C. HOLMAN
Acting Warden

Feb. 7, 1964

Dear Mrs. Rachel Anglin:

Your letter concerning the death of Alfred arrived in today's Mail. Unfortunately, I have no tangible information concerning the questions you asked. And, as I am resigning from Prison Ministry, effective the 14th of this month, I will not be able to secure the information you desire.

I am turning your letter over to Deputy Warden Wells and I'm sure that he will forward you all available information. May God bless you and comfort you.

Sincerely yours,

R. S. Watson, Chaplain
Kilby Prison
Montgomery, Ala.-36110

Appendix F

"Alcatraz"
by
Ellsworth R. "Bumpy" Johnson

Six feet of chambered stone
The nation gives us for a home,
Ten feet from top to floor
A barred-in gate serves as a door.

A special jail for special men
That someone hopes won't rise again,
Yet be man low or be he great
No can controls a strong man's fate.

So here we sit and watch them pass
The weak and strong of Alcatraz;
The weak will perish ere they start
But the strong will play a greater part.

What prompted germ of thought in man
To etch, blueprint and build this plan?
This special jail for special men;
From a bureaucratic dreamer's pen.

Fools in high places should not dwell
For they make life a living hell,
And leave behind them when they pass
A monument like Alcatraz.

Appendix G

A Final Word About Clarence "Joe" Carnes
by Joseph M. Brandenburg, Jr., Deputy Chief U.S. Probation Officer Kansas City Missouri

I helped bury Clarence Carnes on October 7, 1988, at the Resurrection Cemetery in Springfield, Missouri. Hopefully, he has finally found the peace that he wanted and searched for most of his life.

Unlike the majority of us, his name will not soon be forgotten. The "Choctaw Kid," "Joe," Clarence Carnes has found a place in our American lore. We have a strange relationship with our anti-heros, our gangsters, our "bad guys." We are fascinated with them, with their exploits and their lives for reasons that only the experts of our American psyche can begin to understand or explain. History and legend will in time dictate Clarence's place with our "bad guys" and in our folklore.

I do not choose to attempt in any way to assist in the development of the lore of Clarence Carnes. In 1973, when Clarence was released after 28-plus years of confinement, I was his parole officer. I continued to be his parole officer until his death in October 1988, in the Medical Center for Federal Prisoners in Springfield, Missouri. In those sixteen years, I came to know Clarence as well or better than anyone, certainly in the latter years of his life.

While I knew him as well or better than anyone, I can't say I completely knew or understood him. After spending most of his adolescence and all of his adult life in federal penitentiaries, he found it necessary and safest for no one to completely know him.

The Clarence Carnes I knew was terrified of living in the "free society"; he didn't know how. I knew the Clarence who survived as the youngest con ever in Alcatraz and one of the youngest in Leavenworth, but did not know how to survive on the streets of Kansas City, the Clarence who was totally unprepared to live with the rest of us. I knew the Clarence who was socialized and reared in our toughest penitentiaries—in a world of hate, violence, and dehumanization, yet was so scared and lonely in the community that he would cry like a small child. The Clarence that had a Piped-Piper-like charisma with young children who saw a gentleness and kindness in him that we adults either could not or would not see.

I knew the Clarence that could not understand why there were often more men of integrity and men of their word in the institutions than in the community that Clarence knew.

Clarence could not understand the extent that people could use and abuse each other and still call themselves "Christians." He often trusted too much, even after people would use him and discard him, and yet he would go back for more.

As a people, we are uncomfortable with shades of grey. We want and need blacks and whites. We don't want good in our bad guys or bad in our good guys. We want our lives and answers simple and pure. What is unsettling to us is that Clarence was like the rest of us. His parents wanted Clarence to have what they did not; they wanted him to have life a bit easier than they. As a youth, he was daring and often stupid. It seems for youth such is a given right of passage.

Clarence was described by Alcatraz officials as one of the most dangerous escape risks to ever have been confined on Alcatraz Island, and I am sure he was. But he was so like us in other ways. The Clarence I knew was often scared, weak, hurt, emotionally drained, startled and hurt by the coldness and cruelty of the people he came to know.

Clarence was sick; he grew old; and yes, he often drank too much. Clarence was a stand-up guy, in the prison vernacular a "con," not an inmate.

Clarence was a lot of things to a lot of people. He is a part of all of us, a part of what we have created. We have a right and responsibility to punish those who break our laws, and we exercise that right and responsibility, but I would suggest that we must take the responsibility for the punishment that we demand. To punish and then be responsible for that punishment is fair and right, and after all, fairness and rightness is what justice is all about.

Clarence was an anti-hero, a complex person, a part of our lore. But to me Clarence was a lot less and yet a lot more too—he was my friend.